TAKING COMMAND

TAKING COMMAND

GENERAL J. LAWTON COLLINS

FROM GUADALCANAL TO UTAH BEACH
AND VICTORY IN EUROPE

H. PAUL JEFFERS

NAL
CALIBER

NAL CALIBER
Published by New American Library,
a division of Penguin Group (USA) Inc.,
375 Hudson Street, New York, New York 10014, USA
Penguin Group (Canada), 90 Eglinton Avenue East, Suite 700, Toronto,
Ontario M4P 2Y3, Canada (a division of Pearson Penguin Canada Inc.)
Penguin Books Ltd., 80 Strand, London WC2R 0RL, England
Penguin Ireland, 25 St. Stephen's Green, Dublin 2,
Ireland (a division of Penguin Books Ltd.)
Penguin Group (Australia), 250 Camberwell Road, Camberwell,
Victoria 3124, Australia (a division of Pearson Australia Group Pty. Ltd.)
Penguin Books India Pvt. Ltd., 11 Community Centre,
Panchsheel Park, New Delhi - 110 017, India
Penguin Group (NZ), 67 Apollo Drive, Rosedale, North Shore 0632,
New Zealand (a division of Pearson New Zealand Ltd.)
Penguin Books (South Africa) (Pty.) Ltd., 24 Sturdee Avenue,
Rosebank, Johannesburg 2196, South Africa

Penguin Books Ltd., Registered Offices:
80 Strand, London WC2R 0RL, England

First published by NAL Caliber, an imprint of New American Library,
a division of Penguin Group (USA) Inc.

First Printing, May 2009
1   3   5   7   9   10   8   6   4   2

LIBRARY OF CONGRESS CATALOGING-IN-PUBLICATION DATA:

Jeffers, H. Paul (Harry Paul), 1934–
Taking command: General J. Lawton Collins from Guadalcanal
to Utah beach and victory in Europe/H. Paul Jeffers.
p. cm.
Includes bibliographical references and index.
ISBN 978-0-451-22687-7
1. Collins, J. Lawton (Joseph Lawton) 2. Generals—United States—Biography.
3. World War, 1939–1945—Biography. 4. United States. Army—Biography. I. Title.
E745.C64J44 2009
940.54'81092—dc22   2008052746
[B]

Set in Horley MT
Designed by Elke Sigal

Printed in the United States of America

For my nieces, Beverly, Barbara, Ginny, and Patty;
my nephew, Larry; and in loving memory
of their mother, Jean Jeffers Detwiler

CONTENTS

"Where the crux of the fighting was is the place I headed for."
—General J. Lawton Collins

GENERAL JOE WHO?

In the rearview mirror of history, the turns, twists, detours, and crossroads encountered by Joseph Lawton Collins as he ventured from boyhood in Louisiana during the Theodore Roosevelt administration to a soldier's life and a role as a three-star general in World War II stand out as if they were marked by signposts with arrows declaring "This way to your destiny."

Forty years after Teddy took office, "Lightning Joe" Collins was a significant figure in the Second World War. First at Guadalcanal and then as commander of the Seventh Corps to the end of the war, he was at the heart of the planning for the invasion of France, commanded the troops that landed on Utah Beach on June 6, 1944, and was at the vortex of the mightiest land battles and countless smaller ones on the way to victory over Nazi Germany.

Yet, six decades after the war in which he led troops in fetid Pacific jungles and in the most momentous events in Europe, and two more decades of distinguished service to his country in and out of an army uniform after the war, most Americans, if asked if they have ever heard of General Joe Collins, are likely to reply with a puzzled look, "General Joe who?"

Although I had heard a little about him when I was a child during the war by following news reports and watching newsreels at the movies, it wasn't until I ventured into studying and writing World War II history that I fully realized his significance. This new appreciation deepened as I wrote the first biography of Brigadier General Theodore Roosevelt, Jr. The eldest son of Teddy and called Ted, he was in his mid-fifties when he waded gallantly ashore on Utah Beach with a pistol in one hand and a cane in the other in the first wave of troops of the Fourth Division on D-day as part of Collins's plan for the Seventh Corps to take Utah and drive inland to capture the vital seaport of Cherbourg.

After the Seventh Corps spearheaded a breakout from the Normandy beachhead, it participated in the closing of the Falaise gap that threatened to thwart the Allied advance, then swept northward into Belgium. After capturing the city of Aachen, the Seventh Corps fought in a fierce winter battle in the Hurtgen Forest, turned back a German northern drive in the Battle of the Bulge, took Cologne, crossed the Rhine River, plunged into the industrial Ruhr Valley, linked up with Russian forces at Dessau on the Elbe River, and helped bring down the curtain on the war in Europe.

Known as a commander who drove his troops hard, Collins exhibited an enthusiasm and a frankness that earned the respect and affection of his men. One war correspondent called him "the GI's general." Participating in a seminar conducted by the Combat Studies Institute at the Command and General Staff College, Fort Leavenworth, Kansas, on May 17, 1983, Collins recalled, "Every day I was out in the field visiting as far as I could the critical point of action. Where the crux of the fighting was is the place I headed for. I tried, and most of the time was able, to visit practically every division during each day."

This desire to be at the center of the fighting was first demonstrated early in the war in the Pacific when he was named commander of the army's Twenty-fifth Division. Because its nickname was "Tropic Lightning," a bolt of lightning appeared on all field orders sent from headquarters above the signature "J. Lawton Collins." When the division was sent to relieve the marines who had landed on Guadalcanal, Collins inspected an area being held by the Twenty-seventh Infantry. As he was studying the terrain through field glasses, a GI in a foxhole spotted him and exclaimed, "By God, there's J. Lightning himself."

As the story of the incident spread throughout the division and in the press, "J. Lightning" became "Lightning Joe" and the nickname stuck.

In a 1944 article in *YANK*, the army's weekly magazine, titled "2-Front Fighter," Sergeant Mack Morris described the two-star commander of the Seventh Corps as "an iron-graying West Pointer." He wrote, "In the Solomons [in the Pacific], he earned himself a reputation for personal combat by prowling around in the jungle, occasionally dueling with Jap snipers. Over here [in France] he has less time for duels, but his corps has become known as a 'spearhead' outfit and his enthusiasm hasn't suffered because of the greater responsibility."

As evidence of how Lightning Joe Collins identified with the ordinary GI, Morris wrote, "Comparing foxholes in the Pacific war and those in France, Collins stated 'I'm not saying that the men in the [European] theater are living in the lap of luxury, but most of the time they can find straw to line their holes with. In the Solomons they could take their choice between a foxhole in the soft mud or a foxhole in the hard coral. I haven't been in a foxhole yet over here. On New Georgia I was in one 15 times in one night.'"

One of only three generals who led troops in combat in both the Pacific and Europe, he was affable, with fair hair, a boyish face, a winning smile, and a Louisiana accent. With a forceful manner and disarming Irish charm inherited from his father, he was among a small coterie of brilliant young officers deemed by Army Chief of Staff George C. Marshall in the years immediately before the war to have the potential to become great commanders. Along with Collins, those tapped by Marshall who were to become household names in wartime America were Dwight D. Eisenhower, Omar Bradley, George Patton, Mark Clark, Jacob Devers, Leonard Gerow, Courtney Hodges, Walter Bedell Smith, Maxwell Taylor, and Lucian K. Truscott, Jr. Joe Collins knew and fought shoulder to shoulder with all of them.

After the guns went silent around the world in 1945, Collins served as deputy to General Eisenhower, chief of staff of Army Ground Forces, chief of army public information, and deputy and vice chief of staff of the army. Elevated to chief of staff in 1949, he held the post as the guns roared again throughout the Korean War. He played a key role in the formation of the North Atlantic Treaty Organization (NATO), and as President Eisenhower's representative with the rank of ambassador to Vietnam in 1954, he advised against American military intervention.

From 1954 to his retirement from public service, he served in various posts related to the postwar European recovery and faced the new challenges of the cold war with NATO. After his retirement from the army in 1956, he became a business executive. In 1969, he watched via TV as the astronaut Michael Collins (the son of his nephew, General James Lawton Collins, Jr.) piloted Apollo 11 in orbit while Neil Armstrong and Buzz Aldrin became the first men to walk on the moon. He published two books, *War in Peacetime*, about being chief of staff during the Korean War, and an autobiography, *Lightning Joe*. He died on September 12, 1987, of a heart attack in Washington, D.C., at the age of ninety-one.

Drawn from official military histories and records, field orders, situation reports, letters, memoranda, Collins's autobiography, memoirs of other World War II generals, press accounts of the war, and official histories of the conflict, this first biography of J. Lawton Collins concentrates on his active military career after graduation from West Point in 1917, during the First World War, the years between the world wars, his service in the second, as chief of staff, and other government assignments during the first term of President Dwight D. Eisenhower. An epilogue deals with the period of his retirement and his reflections not only on his life but on the state of America's military in a world that was dramatically different from the one he'd helped to free from tyranny in World War II. With an undiminished optimism, he wrote that his experiences left him with "abiding admiration and affection for the Army of the United States and its men and women who, I am sure, no matter what dangers the future holds for us, will always live up to our nation's trust."

Citing Collins as one of the most outstanding field commanders in Europe and "the most aggressive" commander of U.S. ground forces, General Omar Bradley wrote in his memoir, *A Soldier's Story*, that Collins brought to the battlefields not only a seasoned and unerring tactical judgment but just enough bravado to make every advance a triumph.

"Such self-assurance is tolerable only when right," added Bradley, "and Collins, happily, almost always was."

STAG DINNER AT THE ALIBI CLUB

A few days after Christmas 1943, as a scattering of snow-flakes sparkled in the beams of the headlights of a taxi gliding to a stop on a Monday evening in Washington, D.C., Major General Joseph Lawton Collins peered through a steamed-up window at the plain façade of a nineteenth-century town house and asked the driver, "Are you sure this is the Alibi Club?"

"Yes, sir. Number 1806 I Street North West."

"There's no sign on the door. No name anywhere that I can see."

"Far as I know, there never has been a sign."

Founded decades earlier by seven members of the capital city's exclusive Metropolitan Club who were seeking an even more private setting for gentlemen, the Alibi Club had been started, in the felicitous words of its first president, Marcellus Bailey, "to relieve the mind of what some call the monotony of domestic life and toll of business."

The club quickly became a bastion for the elite and powerful of the nation's capital and remained a refuge from the prying eyes of the curious and the press.

Stepping from the cab, Collins tried to remember the last time he felt snowflakes on his face. There'd been snow on the ground at West Point, but none in the air, when he and his wife, Gladys, spent Christmas Day with their daughters, Nancy and Gladdie, and their son, Jerry, in his plebe year at the Military Academy. The reunion was a surprise. Gladys hadn't learned her husband was coming home from duty in the Pacific until the day before he arrived. Lucky to grab space on an army transport from tropical New Zealand and then a direct flight from the West Coast, he landed at National Airport on December 23, only to learn that Gladys and Nancy had gone to New York to pick up Gladdie at Vassar and go on to visit Jerry. At West Point's Thayer Hotel for the Collins family's first meal together in two years, he found that the girls he had left at home were now vivacious teenagers. Jerry looked perfectly soldierly in his cadet's uniform.

Two days later in an Arlington, Virginia, office in a gigantic five-sided building known as the Pentagon, which didn't exist the last time Collins was in Washington, U.S. Army Chief of Staff George C. Marshall informed Collins he wanted to hear everything about the fight for Guadalcanal. While Marshall settled back in his chair to listen to all that the major general who had commanded the Twenty-fifth Division for more than a year said in describing the first American defeat of the Japanese on land in the Pacific, Collins observed nothing in Marshall's demeanor to indicate that he was disappointed with President Franklin Roosevelt's decision not to put Marshall in command of the planning and execution of the long-anticipated invasion of France. On Christmas Eve, FDR had announced that the Supreme Allied Commander would be Marshall's protégé, General Dwight D. Eisenhower.

Well acquainted with both men, Collins had known Marshall much longer but recognized the virtues in each. Eisenhower had demonstrated not only that he was a brilliant military planner but the possessor of a natural charm and affability symbolized by his nickname, "Ike." They were certain to be assets in negotiating perilous tides to hold together a potentially fractious coalition built upon personalities known as the "Allies." Marshall was a somber figure who was strictly business. A stickler for proprieties, he addressed a man only by his last name. To Ike, Collins was Joe. With Marshall he was Collins.

While Roosevelt, as the senior figure of the Allies and commander in chief, got to choose the top man for the invasion, Marshall had the responsibility of approving the field commanders. Consequently, when Collins completed summarizing the final stages of the first American land campaign against Japan, he ventured to Marshall that he was confident he could move up a rung from division commanding officer to CO of a corps. Marshall replied that he'd raised that very question in Australia with the commander in the Pacific theater, General Douglas MacArthur. With what Collins described as a rare twinkle in his eyes, Marshall added that the general had replied, "But Joe Collins is too young."

Collins had graduated from West Point in 1917 and was now four months shy of forty-eight. When the United States entered World War I, he served at various domestic posts and in 1919 took command of the Third Battalion of the Twenty-second Infantry Regiment in France and was assistant chief of staff of supply for the American occupation forces in Germany (1920–21). For the next few years he attended and taught in various army schools. Promoted to major, he was executive officer of the Twenty-third Brigade, Manila, and assistant chief of staff for intelligence in the Philippine Division (1933–34). Named lieutenant colonel in June of 1940, he was appointed chief of staff, Seventh Corps, in the temporary rank of colonel (January 1941). Following the attack on Pearl Harbor, he was designated chief of staff to General Delos C. Emmons and traveled with him to

Hawaii and assisted in the reorganization of the islands' defenses. Appointed commanding general of the Twenty-fifth Infantry Division in May 1942, he led it in securing Guadalcanal.

Marshall closed the meeting by telling Collins his presence was desired at a reception Marshall was giving for Eisenhower on January 3. The stag dinner at the Alibi Club was to be, as the historian Mark Perry wrote in *Partners in Command*, Eisenhower's official "coming out party." The guest list was stellar. From the administration were Secretary of War Henry L. Stimson, Undersecretary Robert R. Patterson, Assistant Secretary John J. McCloy, and Director of War Mobilization James F. Byrnes. On behalf of the Congress were Senators Warren Austin and Wallace H. White and three representatives, Andrew J. May, Walter G. Andrews, and R. Ewing Thomason. Needing no government title, the financier Bernard Baruch was an FDR confidant and a friend of Marshall's.

At the dinner, reporting the status of the war against Nazi U-boats in the North Atlantic would be former Chief of Naval Operations Admiral Harold R. Stark. The air force was the province of General Henry H. "Hap" Arnold. To cover the campaigns in the South Pacific, Marshall would call on General George Kenney to describe an airborne attack carried out in the Markham Valley of New Guinea and the operations in New Britain. Going first after dinner, Collins would discuss the wrapping up of Guadalcanal and a campaign in New Georgia.

Marshall and Eisenhower welcomed the guests at the door. Each was greeted with the Eisenhower smile that would become as familiar to the American people for the duration of the war and long after it as the rakish upward tilt of FDR's long cigarette holder, British prime minister Winston Churchill's cigar, Douglas MacArthur's corncob pipe, and George Patton's brace of ivory-grip revolvers.

After dinner, Eisenhower reported on the victories in 1942 of

Operation Torch in North Africa, the success of Operation Husky in Sicily in 1943, the invasion of Italy at Salerno and subsequent landing at Anzio, and the costly fight to break out from the bridgehead to breach the tenacious German defenses blocking a drive northward to take Rome. The invasion of France, known to insiders as Operation Overlord, to confront Adolf Hitler with a western front and relieve the burden on Russia in the east was mentioned only in the vaguest of terms. At the conclusion of Ike's remarks, Marshall led the guests in lifting glasses in toasts to Roosevelt and Eisenhower.

The next morning, Collins and Gladys left the capital for White Sulphur Springs, West Virginia. A secluded resort where people had been "taking the waters" since 1778, it had a hotel, the Greenbrier, and small guest cottages. Taken over by the army to serve as a military hospital, it was also a place for visitors who had army business to elude the prying eyes of the press, and possibly spies. It was also an ideal out-of-sight spot for Marshall to sequester visiting generals.

Collins and Gladys had been there only a day or two when they were invited to dinner at the house of the commander of the hospital, Colonel Clyde McK. Beck. Stating it would be a small, informal party, Mrs. Beck stressed that guests be on time. Her reason for this was revealed when the last guests arrived. Surprised to see General and Mrs. Eisenhower enter the room, Collins had the impression that Ike was just as taken aback to see him.

This feeling was validated when Ike exclaimed, "Why, Joe! I didn't know you were down here. I understand you are coming over to join us!"

Startled to learn in this offhand manner that he was evidently to be transferred to Ike's European theater, Collins assumed that Marshall had dismissed MacArthur's view that Collins was too young to head a corps and had said so to Eisenhower.

Acutely conscious of the need for security, even at a Green-brier cocktail party where everyone knew everyone, Collins said to Ike, "Thank you very much!"

The evening passed with small talk, capital gossip, and chats about army colleagues.

Recalling the moment in his autobiography, Collins wrote that as much as he enjoyed the privilege of commanding the Twenty-fifth Infantry Division in the South Pacific, he knew that the decisive battles of the war would be in Europe and he wanted to participate. The orders assigning him to Eisenhower's command were issued on January19, 1944, but before he could leave he had to pass a physical examination. He did so, but after the exam he was struck with chills and fever, indicating a recurrence of malaria he had contracted in the Pacific. Rushing to the house that Gladys had acquired, he gulped quinine pills he'd brought from New Guinea, and went to bed. When she returned from a shopping sojourn and saw him with covers up to his ears and an ice bag on his head, her face turned pale with shock.

After taking quinine for three days, Collins had a final checkup and showed no trace of fever. Without mentioning the episode to the medical officer, he continued the quinine, but at reduced dosages, and never had a recurrence. On January 26, 1944, he kissed Gladys and Nancy good-bye and boarded an army plane for England to begin his greatest adventure since he'd left home in 1913 to follow in his brother's footsteps to the United States Military Academy.

CHAPTER ONE

THE NATURAL

B orn on May 1, 1896, Joseph Lawton Collins was the fifth son and the tenth of eleven children of Jeremiah Bernard Collins and the former Catherine Lawton. Emigrating at age fifteen with his parents from Ireland in 1862 to Ohio, Jerry soon found himself in an army uniform as a drummer boy in the Ohio militia in the Civil War but saw no combat. After heading to Texas to help move a herd of horses to replace cavalry mounts that were lost during the war, he settled in New Orleans and worked for a grocer, James Lawton. Eventually running the stables and managing delivery wagons, he courted and wed the boss's daughter. After establishing a dry-goods store with a pub in the back in the Algiers area of New Orleans on the west bank of the Mississippi River, they had their first child (December 10, 1882) and named him James after her father.

When Joseph entered the family fourteen years later, James was in high school. Describing James as the older brother all the Collins children looked up to, Joseph wrote, "The most cherished periods of my childhood were long summer vacations. Barefooted, and wearing blue overalls, sleeveless cotton shirts, and soft straw

hats, my younger brother Bernard and I played together inces-
santly, whether it was building tree houses in the back yard, playing one o'cat baseball with neighborhood kids (using a small red
rubber ball and a broom handle for a bat), fishing for crayfish in a
ditch alongside Southern Pacific Railroad maintenance shops, or
shooting marbles on the smooth-packed mud borders of the side-
walks. Few of the streets were paved when we were small boys,
and following the frequent heavy rains they developed into wonderful mud holes. I still remember the exquisite feeling of sticky
Louisiana blue clay oozing between my bare toes as we splashed
through those mud holes."

Accompanying his father on wagon trips to wholesale produce markets in New Orleans to purchase supplies for the store,
Joe boarded a paddle-wheeled ferry to cross the Mississippi,
swirling along within its retaining levees at five miles an hour, ten
feet or more above the level of the city streets. Creole and Italian
voices mixed with the shrill cries of street vendors, the stomping
of horses' hoofs, and the rattle of wagon wheels to produce a ca-
cophony that was music to a boy of ten. With the wagon loaded
till its springs creaked, they clomped back to the Canal Street
ferry and on home with Jerry singing old Irish ditties.

While Jerry Collins was an Irish immigrant who made his
way to Louisiana, Catherine Lawton sprang from deep Southern
roots and a family with such strong ties to the Bayou State that an
uncle, Martin Behrman, became the forty-sixth mayor of New
Orleans and served sixteen years. Born in New York, he had come
to the city as an infant. Orphaned early, he began as a clerk and
salesman for several produce and grocery firms. Entering Democratic Party politics as a ward worker, he took part in the 1888
gubernatorial campaign of Francis T. Nichols and in 1898 was a
delegate to the Louisiana state constitutional convention. Prior to
his election as mayor in 1904, he held minor elective and appoint-
ive offices, including the presidency of the Board of Assessors and

State Auditor, and rose to power as the leader of the city's fif-teenth ward (Algiers).

These political connections would prove directly beneficial to the eldest and youngest Collins boys by helping them get appointed to West Point.

Although the only evidence of military experience in the Collins family had been Jerry's service as a drummer in the Civil War, James grew up with hopes of attending the U.S. Military Academy. When he left home for West Point in 1903, Joseph was seven years old. Graduated in 1907, James saw action against the Moros in the Philippine Insurrection and in 1916 served as an aide to General John J. Pershing in a campaign known as the Punitive Expedition against the Mexican rebel and border raider Pancho Villa. With U.S. entry into World War I and Pershing appointed commander of the American Expeditionary Force, James served as his aide-de-camp.

Joseph followed his brother to West Point in 1913 with aspirations of graduating near the top of his class. Recalling that he was one of the rare cadets who enjoyed the arduous customs of the Academy, he wrote that he planned to join the Corps of Engineers but quickly realized he was more interested in the humanities. "What appealed to me most about West Point, aside from its setting and tradition," he said, "was its high standard of integrity, its emphasis on duty and honor, and its dedication to the service of the country. I treasured the qualities of fellow cadets, including the diversity of their points of view, which reflected that they came from every state in the Union and all walks of life. Though I loathed close-order drill, and years later devised a new drill that eliminated most of its dull routine, I never failed to be moved by the dress parades nor lost the thrill that crept up my spine as 'The Star-Spangled Banner' was played at retreat and the flag fluttered down at Trophy Point."

Among his classmates were future World War II generals

Mark Wayne Clark, Matthew B. Ridgway, and Alfred Gruenther. Two years ahead of them and graduating in 1915 were his future bosses, Dwight D. Eisenhower and Omar N. Bradley.

Although the *New York Times* headline for a story on the graduation of the West Point Class of 1917 declared "139 New Officers Graduated for War," Joseph was not rushed off to join his brother James in the Allied Expeditionary Force in France. Assigned to the Twenty-second Infantry and quickly promoted to first lieutenant in May 1917 and to captain in August, he was sent to the Infantry School of Arms at Fort Sill and served with his regiment at various locations. Promoted to temporary major in September 1918, he was named the commander of the Third Battalion, Twenty-second Infantry, and at last sent to France. With the war over, he arrived in Brest and his unit moved by railroad to Château-Thierry, then joined a motor tour of the U.S. battlefields of Cantigny, Saint-Mihiel, and the Meuse-Argonne. The sojourn ended in Paris and a reunion with James, who was now secretary of the General Staff at General Headquarters at Chaumont. After sightseeing, the brothers drove there in time for dinner at Pershing's personal mess. Announced by an orderly, Pershing stood momentarily at the head of the stairs leading down from his living quarters. Joseph noted, "He was a stunning, commanding figure in his beribboned uniform, tall and erect, perfectly groomed from his iron-gray head of hair to his polished Peale boots."

Leaving Chaumont to rejoin his unit to continue the tour of bases, with stops to visit supply depots and other installations that had supported the American advance into Germany, Joseph arrived at the junction of the Moselle and Rhine rivers and entered the ancient city of Coblenz to find the American flag flying above its battlements. A quarter of a century after the raising of the Stars and Stripes as a symbol of the defeat of Kaiser Wilhelm's Germany, Joe Collins, as three-star commander of the U.S. Army

Seventh Corps, would order the hoisting of the flag in Germany to signify the vanquishing of the Nazis.

After commanding the Third Battalion, Twenty-second Infantry, throughout 1919, he was shifted in 1920 to command the Eighteenth Infantry Regiment of the First Division of the American occupation forces in Germany. When the division departed for home, he found himself no longer with a battalion to command and reduced in rank from temporary major. But because he had been made a permanent captain effective June 25, 1919, he remained in France. Twelve years would elapse before he would again achieve the rank of major, and eight more years before he became a lieutenant colonel at age forty-four.

Not having had command of troops in action in the World War and confident there would be no more large-scale wars, he believed he would get nowhere in the army and gave thought to resigning from the service and studying law. Knowing several friends in New York who had left the army and were back in law practice, he wrote to Columbia University and on the strength of his West Point diploma was accepted for law school for the academic year 1919–20.

When he wrote to his close friend George Welch to get his reaction, Welch replied, "Joe, you are crazy. We can hire any number of good lawyers in New York for $200 a month. Unless you marry the boss's daughter, the prospects for a young lawyer in New York are not good. Your métier is the Army. Stick to it."

While weighing the pros and cons of quitting the army, Collins was called in by his battalion commander. Lieutenant Colonel Charles L. Wyman told him that he had just written an efficiency report stating that Collins was the most promising officer with his length of service that he knew. The report noted, "He is a natural and should enjoy a great career."

Recognizing that except for a lack of combat experience he'd been fortunate in having interesting and challenging assignments, had never been required to do anything that was contrary to his personal standard of conduct, and unsure that this would always be the case in the legal profession or the business world, he weighed Wyman's report and reconsidered the idea of quitting the army. These factors, combined with a desire to see more of the continent before going home, resulted in a decision to give the army a try for another year.

With the permanent grade of captain, he had taken command of Company L, Eighth Infantry, which had moved into former French barracks near the Moselle River at Coblenz. This meant a reunion with his sisters Agnes and Margaret. Members of a volunteer unit of the National Catholic Welfare Council, they were serving with the American army in France. When the World War ended, their unit had moved up to Coblenz. A Newcomb College graduate who had taught in New Orleans, Agnes had become a teacher in the high school organized for U.S. soldiers under the army educational and vocational training program.

"Having two sisters with me," Collins wrote, "provided a homelike atmosphere to our billet and added greatly to the pleasure of my stay on the Rhine. They both loved to travel, as I did, and we made two trips to France, Switzerland, Austria, and Italy. Paris, Vienna, and Rome, with their wonderful shops, museums, great cathedrals, and music halls, were of course the chief attractions, though the mountains and lakes of Switzerland had a special appeal to me, perhaps because of my fondness at the time for the poetry of Byron and Coleridge."

The last vestige of thoughts of leaving the army evaporated on his first evening in Coblenz after he had moved there from the Rhine bridgehead in November 1919. Attending a Third Battalion officers' dance, he was, as he wrote in his memoir, "attracted to a lovely girl in evening dress, which enhanced her fresh beauty." He asked an aide, "Who is the pretty girl?"

The assistant replied, "Gladys Easterbrook. Would you like to meet her?"

Collins exclaimed, "Would I!"

With other young bachelors converging on her from all directions, he beat them to her side and was introduced. Just as the music resumed, he asked, "May I have this dance?"

Before the evening ended, they had several dances and Collins had persuaded her father, Chaplain Edmund P. Easterbrook, who was chaperoning his daughter, to leave her in the hands of old friends, Colonel and Mrs. Calvin P. Titus. At the end of the dance, they gave their permission for Collins to walk her home.

Recalling that night, Collins wrote, "A full moon shone overhead and added its magic to an enchanting evening. As we strolled along I learned that Gladys loved to ride horseback, so before saying good night, we made a date for a ride the next Sunday afternoon. I walked to my billet in a trance. Without realizing it, my last lingering thought of resigning vanished in the moonlight."

Two long years of courtship followed. Collins was Catholic, and Gladys was the only daughter of a Protestant minister and his devout Calvinist wife, both of whom were born in England. Because of these religious differences, Joseph and Gladys had three marriage ceremonies on July 15, 1921. The first was a civil union conducted by the city's mayor. The second was by Gladys's father in the chapel of the Kaiserin Augusta's palace. The last was in the billet of his sisters by an "understanding" Catholic chaplain. The decision to be married in Coblenz had been precipitated by War Department orders to Collins to report in August 1921 to the U.S. Military Academy at West Point as an instructor.

The result was a twelve-year round of assignments as an instructor or student in the army's school system.

Reporting for duty at West Point on August 25, 1921, he expected to teach French and was surprised to be assigned to the chemistry department. Looking back on the West Point experience, he wrote, "It provided stability for the early years of our marriage at a time when conditions in the postwar Army were almost chaotic. Our son Joseph Easterbrook, whom we called

Jerry, was born during our third year at the Academy, adding joy to our already happy life, and making West Point truly our first home."

After four years at the Academy, Collins spent a year at the company officers' school at Fort Benning, Georgia, and in 1926 was offered a choice of attending the Army Air Corps Tactical School or the Field Artillery School. Electing the latter, he reported to Fort Sill, Oklahoma, and spent another year learning the capabilities and limitations of artillery, which would serve him very well as commander of the Seventh Corps in World War II.

Thirty years old in the rank of captain, with a wife, a young son and daughter (Gladys), and another child on the way, and all thoughts of giving up the army abandoned, he graduated from the Artillery School in 1927. Trading in a six-year-old Ford auto for a two-door Oakland sedan, they traveled rough and muddy country roads to Columbus, Georgia, and the nearby Infantry School of Fort Benning. Two days after their arrival on August 3, 1927, Nancy was born in the post hospital. The family settled into a small frame cottage in a grove of tall oak trees that was within walking distance of the Infantry School.

As Collins delivered his first lecture, he saw for the first time a man who would not only influence the military careers of Joseph Lawton Collins, Dwight D. Eisenhower, and a host of other middle-grade officers but direct the conduct of the Second World War, inscribe a new chapter in American military history, shift the direction of U.S. foreign policy in the postwar years as secretary of defense and secretary of state, and be awarded the Nobel Peace Prize. Quietly slipping into the classroom as Collins began his lecture, Lieutenant Colonel George Catlett Marshall had just taken over as assistant commandant of the Infantry School and brought with him to Fort Benning, in the words of Collins, a reputation as a "grave, humorless man, who was all business."

Born on December 31, 1880, in Uniontown, Pennsylvania, Marshall had enrolled at the Virginia Military Institute, from which he was graduated in 1901 as senior first captain of the Corps of Cadets. After serving in posts in the Philippines and the United States, he graduated with honors from the Infantry-Cavalry School at Fort Leavenworth in 1907 and from the Army Staff College in 1908. After distinguishing himself in a variety of posts over the next nine years, he earned an appointment to the General Staff in World War I. Sailing to France with the First Division, he achieved fame and promotion for staff work in the battles of Cantigny, Aisne-Marne, Saint-Mihiel, and Meuse-Argonne. After serving as aide-de-camp to General Pershing from 1919 to 1924, he was in China from 1924 to 1927 and was an instructor in the Army War College in 1927.

On the Saturday afternoon following Collins's lecture, while Collins was raking leaves in front of his cottage, Marshall walked by. Of this second encounter, Collins wrote, "He stopped to chat, and as he seemed to linger, I invited him in for a cup of tea. I said Mrs. Collins probably was not dressed for visitors, but he accepted without hesitation. Gladys served us tea, and the Colonel sat and visited for some while in a relaxed, informal fashion. Thereafter I always felt at ease with this remarkable man."

Though Marshall's predecessors had launched the new Infantry School at Benning in 1918, his arrival marked its coming of age. Collins noted that Marshall brought a fresh outlook on problems of the infantry, and to the army, to which he evidently had given considerable thought. He also came with matured judgments as to what he wanted to accomplish, including shaking the infantry out of its conservative ways by developing innovative ideas and methods. While making it clear to the faculty and students that these principles and methods were all subject to challenge, he retained the system of having approved or preferred solutions to the problems presented to student classes. In one of his earliest directives to the faculty, he stated that any student's solution to a problem that differed markedly from the approved solution, yet made sense, should be published to the class.

"Despite Colonel Marshall's seemingly forbidding appearance," wrote Collins, "he was always accessible. Anyone with a new idea, a new method or procedure, could get a hearing and was encouraged to come up with a specific project to develop his theory. [He] frequently sat in on faculty lectures and listened in on the discussions, getting a feel for students and instructors. As he came to know the faculty, he gradually made changes. By the end of his first year he had changed the heads of the sections of the academic department, with marked improvement in several instances. He waited until he could get Lieutenant Colonel Joseph W. (Vinegar Joe) Stilwell to head Tactics. Then he shocked the infantrymen at Benning, and demonstrated his unorthodox approach, by selecting a medical officer, Major Morrison S. Stayer, who had a talent for administration, to take over Logistics. To lead Weapons, Marshall lifted Omar Bradley from the ranks of Tactics."

One of the assignments given to Collins was a review of the infantry close-order drill system that had been in use since the Civil War. Although his recommendations for streamlining the system were turned down by the army, they would be adopted when Marshall became chief of staff in 1939 and, as Collins noted, "saved hundreds of thousands of hours training soldiers in World War II."

After four years at Benning, Collins received orders to report to the Command and General Staff School at Fort Leavenworth, Kansas, as a student. He arrived on August 29, 1931. With a two-year program, the school had been designed to give students, mostly captains and majors, tactical training with units of combined arms that included infantry, artillery, tanks, engineers, and supporting aircraft, so that someday they might be competent to command a division, and meanwhile be qualified to serve on the general staff of a division or higher unit.

Collins noted, "Having no troops available for practical test-ing and training, the school was forced to rely on theoretical map problems. The situations ran the gamut of attack and defense, with differing opposing forces, and included problems in pursuit of a defeated enemy, withdrawals, and special operations such as river crossings and amphibious landings on hostile shores."

After four years at Benning under the innovative, experimen-tal testing and proving atmosphere created by Marshall, Collins found instruction at Leavenworth stereotyped. He believed this was done deliberately, particularly in staff exercises, because the army had little experience in large-scale operations between the Civil War and World War I and authorities evidently wanted to establish a pattern for staff functions dealing with personnel, logistics, intelligence, and operations. This would simplify the training of large numbers of officers, most of whom in a time of war would have to come from the National Guard and Reserves.

The second year at the school was devoted chiefly to logistics of large units, corps, armies, and groups of armies. Because most of this was new to Collins, he found logistics fascinating and the instruction first-rate. "For the Army as a whole," he wrote, "the courses at the Command and General Staff School were probably the most important in the system of military education, and were to prove invaluable in World War II. It was at Leavenworth that Eisenhower and Bradley and most of our senior commanders in that war, few of whom had ever commanded a combat unit larger than a battalion, learned the techniques of large units."

Near the end of his second year he was called to the office of the commandant and wondered what he had done wrong. The commandant asked him to be seated and said that he had been following Collins's academic work and had decided to present a request to the War Department asking that Collins be detailed as an instructor.

Disappointed, Collins replied, "General, I have been teach-ing or being taught for twelve consecutive years at West Point,

Benning, Sill, and Leavenworth. I am afraid if I were to remain here as an instructor for four more years I would lose any practical ability I might have."

Thumping his desk, the commandant exclaimed, "By God, Collins, you are right!"

The result was a transfer to the Philippines.

Looking back on the dozen years he spent either as an instructor or student, retired Lieutenant General Collins told a seminar in 1983 at the Command and General Staff School, "I am a great believer in the Army school system. The thing that made the Army [of World War II] a success was this school system. If it weren't for the Army school system I don't know what in the world we would have done."

With a month's leave, Collins and his family drove from Kansas to the West Coast and visited Gladys's brother and his family in Seattle, Washington. After arriving in San Francisco to board the army transport *Grant*, they departed on a three-week voyage to the Philippines on August 4, 1933, for the beginning of his first overseas assignment since his tour of duty in France. During a stopover in Hawaii, Collins accepted an invitation from a classmate at West Point for an aerial tour of the islands. "As the sole passenger," he recalled, "I rode with the pilot in the cockpit, which afforded a clear view of islands from Oahu to Hawaii. It was a gorgeous day. I was fascinated with the infinite variety of sapphire and emerald coloring of the water along the reefs which lined the shore below us, and the varying shades of green of the island jungles, waving palm trees and fields of sugar cane, as they reflected the bright sunlight." Eight years later, he would see Pearl Harbor in ruins.

Continuing across the Pacific on the *Grant*, he arrived in Manila Bay on the morning of August 26, 1933, and sailed past the island of Corregidor and the Bataan peninsula to begin a three-year assignment with the Philippine Division. With ample time off, he made trips to China and Japan at a time when the Japanese were expanding their Asian empire by invading Korea and Manchuria. Meanwhile, Adolf Hitler's Nazis were consolidating their power in Germany and rapidly building an army, navy, and air force in violation of the terms of the agreements that had ended the First World War.

When Collins arrived in the Philippines, he found that the American forces had been reduced to a single understrength division. It consisted of the Twenty-third Brigade and service troops, stationed at Fort William McKinley on the southern outskirts of Manila; the Twenty-fourth Field Artillery Regiment at Fort Stotsenberg, about fifty miles north of Manila; a separate Twenty-sixth Cavalry Regiment, also at Stotsenberg; the Thirty-first Infantry, a U.S. Regular Army regiment in Manila; and Coast Artillery units manning the fortifications on Corregidor and adjacent small islands guarding the entrance to Manila Bay. Except for the Thirty-first Infantry, these units consisted of native Filipino volunteers, called Philippine Scouts, with an officer corps that was a mixture of Americans and Filipinos. Although they were fine, well-disciplined, loyal troops, they would be incapable of resisting a Japanese invasion.

As was inevitable with troops in peacetime, Collins observed, the combat training in the Philippine Division and defense planning had slackened. Training had been allowed to take second place to the administration and maintenance of barracks, roads, and facilities at posts, camps, and stations. The troops were forced to spend half their time performing these essential chores with consequent deterioration of their readiness for combat.

Should there be a Japanese attack on the islands, a War Department plan to defend the Philippines, with the code name Orange, anticipated that the main attack would be launched across the beaches of Lingayen Gulf, north of Manila, with a secondary landing to the south or southeast of Manila Bay. The plan estimated that the Japanese would attack the islands with a minimum of four divisions, supported by strong naval forces. It also recognized that the American forces then located in the Philippines could not be reinforced from Hawaii or the United States in less than forty-five days and might require six months. Under these woeful circumstances, while the basic plans of the department and the Philippine Division called for the division to meet the enemy at the beaches and prevent his landing, a much more realistic auxiliary plan provided for delaying to the maximum practicable extent the advance of the enemy from his landing beaches until the division was forced to withdraw to the Bataan peninsula, covering Corregidor and the sea entrance to Manila Bay. Bataan was to be held until the arrival of reinforcements. But details of these plans had not been worked out on the ground or tested in field maneuvers, for which funds had never been provided by the War Department or Congress.

A first step to change this situation, Collins noted, was taken in exercises held in January 1934. Because it was too late to make any major changes in the program, the plan for the exercises called simply for the movement of the Twenty-third Brigade and other elements of the Philippine Division by barges across Manila Bay to Bataan.

"Those of us who worked on plans for the defense of the islands," Collins recorded in his autobiography, "had no illusions as to the adequacy of our planning, or the ability of the forces available to make these plans effective."

General Cortland Parker, the department commander, wrote on February 28, 1934, to General Douglas MacArthur, then chief of staff of the army, pointing out the inadequacy of the army and navy forces allotted to the defense of the Philippines. Parker warned, "There is no possibility of stopping an Orange invasion with the forces that will be available in the extremely short period of preparation." Asserting that strategy depended directly on national policy, he continued, "When this national policy is lacking for a given situation there can be no strategy. Under existing conditions, a crisis will have to be met by the Army and Navy as has always been the case in our past history, by improvisation instead of the preparation which a definite policy invariably assures."

Eight months after Collins ended his tour of duty and left the Philippines on March 22, 1935, responsibility for the defense of the islands passed into the hands of General Douglas Mac-Arthur. Leaving the post of U.S. Army chief of staff in 1935, he was appointed military advisor to the government of the Philippines and brought with him as his chief of staff Major Dwight D. Eisenhower. When the Japanese attacked the Philippines in December 1941, Eisenhower was back in the United States and in charge of planning for the inevitable conflict in the War Department, while MacArthur and his small force of Americans and Filipinos eventually fell back to Bataan. Using the plans devised by Collins and others, they finally retreated to the island of Corregidor in Manila Bay.

After MacArthur was personally ordered by President Franklin D. Roosevelt to leave the embattled but ultimately inadequate Corregidor fortress, with a pledge to return with a liberating force, the remaining defenders made a last valiant stand against overwhelming Japanese forces. Under command of General Jonathan Wainwright, with whom Collins had served briefly in France, they were forced to capitulate and many died from exhaustion or wounds or were massacred by the Japanese in what became infamous as the Bataan Death March. "It was a source of great satisfaction to me, as I read the dispatches of the fighting on Bataan," wrote Collins in his memoirs, "that our work was of some help to the gallant men who fought there."

After completing his service in the Philippines, Collins and his wife visited China, Japan, Siam, Indochina, and Cambodia en route to the United States. Hoping to be assigned to the Army War College, Collins was disappointed to learn that his name was not on the list, but was assured that he'd be appointed to the next class. In the meantime, he was to attend the Army Industrial College in Washington, D.C. Established in 1924 to teach officers the intricacies of coordination between civilian industries and the military when mobilizing for war and the complexities of supplying materials in wartime, it was located in the old Munitions Building on Constitution Avenue. It offered lectures by the foremost leaders of American industry and classes in supply and cost and management control. As the course neared its end, Collins had so excelled in every aspect of the training that he again found himself being asked to stay on as an instructor. He explained that he preferred to attend the War College. The desired appointment came in the fall of 1937.

Settled with Gladys and the three children in a rented house on Thirty-fifth Place in northwest Washington, he commuted to the War College at Fort Humphreys (later Fort McNair) on the Potomac River. In a nine-month course, the program covered political and economic aspects as well as the military considerations involved in wartime mobilization, military intelligence, command relations between the army and navy, coordination with wartime allies, and strategic planning for war and national emergencies. At the end of the course, he was again asked to stay on as an instructor and accepted the offer.

In his second year of teaching, two events on the same day changed the course of his life. On September 1, 1939, Hitler sent his army and air force smashing across the Polish border, and George C. Marshall took office as army chief of staff. When Britain and France issued an ultimatum that if the Germans did not withdraw by September 3, they would declare war on Germany, Hitler ignored the demand and the Second World War began.

A few days later, Collins received a phone call from the War Department. Lieutenant Colonel Orlando P. Ward of the General Staff told him to get out the revised drill regulations Collins had produced at Marshall's request at Fort Benning, which had been turned down by the War Department at the time.

"He wants to put them into effect without delay," Ward continued. "Check them over again and submit them directly to this office."

Within weeks, the drill regulations were made mandatory and were used to train millions of soldiers throughout and after World War II.

After Congress authorized expansion of the size of the army for possible American entry into the war, Marshall directed its reorganization. To deal with an urgent need for a cadre of officers to train and command them, he ordered suspension of the Command and General Staff School and closing of the War College. The result for Collins was assignment in June 1940 to the secretariat of the General Staff in Marshall's office. Among others on the staff that Collins described (in one of the great understatements of the entire war) as a "high-caliber group" were Omar Bradley, Walter Bedell Smith (known as "Beetle," and later chief aide to Eisenhower), and Maxwell Taylor. Along with the assignment, Collins received temporary promotion to the rank of lieutenant colonel.

In December 1940, Colonel Ward informed Collins that Marshall had instructed Ward to have Collins permanently assigned to the General Staff. Collins asked to speak to Marshall about this before any orders were issued. At the meeting, Collins stated that if war came, he did not wish to be stuck in a staff job, but wanted a combat command.

Marshall replied, "All right, Collins, I will let you go."

A few days later, Marshall told Collins that he (Marshall) had recommended Collins for the post of chief of staff to General Frederick Smith in the organization of three National Guard units into a new army group, designated the Seventh Corps, under Lieutenant General Ben Lear, commander of the Second Army, based in Tennessee. Collins and Smith departed Washington for Memphis on January 3, 1941. Consisting of the Twenty-seventh Division of the New York National Guard, the Thirty-fifth Division of the Kansas, Missouri, and Nebraska National Guard, and the Thirty-third Division of the Illinois National Guard, the new Seventh Corps would be based at Birmingham, Alabama. With headquarters established in a new office building in a suburb of the smoky city of steel mills and coal mines, Collins found a spacious house above the smoke on a mountain slope nearby and brought Gladys and the children down from Washington.

Training of the new corps began at nearby Fort McClellan and culminated in three maneuvers. The first of these was held in Tennessee in June 1941, followed by an exercise in Arkansas in August. The largest, in Louisiana, in September 1941 was designed to test the readiness of the U.S. Army for full-scale warfare. Under the overall command of General Leslie McNair and Collins's West Point classmate Lieutenant General Mark W. Clark, the Louisiana maneuvers were to be the largest ever held and consisted of a free, two-sided exercise pitting the Second Army, under General Ben Lear, and the Third Army, under Lieutenant General Walter E. Krueger, supported by more than one thousand airplanes and the first use of paratroopers. Another first was to be a test of the army's experimental armored corps consisting of the First and Second Armored Divisions commanded by Major General George S. Patton. In the same experimental category as the use of tanks was the employment of three of the newly organized "triangular" infantry divisions of the Regular Army, operating alongside four regiments made up of divisions of the National Guard. A fair number of antitank units, some experimental, were available for the first time, as was a supply of dummy antitank mines. The troops would total almost 400,000 men. In an attempt to improve the assessment of the effects of aerial bombardment and armored, artillery, and infantry fire, General Headquarters (GHQ) had prepared a new Umpire's Manual, and umpires had been trained. In the area chosen there would be room for maneuvers off the roads, and funds to meet any claims for damages to fences and crops, so as to eliminate most excuses for troops remaining road-bound in the face of attacks from the air.

"Along with all other participants," Collins wrote, "the VII Corps looked forward to an interesting fortnight in the field. We were not disappointed. GHQ had planned the exercises in two phases. During the first period, the Second Army was to move southwesterly from the vicinity of Shreveport and engage the Third Army advancing from the Texas-Louisiana border west of New Orleans. Depending on how this action developed, the second phase was to require the Third Army to drive the Lear forces back north and capture Shreveport by the end of the maneuver period on September 28."

News of the planned maneuvers stirred intense public interest. As the press descended on Louisiana, reporters looked for a winner between Lear and Krueger, both of whom had come up from the ranks of the army and had reputations of being tough competitors. The participation of an armored corps under Patton, who had already become a popular swashbuckling figure, further whetted the interest of the newsmen.

"These objectives were not intended by General McNair," noted Collins, "who was more interested in gauging the progress of the troops in their training, the development of skills in such difficult operations as river crossing, and their ability not only to exploit but to counter armored forces, and to meet the threat of aerial attacks."

At the opening gun the Second Army was northeast of the Red River near Alexandria, with the Third Army some distance to the south and southwest. Missions assigned to the two armies required each of them to attack. The Third Army had no way of knowing the intentions of its opponent but evidently expected to find it in a defensive position north of the Red River. Lear decided to hold the north bank of the Red River with a light covering force and cross the bulk of his army to the south side so as to position it on the left flank of the Third Army as the latter prepared to attack north across the river. The crossings were not immediately discovered by the Third Army. Consequently, the Second Army was favorably positioned to strike the left flank of the Third Army as it was crossing, or preparing to cross, the river. For some reason Collins was unable to fathom, Lear did not launch his attack at once. The Third Army was able to regroup, change its front so as to checkmate the Second Army, and then, with its greater strength, force Lear's army to withdraw.

For the second phase of the exercises, the two armies were reconstituted by GHQ. One of the chief interests of GHQ in this phase was to test the ability of the antitank weapons to neutralize armor. The mission assigned the Second Army was to cover Shreveport. The heavily wooded terrain, crisscrossed by swampy tributaries of the Red River, was not well suited for tank operations. It favored antitank mines and weapons, including aircraft, in support of the delaying positions in back of the many streams. Not even Patton with his Second Armored Division could make a breakthrough, though the Third Army gradually drove the Second back.

"If the maneuver had been allowed to continue past its planned termination date on September 28," noted Collins, "Shreveport would have been captured by the more powerful Third Army. But the exaggerated notion of the invulnerability of armor was dissipated."

When more than two hundred reporters and photographers converged for the war games, many were veterans of genuine combat, including United Press's Richard C. Hottelet, fresh from a German prison, Leon Kay, who saw the Nazi invasions of the Low Countries in 1940 and the Balkans, and CBS's Eric Sevareid, who had been in London during German air raids. Showing a cordial personality and public relations savvy as a commander that would capture the affection of war correspondents and through their stories introduce "Ike" to the American people,

Eisenhower converted his tent into a kind of resort for reporters covering the maneuvers and amused them with unprintable stories about New Orleans whores with whom some of his troops had sported. The columnist and radio commentator Drew Pearson in his "Washington Merry-Go-Round" said in his account of the maneuvers that credit for the war games strategy that routed the Second Army belonged to Colonel Eisenhower.

Evaluating the Louisiana field exercises in his autobiography, Collins noted that they had afforded highly valuable training, particularly for the staffs and commanders of the larger units, from divisions up to armies. He wrote, "Many of us were participating in large-scale, free, two-sided maneuvers for the first time under tactical situations requiring coordination of infantry and armor, air and ground forces, in attack and defense. Experience was gained in two of the most difficult military operations, withdrawals and river crossings, requiring coordination between engineer and ground troops in building and demolition of bridges, erection of tank obstacles, and the laying and clearing of minefields. Advantage was taken of the opportunity to experiment with different combinations of infantry, armor, and antitank units in corps and armies. The new triangular divisions proved more flexible and manageable than the square divisions, leading ultimately to the triangular organization for both the Regular Army and National Guard."

This logistical experience gained by all units participating in the Louisiana exercises was also of value at least equal to tactical and organizational gains. For the first time in any field maneuvers, a full-scale logistical framework was provided, including quartermaster, engineer, signal, ordnance, and medical troops and supplies.

This offered a unique opportunity in a time of peace to measure the tremendous task of moving, feeding, and providing shelter and medical care for 400,000 men in the field.

The maneuvers also sorted out the best and the least capable leaders in the officer corps, especially in the upper echelons. Among the senior men who came to the fore were Patton, already marked for high command by General Marshall, and Eisenhower, who was the chief of staff of the Third Army. Always highly regarded within the army, he was then almost unheard of outside it. Other stars were McNair and Clark.

Exhilarated by taking part in the Louisiana maneuvers and generally satisfied with the performance of his Seventh Corps, Collins returned to Alabama to contemplate the lessons learned and resume his duties. Although President Roosevelt repeatedly assured the people of the United States that he had no intention of taking the country to war, Collins was convinced that American involvement was inevitable. By the autumn of 1941, Hitler had taken all of Europe and invaded the Soviet Union, leaving Britain to stand alone while expecting a German invasion and enduring continual bombing raids on London by the German air force. In the Far East, Japan continued its aggressive expansion, determined to create what its militant leaders called a greater co-prosperity sphere by dominating the entire Pacific. At the same time, Japanese diplomats were meeting in Washington with U.S. State Department officials to discuss increasing tensions in American-Japanese relations.

On Sunday, December 7, 1941, Collins was changing clothes at home after a round of golf at the Mountain Brook country club when he heard a radio bulletin that Japanese planes had attacked the U.S. Pacific Fleet and other military and air force installations at Pearl Harbor, Hawaii. After shouting the news to Gladys downstairs, he added, "This means war." The next day, they listened to a radio broadcast of President Roosevelt informing Congress that since the dastardly surprise attack a state of war existed between the United States and Japan. The president vowed that the United States would gain an inevitable triumph. A day after the speech, Adolf Hitler joined Germany's ally Japan by declaring war on the United States.

On December 12, Mark Clark phoned Collins and told him that the Seventh Corps was to move immediately to the West Coast to provide a defense of Northern California under the command of General John L. DeWitt. That evening, Collins and Gladys made plans for the family to join him in California when he found a place to live and arranged schooling for the children. The next morning, he kissed Gladys and the children good-bye. He would not see them again for two years.

CHAPTER TWO

I AM IT

Boarding a small airplane with the commander of the Seventh Corps, General Robert C. Richardson, Jr., Collins headed west. They were forced to land in Oklahoma City by rough weather that extended to California, but continued the trip by train and upon arrival in San Francisco headed south to San Jose to make arrangements to establish the Seventh Corps headquarters there. After checking into a hotel, Collins and Richardson went to the San Jose armory to meet Major General Isaac D. White, commander of the Seventh Division. As the two generals conferred, Collins received a telephone call from the army's West Coast headquarters at the Presidio in San Francisco.

Breathless with excitement, Colonel James J. Bradley, chief of staff to General DeWitt, exclaimed, "Joe, pack up your bags at once and return to San Francisco. You are relieved as chief of staff of the Seventh Corps and appointed chief of staff of the Hawaiian Department under General Delos Emmons. He is here now. You are to report to him by six o'clock and will probably fly to Hawaii tonight."

Upon arrival at the Presidio, Collins learned that the abrupt

★   *37*   ★

change in plan was the result of the death of Major General Herbert A. Dargue, whose plane crashed in stormy weather on his way to Los Angeles for assignment to Hawaii to take command of the armed forces in the islands. Forced to reshuffle his plans, General Marshall chose General Emmons to replace him, with Collins as his chief of staff. After Collins and Emmons met for the first time and dined in the officers' club at Hamilton Field, they boarded a B-24 bomber that evening and took off for Hawaii. Arriving on the morning of December 17, 1941, they saw the devastation wreaked on Pearl Harbor, on the Pacific Fleet, the air force at Hickam Field, and the Ford Island naval base.

Describing Emmons as "an excellent choice" to take over in Hawaii because of his long army service and familiarity with Hawaii, having served there as air officer from 1934 to 1936, Collins wrote of his new boss, "Emmons had an astute, keen mind, was self-contained, sure of himself without being cocky, and always gave the impression of knowing what he wanted to do and how to do it, though he had no exaggerated idea of his own ability. He was easy to work with and we got along handsomely."

Stating that he was not interested in routine administrative work, Emmons told Collins to handle the staff and manage the business of the headquarters as he saw fit. Emmons would make all major decisions and determine questions of policy. As chief of staff, Collins was also to be coordinator of the ground defenses of the islands and supervise the operations of two Hawaiian National Guard regiments.

Promoted to the rank of brigadier general in February 1942, he continued as chief of staff to Emmons. On that day, General Eisenhower, now head of the War Plans Division of the War Department, phoned Emmons to politely inquire if Collins could be spared to replace Major General Maxwell Murray as commander of the Twenty-fifth Division. Emmons concurred and suggested that with the new assignment Collins be promoted to major general. Orders assigning Collins to the combat command arrived on

May 6. On the same day, Collins heard a radio report that the Japanese had announced that on the following day General Jonathan Wainwright would broadcast the surrender of the American and Filipino troops that had been holding out for six months against an overwhelming Japanese force on Corregidor. Anxious to verify the authenticity of the voice on the broadcast, the War Department asked Collins if there was anyone in the Hawaiian Department who knew Wainwright well enough to identify his voice. Having served in France as Wainwright's assistant, Collins certified that it was Wainwright. When he'd done so, he wept.

Consisting of the Twenty-seventh Infantry, called "the Wolf Hounds," the Thirty-fifth Infantry, and the 161st National Guard Infantry Regiment, the division engaged in six months of intensive training. Based on Collins's belief that the division would soon be ordered to leave Hawaii for a combat assignment, the preparation consisted of field exercises with close air support and amphibious landings through the heavy surf on the Waiana beaches using landing craft borrowed from the navy and marines. With no ships from which to practice debarking, the men climbed down barracks walls carrying full equipment packs on their backs.

Concerns that the Twenty-fifth Division might be required to repel a Japanese invasion of the Hawaiian Islands were allayed by the defeat of a Japanese attack on Midway Island by the U.S. Navy in June in which four Japanese aircraft carriers were sunk, leaving the Imperial Japanese Navy crippled and in retreat. In a battle that was a turning point in the Pacific war, the American victory paved the way for the United States to go on the offensive, beginning with a U.S. Marine Corps assault to drive Japanese forces from the tiny island of Guadalcanal.

As Collins hoped, orders came from the War Department in late October 1942 that transferred the Twenty-fifth Division to General Douglas MacArthur's Southwest Pacific theater. Upon receipt of the orders, Collins was called to a meeting

with the commander of the Central Pacific area, Admiral
Chester W. Nimitz. After congratulating Collins on his new
assignment, Nimitz said, "Collins, you may think you are going
to MacArthur's command, but I want to warn you that I am not
going to let you get away. You have too fine a division to lose from
this theater. The First Marines will soon be needing relief on
Guadalcanal, so don't be surprised if your orders are changed
while you are en route to Australia."

With almost bewildering speed in a period of months, Collins
had gone from being an instructor at the War College as a lieutenant colonel to chief of staff of the Seventh Corps in Northern
California as a colonel, then to chief of staff of the Hawaiian Department as a brigadier general. Now he was a major general in
command of the Twenty-fifth Division with orders to sail for
Australia to join MacArthur's Southwest Pacific command, with
the likelihood voiced by Nimitz that orders could be changed to
divert the division to Guadalcanal to relieve the marines who had
landed on the island on August 1, 1942.

After the Japanese moved into the Solomon Islands in March
1942, their purpose in taking Guadalcanal was to build an airfield
near the mouth of the Lunga River and solidify a base on the island as part of their plan to conquer Australia and New Zealand
and gain dominance of the South Pacific. To stop the Japanese
advance, the U.S. Joint Chiefs of Staff deployed the marines and
on August 1, the First Battalion, Fifth Marines, quickly followed
by the Third Battalion, landed in complete surprise to the Japanese at Lunga Point and established a beachhead without opposition. Their objective was to seize the nearly complete airfield at
Lunga Point and an anchorage at nearby Tulagi. Action ashore
went well, and Japan's initial aerial response was costly and un-
productive. But two days after the landings, the U.S. and Austra-
lian fleets were dealt a serious defeat in the Battle of Savo Island.
A lengthy struggle followed, with its focus the Lunga Point airfield that the marines had taken and renamed Henderson Field.

Although it was regularly bombed and shelled, planes were still able to fly, ensuring that Japanese efforts to build and maintain ground forces were prohibitively expensive. Ashore, there was hard fighting in the heat of dense jungles, with the Americans aided by local inhabitants discovering the weaknesses of Japanese ground combat doctrine.

At sea, the campaign featured two major battles between aircraft carriers that were more costly to the Americans than to the Japanese and many submarine and air-sea actions that gave the Allies an advantage. Inside and just outside Tulagi, five significant surface battles and a few skirmishes proved U.S. superiority over Japan's navy. Meanwhile the ground campaign would remain in doubt for nearly four months.

Sailing from Hawaii in three convoys beginning on November 25, 1942, Collins's Twenty-fifth Division was well under way on November 30 when an order was received from the Joint Chiefs of Staff to proceed not to Australia and MacArthur's command but to Noumea, New Caledonia, eight hundred miles to the north, to prepare to relieve the First Marine Division on Guadalcanal.

Reinforced in the autumn by two regiments of the recently formed U.S. Army Americal Division under the command of Major General Alexander "Sandy" Patch, the Americans had extended their bridgehead east and west, but at a cost of more than twenty-seven hundred casualties, which in the eyes of the Joint Chiefs of Staff in December 1942 had earned the marines respite and relief.

Although Americans on the home front read accounts in newspapers or listened to reports on the radio of the hard fighting on Guadalcanal, the War Department kept the details of the battles in the jungles and the full extent of the toll on the marines secret.

When Collins and his division anchored in Noumea's harbor on December 10, he reported to Admiral William F. Halsey. Welcomed with a grin and hearty handshake from the bushy-browed commander of the South Pacific area, whose guff manner had earned him the nickname "Bull," Collins was shaken by Halsey's forceful assertion that instead of a three-day stopover that Collins requested, he and his men were to sail to Guadalcanal the next morning. That evening, Collins dined with Halsey and the commander of the marines on Guadalcanal, Major General A. Archer Vandegrift, who was on his way to Australia in advance of the marines. Vandegrift presented a somber picture of conditions on the island and warned Collins of a tough fight ahead. To see for himself and prepare for the arrival of his troops on December 17, Collins and a small staff flew to Guadalcanal and met with General Patch.

Born at Fort Huachuca, Arizona, on November 23, 1889, he was the son of Colonel Alexander M. Patch. Although his father had been a cavalryman and Patch learned to love horses and rode expertly, Patch chose the infantry. A West Point graduate a year before Collins, he joined the Cadet Corps, struggled to make good grades, shone as a pole-vaulter for the track team, boxed, made wry, quiet wisecracks about himself, and picked up the nickname "Sandy."

For his class's Twenty Year Book in 1933, Patch wrote a story entitled "How I Became a Hero." Describing himself as an eager young captain who wanted desperately to be a single, lone, magnificent sort of hero, he said not one word about his World War I record of combat on the Aisne and Marne, at Saint-Mihiel, and in the Meuse-Argonne. After the war, he taught recruits at Fort Bragg, machine-gun operations at Fort Benning, and military science at Staunton Military Academy. After attending the Command and General Staff School, he was graduated from the Army War College. Sent by General Marshall to the French island of New Caledonia in the Pacific after Pearl Harbor, he took command of diverse units originally on their way to the Philippines and forged a division that he named the Americal [America-

Caledonia] Division for the purpose of relieving the marines on Guadalcanal and finishing the job of clearing the Japanese from the island.

Described as being capable of hot impatience, he also exhibited a calmness while handling problems that one observer called "deliberation that nothing could hurry." A war correspondent depicted a commander with a gaunt, hard face with deep worry lines who mixed easily with his troops and chatted with them while rolling a cigarette from a sack of Bull Durham.

As Patch invited Collins and his staff into his underground command post at the edge of Henderson Field, an air-raid alert sounded. Unruffled, Patch said, "Don't let that disturb you, Collins. Happens all the time."

As overall commander of U.S. forces on Guadalcanal, with orders from Halsey to "eliminate all Japanese forces" on the island, Patch would have under him the Americal Division, Collins's Twenty-fifth Division, and the Second Marine Division, due to land at the same time as the Twenty-fifth (January 4, 1943). The Twenty-fifth's mission was to relieve the 132nd Infantry Division on Mount Austen and seize and hold a line to the west in preparation for a coordinated attack designed to satisfy Halsey's order to eliminate the Japanese from Guadalcanal.

In a series of reconnaissance flights over the terrain, Collins recognized that the rough, broken ground would have a dominating influence on the plan of attack and make supply and communication extremely difficult. Steep slopes above the Lunga River south of Mount Austen limited operations in that direction, while three forks of the Matanikau River divided the division's zone of action into three areas. These consisted of Mount Austen, a region between the southeast and southwest forks that became know as the Sea Horse because of its shape, and a twisting ridge between the southeast and southwest forks that someone decided looked like a galloping horse and so named it.

Rising fifteen hundred feet, Mount Austen overlooked Henderson Field and the landing beaches and provided observation over approaches to Guadalcanal from the north. The Japanese were dug in in an area that became known as the Gifu Point that would have to be eliminated to ensure envelopment of the south flank of the Japanese positions. The Sea Horse was like an island bounded by the southeast and southwest forks of the Matanikau and their tributaries.

"To have attacked it from the east," Collins wrote, "would have required frontal movements in and out of the southeast fork, over its steep, jungle slopes. Instead, it would have to be taken from the south, in connection with a southern envelopment. A similar terrain analysis applied to the Galloping Horse area in the northeast part of the division's zone. To avoid a frontal attack across the southwest fork of the Matanikau it would be necessary to attack from the north by crossing the northwest fork near its junction with the main stream of the Matanikau."

These movements against Mount Austen, the Sea Horse, and the Galloping Horse would leave a wide gap on the northwest slope of Austen, which would afford excellent positions for placing artillery. Deciding not to launch frontal attacks but to go after the open ridges in flanking maneuvers and keep out of the low jungle area, Collins believed that if Mount Austen could be cleared and the Sea Horse and Galloping Horse ridges taken, his force could trap the Japanese in the pocketed valleys of the Matanikau, where they would be forced to surrender or be destroyed by artillery and mortar fire, with minimum losses of American lives. This analysis dictated an attack by the Twenty-fifth Division with two regiments abreast and a third in reserve.

In Collins's first field order, the Thirty-fifth Infantry was to reduce the Gifu strongpoint, envelop the south flank of Mount Austen, seize the Sea Horse by attack from the south, then continue the attack to the west. The Twenty-seventh Infantry was to pass through positions of the Eighth Marine Regiment and a reconnaissance squadron of the Americal Division, seize the Galloping Horse ridges, and clear the area north of the southwest fork of the Matanikau. The 161st Infantry was to assemble in a central position as division reserve. The Third Battalion, 182nd Infantry, attached to the Twenty-fifth Division, was to occupy an area in the gap between the Thirty-fifth and Twenty-seventh regiments to guard their flanks and cover the division artillery.

With the division poised to launch its first attack on January 10, 1943, Collins went to his command post on a hill designated No. 49, which offered a clear view of the open to the west to Hills 97, 98, and 99. With thirty years in the army, this would be his first experience in combat.

After a thirty-minute artillery preparation, the Twenty-seventh Infantry jumped off with two battalions abreast, the First Battalion (under Lieutenant Colonel Claude Jurney) on the right, with the mission of seizing Hill 57, and the Third Battalion (led by Lieutenant Colonel George E. Bush) on the left, for Hill 52. The Second Battalion (under Lieutenant Colonel Herbert V. Mitchell), in reserve, was to relieve elements of the Second Marine Division on Hill 55.

"Following the artillery preparation," Collins recorded, "P-39 fighters from the Thirteenth Air Force and Marine dive bombers dropped Navy depth charges on the area. The combined effect on the Japanese in front of the First Battalion, Twenty-seventh Infantry, was overwhelming. Whereas the Eighth Marines had encountered stiff resistance in the water hole, the First Battalion met almost no opposition in breaking through to the north slopes of Hill 57."

An army historian noted that this was not the case with the Third Battalion on the left. Hill 52, the initial objective of the battalion, was actually a ridge athwart the shoulders of the Galloping Horse, facing northeast. The grass that normally covered the entire horse had been burned off by artillery fire, affording the Japanese, dug in on the reverse slope of Hill 52, open fields of fire covering all approaches to the hill. Colonel Bush, jumping off from Hill 54, decided to make an attack with Companies I and L abreast in a double envelopment of Hill 52. Halted by deadly cross fire, the battalion had to throw in Company K, under the cover of woods on the right of Company I, to envelop Hill 52 from the north. Preceded by artillery and aerial bombardment in midafternoon, Company K drove the Japanese off Hill 52 by late afternoon and consolidated the position for the night.

The following morning, the Third Battalion resumed the attack but made little headway, while taking casualties throughout the day. Men were exhausted from the continuous uphill fighting, the oppressive heat, and lack of water. The Galloping Horse ridges were devoid of water, which had to be hauled forward with the rations under cover of darkness. Colonel McCulloch decided to halt the attack for the night and pass the Second Battalion through the Third on January 12.

"I had gone up to Hill 50 on the eleventh and had discussed the situation with Colonel Bush," Collins wrote, "and while I was talking with him, men of Mitchell's Battalion in reserve on Hill 50 began firing indiscriminately into the woods to their right, claiming that they were receiving fire from snipers in the trees. Bullets were clipping through the tops near us, but I was convinced that this fire was coming from Colonel Jurney's battalion on Hill 57 to the northwest. Mitchell was finally able to stop the firing, and the 'Jap' fire ceased. After, I had the regimental and battalion commanders pass the word among the men that I would pay ten dollars to any man who could prove he had shot down a Japanese firing from up in a tree. The offer cost me not a penny throughout my stay in the South Pacific, but it helped put down the silly claims of snipers in the treetops."

The Second Battalion, Twenty-seventh Infantry, relieved the Third Battalion on January 12 and renewed the attack at six thirty a.m., following an aerial bombardment and heavy artillery preparation. G Company was able to capture an area north of Hill 52 and established contact with the First Battalion on Hill 57, but F

Company, trying to outflank the next ridge west of Hill 52, was caught in the cross fire of machine guns from the ridge northeast of Hill 53. F Company was able to occupy the first ridge, but neither F nor E Company on its left was able to advance in the face of heavy fire. During this action Lieutenant Robert M. Exton was mortally wounded. To honor him, the ridge was named for him.

The determined Mitchell withdrew F Company from Exton Ridge and directed F to outflank it from the north, gaining a foothold, but a concealed enemy strongpoint stopped any further advance.

"Realizing the importance of the Second Battalion's attack," Collins wrote, "I joined Colonel Mitchell at his CP on Hill 52, where H Company had established its machine guns and 81mm mortars as a base of fire to support the attack. Meanwhile Mitchell had committed his reserve Company E to the left of F Company on Exton Ridge, from which it joined the attack of F Company. The two companies became intermingled. Captain Charles W. Davis, the battalion executive, in a rare display of bravery beyond the call of duty, volunteered to go forward to straighten out the companies and locate the strongpoint that was holding up their advance."

Collins watched breathlessly as Davis, running like a halfback, dodged back and forth to avoid the fire directed against him as he advanced over open ground. He made it to the ridge beyond Exton. After untangling Companies E and F, he scouted the Japanese strongpoint. Accompanied by Captain Paul K. Mellichamp, Collins's former aide on Oahu, and Lieutenant Weldon S. Sims, he crawled along the east side of the ridge until he was able to locate the enemy strongpoint. When Sims raised his head above a protecting ledge to confirm its location, he was shot. His companions pulled his body back but were unable to save him. They honored him by giving his name to the ridge where he was killed.

Davis and Mellichamp crawled back to F Company's position, from where Davis radioed for fire from the 81mm mortar platoon of H Company. No more than fifty yards separated Davis and Companies E and F from the Japanese. The mortar platoon leader, Sergeant Rex P. Henry, using the bandaged head of Lieutenant Exton as a reference point, coolly drew back his fire after an opening round well beyond Sims Ridge.

Captain Davis relayed his bearings to adjust the fire until shells, exploding on the crest of the ridge and its reverse slope, where the enemy was, showered Davis and the troops with dirt, rocks, and shell fragments but failed to destroy the strongpoint. Colonel Mitchell moved up to Sims Ridge under cover of this fire to take direct command. At this time his men had exhausted their drinking water and were on the verge of collapse. Mitchell had the companies organize for all-out defense against an expected counterattack. He and Davis remained overnight on Sims Ridge as they planned the next day's attack.

Collins returned to his CP by jeep and was back on Hill 52 early the next morning with Colonel McCulloch to see the windup of the attack, which had a dramatic effect. In a plan that Davis devised to break the stalemate, Mitchell took part of E Company down the east slope of Sims Ridge to the south end of the ridge and prepared to attack the ridge from the south, while Davis and a few volunteers crawled to within ten yards of the Japanese strongpoint, covered by mortar fire hitting just beyond them.

"At Davis's signal to the mortars to cease firing," Collins recalled, "his party and E Company under Mitchell charged the strongpoint. Davis jumped to his feet and fired one burst from his rifle, which jammed. He switched the rifle to his left hand, drew out his pistol and began shooting the startled Japanese in the strongpoint. While still firing, Davis waved his men forward with his rifle. Spurred on by his fearless example, they swarmed over the ridge and routed the defenders. As Davis led the charge he was in full view of us at the OP and most of the Second Battalion. His action had an electrifying effect on the battalion, which stormed over not only Sims Ridge but Hill 53, the last Japanese stronghold on the Galloping Horse, which seemed itself to be prancing in victory."

Colonel McCulloch and Collins went forward to Hill 53 to congratulate Mitchell on the victory of his battalion. They found him surrounded by his exultant soldiers. When Collins shook his hand and congratulated him, Mitchell replied with tears in his eyes, "It wasn't me, it was Davis and his men that did it."

Collins recommended Mitchell and his party of volunteers for the Distinguished Service Cross. Captain Davis received the Congressional Medal of Honor.

While the Twenty-seventh Infantry was distinguishing itself on the north flank, Collins noted, the Thirty-fifth Regiment had initiated the envelopment of the Japanese south flank. The Third Battalion led off at 6:35 a.m., January 10, along the watershed south of Mount Austen, without firing a shot or encountering the enemy. With no trail along the ridge, it was necessary for the leading company to slash through the jungle with machetes and bayonets. It was hard to gauge direction until sometime in the afternoon when patrols advancing ahead of the company found a trail crossing the ridge from the west, with a fork following the ridge toward Hill 43 and another dropping down into a deep ravine to the northeast. A Japanese supply party was seen halted on the upper trail and a bivouac area in a ravine. The Japanese were unaware of the approaching Third Battalion, which had come upon the supply line supporting Gifu and Japanese positions on the Sea Horse. When an attack was ordered to cut and block the Japanese supply line to the west, the Japanese were caught by surprise and wiped out.

Companies K and L advanced north with sporadic resistance to a knoll south of Hill 43. Realizing their plight, the Japanese in the ravine counterattacked to reopen the supply line but were driven back. By dark, the head of the ravine was secured by Company I, while Companies K and L dug in on a knoll five hundred yards south of Hill 43. Colonel James Leer's First Battalion closed up on the Third for the night. In the morning Mullen resumed the attack and by dark had control of the entire Sea Horse, including Hill 44.

Collins noted, "Encirclement of the Japanese in the southeast fork of the Matanikau was complete. When it became evident that the Third Battalion alone would capture the Sea Horse, Colonel McClure directed Leer to attack to seize the XIV Corps objective overlooking the southwest fork of the Matanikau. The First Battalion made slow progress through the heavy jungle on the twelfth but was pinned down about a thousand yards west of the jump-off. In the interim the Japanese in the ravine launched another counterattack but were beaten back. It was not until January 16, after machine guns and 81mm mortars had been brought forward to Hill 43 to join the artillery in support of Leer's Battalion, that it was able to overrun the last opposition on the high ground above the Matanikau."

When Collins arrived back at his command post at the end of the day, the artillery commander, Stanley Reinhart, was waiting for him as he got out of his jeep.

Furious, Reinhart declared, "General, I heard that you ordered my artillery to cease fire this afternoon. I'll have you understand that you don't do that to my artillery!"

"Look, Stanley," Collins replied, "it is not your artillery. It's mine as well. There is only one overall commander in this division and I am it. I command the infantry, the artillery, the engineers, the quartermaster, and the medicos."

Artillery preparation for the final assault on Gifu Point had been planned for the morning of the seventeenth but was held up until afternoon to allow an appeal to the defenders to surrender, spoken in Japanese over a loudspeaker by a psychological warfare specialist from the Fourteenth Corps. They were allowed time to consider, but none gave up. Two days of dogged fighting finally closed the ring around Gifu, but failed to break its tough shell until Collins borrowed three light tanks from the Second Marine Division. Two broke down on the steep climb up the hill but one made it to the top. Captain Teddy Deese of the Twenty-fifth Division's Reconnaissance Troop, and two of his men, volunteered to man the tank. Deese drove it, with a wedge of fifteen men to secure his flanks, into the Japanese position in front of G Company until the tank's 37mm gun was poking directly into the mouth of a machine-gun emplacement. One round knocked it out. Wheeling the tank around, he charged and destroyed eight more emplacements, forming a small but important salient. Darkness in the thick jungle closed in before this could be exploited.

That night about one hundred Japanese tried to break out of the trap that had closed around them. In a "banzai" charge, they threw grenades and fired automatic weapons, but the Americans opened up with machine guns and stopped them. When dawn broke, they found eighty-five bodies, including the Japanese commander. By nightfall Mount Austen was free of enemy troops. Reduction of the Gifu had cost the Second Battalion sixty-four men killed and forty-two wounded.

Destruction of the Gifu strongpoint had engaged five battalions of infantry and lasted over one month. Finally the last effective enemy force east of the Matanikau River had been eliminated, and the Thirty-fifth Infantry became the reserve of the Twenty-fifth Division, which was advancing rapidly to the west.

A January offensive by the Fourteenth Corps gained about three thousand yards of ground and a western line, running from the coast west to the southwest Matanikau fork, had been firmly established. The south flank, extending east to Mount Austen, was now secure. In the opinion of the corps commander, General Patch, Collins's Twenty-fifth Division had performed brilliantly. A citation dated March 7, 1943, stated, "It was largely through the sustained drive of the 25th Infantry Division that the last vestige of organized Japanese resistance on Guadalcanal was crushed and possession of this strategically important island, so vital to projected operations, finally wrested from the hands of the Japanese on 9 February 1943."

Stirred to wrath by the attack on Pearl Harbor, the mothers and fathers of the United States had sent their sons to an island they'd never heard of in the vastness of the Pacific Ocean to inflict defeat on the empire of Japan and begin a drive from one obscure island to the next, like a giant hopscotch game, until they reached Japan itself and ended the war.

The total cost of the Guadalcanal campaign to the American ground combat forces was 1,598 officers and enlisted men killed, 1,152 of them marines. The wounded totaled 4,709, and 2,799 of these were marines. Marine aviation casualties were 147 killed and 127 wounded. The Japanese in turn lost close to 25,000 men on Guadalcanal, about half of whom were killed in action. The rest succumbed to illness, wounds, and starvation. At sea, the comparative losses were about equal, with each side losing about the same number of fighting ships. The Japanese loss of two battleships, three carriers, twelve cruisers, and twenty-five destroyers was irreplaceable. The Allied ship losses, though costly, were not fatal; in essence, all ships lost were replaced. In the air, at least six hundred Japanese planes were shot down; even more costly was the death of twenty-three hundred experienced pilots and air crewmen. The Allied plane losses were less than half the enemy's number and the pilot and aircrew losses substantially lower.

"We struck at Guadalcanal to halt the advance of the Japanese," General Vandegrift said. "We did not know how strong he was, nor did we know his plans. We knew only that he was moving down the island chain and that he had to be stopped. . . . We needed combat to tell us how effective our training, our doctrines, and our weapons had been. We tested them against the enemy, and we found that they worked. From that moment in 1942, the tide turned, and the Japanese never again advanced."

A captured Japanese document stated, "It must be said that the success or failure in recapturing Guadalcanal Island, and the vital naval battle related to it, is the fork in the road which leads to victory for them or us."

"Having sent General Patch to do a tailoring job on Guadalcanal," said Halsey, "I am surprised and pleased at the speed with which he removed the enemy's pants to accomplish it."

Presenting the Medal of Honor to Vandegrift, President Roosevelt expressed the gratitude of the nation to all of the forces at Guadalcanal.

The men of the Twenty-fifth Division soon found themselves assigned to guarding beaches, as well as clearing them of a jumble of surplus equipment, ammunition, and other supplies that the marines and army units had no time to sort out and store before moving into combat. Collins was anxious to maintain the fighting edge they had honed in Hawaii and sharpened in fighting on Guadalcanal. After a series of critiques of the division's actions in the battle, he decided to get the troops back in fighting shape by resuming their combat training as soon as it became apparent the Japanese would not be able to mount a counteroffensive. With the approval of Major General Oscar W. Griswold, who succeeded Patch in April of 1943 in command of the Fourteenth Corps, he selected an area east of Koli Point as a combat range and conducted exercises that included firing all supporting weapons close to frontline troops, and with cooperation of air units on the island perfected the technique of close aerial support.

Health conditions on Guadalcanal proved almost as much a hindrance to operations as were the Japanese, Collins noted. The swampy streams were breeding grounds for the anopheles mosquito, which transmits malaria. Atabrine, or quinine, taken daily as a suppressant of the disease, proved not to be a preventative. All that was needed to receive the disease was a bite from an infected mosquito. Collins was infected within twenty-four hours of his arrival on the island. Confined to his screened tent rather than going to the hospital, he took thirty grains of Atabrine daily for a week, followed by thirty grains of quinine a day for a second week, then a lesser amount of another drug for a week. With the division back in trim, he took a three-week leave in New Zealand at an army rest center. Returning to Guadalcanal, he was presented with the Twenty-fifth Division's next challenge. Describing the situation in his autobiography, Collins wrote, "Having checked at Guadalcanal the Japanese advance toward Australia and New Zealand, the Allies in the south and southwest Pacific areas now sought to capture the Japanese air and naval base at Rabaul, on the Island of New Britain, in the Bismarck Archipelago. The prior capture of the airstrip of Munda on New Georgia was essential. But Major General Noboru Sasaki, the tough commander of Japanese army and Japanese navy forces in the New Georgia group of islands, which included Vella Lavella, Kolumbungara, Arundel, and a host of islets around the island of New Georgia, was determined to protect Munda."

Part of Operation Cartwheel, which envisioned relentlessly driving the Japanese back by "island hopping" through the South, Southwest, and Central Pacific all the way to Japan, the assault on New Georgia began on June 30, 1943, with a landing by the Fourth Marine Raider Division. At the outset of the campaign, Collins was told that the Twenty-fifth Division was to remain at Guadalcanal for possible use in an assault against the Japanese on the island of Bougainville. This plan changed after the Forty-third Division landed near Munda and became bogged down short of its objective. Grudgingly, Admiral Halsey gave the division to the Fourteenth Corps for duty on New Georgia. On August 1, 1943, Collins moved his headquarters to the island. When the airstrip at Munda was finally taken, he was ordered to employ the division to pursue the fleeing Japanese. After difficult going through jungles and swamps, they followed the enemy force to an area known as the Piru Plantation on the banks of a narrows separating New Georgia and Arundel Island. Driven from the plantation by the Twenty-seventh Infantry, the Japanese fled across the narrows, leaving New Georgia in American hands.

The fight for the island resulted in a popular song that gave the American people a glimpse of the battle for New Georgia and introduced a hero. On July 31, 1943, twenty-five-year-old, five-feet-two, 125-pound Private Rodger Young was a member of the 148th Infantry Regiment of the Thirty-seventh Division. When his squad was pinned down by a hidden Japanese machine-gun nest protecting the Munda airstrip, Young was wounded by the initial burst of fire. Spotting the location of the gun, he crept toward it while ignoring pleas and a direct order to stop. Firing his rifle to attract the fire of the enemy, he crept forward and was wounded a second time. When he was close enough, he began throwing hand grenades and was hit again and killed. His heroic efforts allowed his squad to make a withdrawal with no additional losses while inflicting casualties on the Japanese. Young was awarded the Congressional Medal of Honor. About a year later Private First Class Frank Loesser, an established songwriter, composed "The Ballad of Rodger Young." Asserting that "they got no time for glory in the infantry," it became an immediate hit.

Near the end of the New Georgia campaign, Collins was visited at his command post by Generals Millard F. "Miff" Harmon and Oscar W. Griswold and Colonel Godwin Ordway, a Collins friend who was an observer sent out by the War Department. Collins joked that in light of the number of observers being sent to the Pacific from Washington, it was about time someone was sent from the Pacific to observe the War Department, and added that his family happened to live in Washington and he hadn't seen them in two years.

With the New Georgia campaign completed, the Twenty-fifth Division was sent to New Zealand for rest, rehabilitation, and a period of retraining before receiving its next assignment to combat. Settled into the spacious country home loaned to the army by the Earl and Countess of Oxford and named Manurewa House, Collins looked for training areas, but he found that New Zealanders were reluctant to have their land and sparse forests subjected to the tramping of thousands of men and torn up by artillery practice. Returning to Manurewa House after a three-day search for a training area, he went through a stack of accumulated official mail and found a letter from General Harmon's chief of staff. It read, "Miff says to tell you that if you are really serious about wanting to get home for a visit, it's all right to go."

After a few hurried phone calls, frantic packing, and little sleep, he managed to catch a direct military flight to Washington, D.C., and eagerly looked forward to a Christmas reunion with his family before returning to the Twenty-fifth "Tropic Lightning" Division. Instead, he found himself heading to England and the war in Europe.

CHAPTER THREE

HE TALKS OUR LANGUAGE

Informed that terrible weather made crossing the North Atlantic too dangerous, Major General Joseph Lawton Collins settled into his seat in a U.S. Army Air Corps transport plane for a long flight via a southern route to Miami, Trinidad, and Marrakesh, with rest stops at Natal and Dakar, to Prestwick, Scotland. Arriving on a stormy night seven days after departing the United States, he boarded a train bound for London and arrived on the morning of February 2, 1944. After checking into the Dorchester Hotel adjacent to Hyde Park, he reported to Eisenhower's headquarters at 20 Grosvenor Square. Collins had no idea what post Ike had in mind, nor did he have any knowledge of the details of a three-year debate between the Americans and British over how to conduct the war against Germany that had begun even before the United States was drawn into the Second World War by the Japanese attack on Pearl Harbor.

As Hitler's swift conquest of Europe left Britain standing alone in the autumn of 1940, American military observers in England concluded that should the United States enter the war, Germany, as the strongest of the Axis Powers of Germany, Italy, and Japan, should be defeated first. In a series of conferences in Washington in February and March 1941, U.S. and British military chiefs agreed that beating Germany took priority. To plan a strategy to achieve this victory, an Anglo-American Combined Chiefs of Staff was created in 1942. In April of that year, General Marshall and presidential aide Harry Hopkins traveled to England with a preliminary plan code-named Bolero, calling for an invasion of France from England in 1943 and pledging that by the spring of 1943 the U.S. Army would have sent 1 million troops to England for the cross-channel attack.

But after Marshall returned to America, reservations about the plan were expressed by the top brass of the U.S. Navy, faced with a war in the Pacific, and by the British, alarmed by German victories over its forces in Libya in North Africa that had raised a threat to Egypt and the Suez Canal.

With Bolero now ruled out, and President Roosevelt insisting that U.S. forces get into action and achieve a victory as soon as possible, Prime Minister Winston Churchill arrived in Washington on June 18, 1942, with a proposal that the American and British launch a campaign in North Africa. He originally wanted an assault on the French Mediterranean seaport of Dakar, but by November the plan for a North African invasion, code-named Operation Torch, called for American and British forces to carry out invasions of French Morocco and Algeria. This success resulted in a campaign that cleared North Africa of German and Italian forces. Stressing that the Allies take advantage of its hold on North Africa, Churchill called for attacking the "soft underbelly of Europe" through southern France for an invasion of Sicily and then Italy, followed by an Allied push into the Balkans to keep the Soviet Union's Red Army from taking Eastern Europe and remaining there after the war. The Allied attack came in Sicily and Italy.

While this Mediterranean strategy was being carried out, General Marshall continued to press for a cross-channel invasion of Europe as soon as possible. When it was at last given the green light as Operation Overlord and scheduled for May of 1944, a decision had to be made as to who would be in command of its planning and execution. At a conference in Quebec between Roosevelt and Churchill, the prime minister stated that if ever a man deserved the appointment, that man was General Marshall. Roosevelt, however, decided that he needed Marshall in Washington, and the post of chief of the Supreme Headquarters, Allied Expeditionary Force (SHAEF), went to Eisenhower. To be field commander in Overlord, Ike chose Omar Bradley.

Born in a log cabin at Clark, Missouri, on February 12, 1893, Bradley graduated with Ike from West Point in 1915 and was assigned to the Fourteenth Infantry that June. During troop duty in the west (1915–19), he was promoted to first lieutenant in July 1916, to captain in May 1917, and to major in June 1918 because of a need for senior officers in World War I. After the war, he had Reserve Officer Training Corps duty in Minnesota and South Dakota (1919–20). While an instructor in mathematics at West Point (1920–24), he reverted to the grade of captain (1920–22), and was returned to major (1922 and 1924). Graduated from the advanced course at the Infantry School at Fort Benning in 1925, he served in Hawaii with both the Nineteenth and Twenty-seventh infantries (1925–27) and was then in charge of National Guard and Reserve affairs for the Hawaiian Islands (1927–28). Graduated from the Command and General Staff School at Fort Leavenworth in 1929, he was instructor in tactics and weapons at the Infantry School (1929–33) and graduated from the War College in 1934. While instructor in tactics and plans and training officers at the United States Military Academy (1934–38), he was promoted to lieutenant colonel in June 1936 and was chief of the Operations Branch of the War Department from 1938 to 1940, then assistant secretary of the General Staff (1940–41). Promoted to temporary brigadier general in February 1941, he was commandant of the Infantry School and set up the Infantry Officer

Candidate Program (1941–42). Promoted to the temporary ranks of major general in February 1942 and lieutenant general in June 1943, he successively commanded the Eighty-second and Twenty-eighth infantry divisions and was personal representative in the field for the commander of the North African Theater of Operations (Ike). He took over command of the Second Corps from George Patton in operations against Axis forces in North Africa and Sicily and was promoted to permanent brigadier general in September 1943.

Self-effacing, polite, courteous, soft-spoken, and a sharp contrast to the flashy Patton, he was first favorably brought to public attention by the correspondent Ernie Pyle, who called him "the soldier's general." Will Lang, Jr., of *Life* magazine noted, "The thing I most admire about Omar Bradley is his gentleness. He was never known to issue an order to anybody of any rank without saying 'Please' first."

In his autobiography, *A Soldier's Story*, Bradley said that he learned of his appointment to command the Overlord forces in a newspaper. On January 18, as he turned through the lobby of the Dorchester Hotel bound for breakfast at the U.S. Army's officers' mess across the street, he stopped to pick up a copy of the four-page *Daily Express*. The clerk at the counter grinned and said, "This won't be news to you, sir." He pointed to a story that stated Eisenhower had announced that in the invasion of France, Bradley was to be America's version of the British general and hero of the war in North Africa, Sir Bernard Law Montgomery.

The Overlord plan as developed to this time envisioned landings on the Normandy coast of France, with the first U.S. division coming ashore to the right of the British at a point twenty miles west of the city of Caen. A second American division was to land on the east coast of the Cotentin Peninsula with the objective of capturing the large port of Cherbourg. Each of these divisions was to sail from England under the command of a corps. The two beaches were given the names Omaha, near Caen, and Utah, positioned for the sweep to the Cotentin Peninsula. The Omaha assault force would be part of the Fifth Corps, under the command of Lieutenant General Leonard Townsend Gerow. The Utah Beach force would be under the Seventh Corps, commanded by Major General Roscoe B. Woodruff. Troops of the Nineteenth Corps under Major General Willis D. Crittenberger would be a follow-up force. But in one of the twists of fate that dotted the career of Joseph Lawton Collins, Eisenhower felt that both Woodruff and Crittenberger would be, in Bradley's words, "cutting their teeth" as combat commanders. With grave doubts that they had sufficient experience to entrust the entire U.S. assault to them, Ike looked elsewhere for his corps commanders. Crittenberger was sent to Italy and Woodruff to the Pacific. At the suggestion of Marshall, Eisenhower and Bradley agreed to consider as replacements Major General Charles H. Corlett, who had distinguished himself as commander of the Seventh Division at Kwajalein in the Pacific, and Collins.

Aware of the openings for corps commanders, Collins arrived at Eisenhower's offices in Grosvenor Square not knowing of Marshall's recommendation or what Ike and Bradley had in mind for him. Both had been a year ahead of him at West Point, but he'd known them slightly. Of the two, Collins knew Bradley better. Having served with Bradley on the West Point faculty in the 1920s and later, Collins felt he was acquainted with him fairly well and admired him. He'd come to know Ike in the Philippines, but not intimately. Now, both men were peppering him with pointed questions concerning his experience in the Pacific.

When Collins stated that in an attack he had always gone for the high ground, Bradley turned to Ike and said, "He talks our language."

Collins was assigned to command the Seventh Corps, the outfit he had organized in 1941 as its chief of staff before being called away and sent to Hawaii and ultimately to Guadalcanal. Of his choice as a corps commander for the greatest invasion of all time, Collins overlooked experiences that had honed him as a leader of troops and modestly stated in his autobiography, "I was lucky to be the right man in the right place at the right time."

Before the assignment was announced, Collins was invited to accompany Eisenhower and Bradley on a trip through an area of Devonshire where some Seventh Corps troops were billeted. During the trip, Bradley outlined the mission of the Seventh Corps in the invasion. It was to land on the east coast of the Cotentin Peninsula between Varreville and the mouth of the Douve River, seize the beach, link with the Fifth Corp west of the Douve, and capture Cherbourg as early as possible.

Collins relished meeting many old friends and others who had served in North Africa and the Mediterranean. Among his old acquaintances was the commander of the Fourth Infantry Division, Major General Raymond Barton, known as Tubby. They'd met after the First World War in Coblenz. Commander of the First Battalion, Eighth Infantry Regiment, during the war, Barton served in the occupation of Germany and was among the last Americans to leave in 1923. An Oklahoman, Barton graduated from West Point in 1912 and as a cadet had excelled in boxing and wrestling. A tough disciplinarian, he had seen the Fourth Division through a long period of training in the techniques of amphibious warfare at Camp Gordon Johnson, Florida, on the Gulf Coast in the fall of 1943, and landed in England in late January 1944. They arrived knowing just where their CO stood and what he expected. "I am your leader," Barton had said in July 1942. "In the not too distant future we will be in battle. When bullets start flying your minds will freeze, and you will act according to habit. In order that you develop the right habits, training discipline must be strict. I know ninety percent of you want to cooperate. I will take care of the other ten percent."

In a *Time* magazine listing of the invasion commanders, Barton would be described as a fifty-four-year-old "genial West

Pointer, former professor of military science at Georgetown," and rated a crack tactician. Collins felt that while a major in Germany, Barton had established himself as a first-class trainer. "He was not a brilliant man," Collins noted, "but was thoroughly versed in the tools of his trade, and had matured into a dependable division commander. I was fond of him personally and so were his men. The division was in splendid shape, sharp and eager to get under way."

No one was more eager for action than a brigadier general attached to Barton's division. One of the most colorful officers in the army, Theodore Roosevelt, Jr., called Ted, was the oldest son of Teddy Roosevelt and had served in the First World War. Following in his father's footsteps as a member of the New York legislature, he was assistant secretary of the navy under President Warren G. Harding. He had run for governor of New York and been defeated by the Democrat Al Smith, who had the support of Ted's distant cousin, Franklin D. Roosevelt. After serving as governor general of both Puerto Rico and the Philippines, Ted was an executive with the book publisher Doubleday. When Japan attacked Pearl Harbor, he appealed to now President Roosevelt to be returned to the army. Despite his age (fifty-four) and arthritis, he was made a brigadier general and deputy to First Division commander Terry de la Mesa Allen, in North Africa and in the Sicilian campaign.

In Normandy, the Fourth Division would be followed in the assault of Utah Beach by the Ninetieth Division and possibly the Ninth. It would be the Fourth's first action in the war, but the Ninth, under Major General Manton S. Eddy, had been in North Africa and Sicily. Drops by the 82nd and 101st Airborne in support of the Fourth Division were being planned by the First Army. These divisions would then pass to Collins's command. In addition, the Seventh Corps included the Fourth Cavalry Group, and a full complement of artillery, tank and antitank battalions, engineers, and other supporting and service units. Most of the corps combat troops were to be billeted in Devonshire or Hampshire, but other elements were scattered from Wales to the area of Chichester, southeast of London.

Visiting them took Collins hours of driving on the narrow roads of rural England, but he felt it was his duty to spend time with the troops in the field to witness their training and to meet and observe each of the units' commanders, down to battalions. As the first to be landing, the Fourth Division initially drew most of his attention.

Whenever possible at these troop inspections, Collins addressed the men in convenient groups to outline his concepts of discipline, proficiency in the techniques of fire and movement of units, and the high standards of performance he expected of them. He expressed confidence they would meet these tests. Particularly impressive was the Eighth Infantry, his old regiment when he was in Germany, and its CO, Colonel James A. Van Fleet. A West Point classmate of Ike and Bradley, Van Fleet had been known to Collins as one of the toughest and most versatile backfield men in an era of fine army football teams. Collins had also seen something of him at Fort Benning. "The trouble was," he recalled, "that General Marshall, while he served as Assistant Commandant at Benning, confused Van Fleet with a man with almost the same name, for whom Marshall had only slight regard. Although Van Fleet had done well over the years, each time during the war when Van Fleet had been recommended to be promoted to the rank of brigadier, Marshall turned him down."

After thoroughly inspecting the Eighth Infantry, Collins called General Bradley and told him they were wasting Van Fleet as a regimental commander, and stated that he should be in command of a division.

Bradley said, "Well, Joe, he is in your corps. Do something about it."

Collins replied, "If Van does as well on D-day as I feel sure he will, I will recommend him at once to be a BG."

The command post of the Seventh Corps was in the little village of Braemore, south of Salisbury in Hampshire. Collins drove down from London through the countryside of Devon and found it left untouched by the war, except that the farms were being tilled and the cattle cared for by women, members of the Women's Land Army Corps. Charmed by the quiet of Braemore, with its many thatched-roof houses, Collins found it an unlikely place for a corps command post, but settled into a large and stately Tudor mansion on its outskirts that provided billets and office space for most of his staff. Although the makeup of the corps staff had changed since his brief command of it in 1941, he felt as though he had come home. He found numerous familiar faces among the current staff, who had crossed the Atlantic to England in October 1943. Only three important posts had to be filled: a replacement for Woodruff's chief of staff, a logistics officer, and an artillery commander. The first two slots were filled as recommended by Bradley with Colonel Richard G. McKee, formerly chief of staff of the Third Army, and Colonel James G. Anding, an experienced logistician. Of most concern to Collins was the artillery CO.

On his way from the United States to join the Seventh Corps was an artillery officer Collins did not know, Brigadier General Charles R. Doran.

"If I had learned one thing in the Pacific," Collins wrote, "it was that the artillery had to conform to the needs of the infantry. This meant that thoroughly competent men, not merely observers, had to accompany frontline infantry and should be competent to place concentrations of fire within a hundred to two hundred yards of those troops, with safety."

Collins found Doran to be an artilleryman of the old order who still clung to the outmoded routines of depending on observers on hilltops, often well to the rear of the front line. He told Doran to outline the location of troops he was supposed to be supporting in every firing exercise and to have battalion commanders, or other experienced observers, adjust fire from within or close to the front lines. In succeeding exercises he saw that Doran was not complying with his wishes and had him relieved. This time Bradley furnished a replacement, Brigadier General Williston B. Palmer. Collins found him a "top notch" artilleryman who gave the Seventh Corps expert support throughout the war.

Because the name Overlord stood for the general concept of a cross-channel invasion of France at specific assault areas on a target date, the planners had decided by September 1943 to apply the new code name Neptune, which encompassed all aspects of the invasion plan. Given the classification "top secret," Neptune documents were circulated for security purposes to a much more limited number of persons than documents bearing the name Overlord. At the heart of Neptune were plans covering the naval component of the invasion. They consisted of the Western Naval Task Force under U.S. Navy Rear Admiral Alan G. Kirk, who reported to the commander of the Allied Naval Expeditionary Force, Admiral Sir Bernard H. Ramsay. In the plan, Task Force B would sail from Dartmouth, Task Force O from Weymouth Bay, and Task Force U from the port of Torquay and other locations to carry the Seventh Corps to Utah Beach. Comprising 865 vessels and craft in twelve convoys, Task Force U would sail farther than the other forces and was commanded by U.S. Navy Rear Admiral Don P. Moon.

A veteran of the Battle of the Atlantic, Moon was a graduate of the U.S. Naval Academy Class of 1916 and ranked fourth in the class. Regarded as brilliant by colleagues, but cheerless, moody, and aloof, he had been withdrawn from duty in the Mediterranean, where he had been preparing for a proposed landing by Allied forces in southern France, to take command of Task Force U. His Operation Neptune headquarters was at Plymouth in an air-raid-damaged stone building near a steep bluff called the Hoe. Legend held that it was here that in the reign of Queen Elizabeth, Sir Francis Drake insisted on finishing a game of bowls before venturing out to sea to defeat the Spanish Armada. Of more significance to Americans, Plymouth was the port from which the Pilgrims had set out for the New World.

When Collins paid Moon a visit, he found the naval commander to be attractive and friendly. They had several mutual friends in the navy, and Moon was aware of Collins's service in the Pacific. During the meeting, Collins proposed that for convenience in their future meetings, Collins move his headquarters closer to Plymouth. Moon offered to arrange for the Seventh Corps HQ to be housed in Quonset huts across the street from Moon's HQ and for Collins and his staff to be billeted at Plymouth's Grand Hotel. After lunch and a guided tour of Plymouth, Collins left the port city assured that a good start had been made toward a sound and friendly relationship with the navy. In March, the operations part of Seventh Corps HQ moved down to Plymouth, while the rear echelon administrative section would remain at Braemore until shortly before D-day.

After visiting all major Seventh Corps units, Collins began a series of battalion combat exercises within the Fourth Division comparable to those he'd carried out with the Twenty-fifth Division in Hawaii, but limited in their extent by the numerous towns and villages in the area. He found a suitable British training facility at Woolcombe in Devon, a British firing range on the river Clyde in Scotland, and on the sprawling Salisbury Plain, where no firing was allowed.

For large-scale amphibious training, the Seventh Corps moved to the coast of Devon close to Dartmouth and the evacuated coastal village of Slapton Sands. In a series of massive exercises designed to be dress rehearsals for D-day, Collins suffered an injury that gave him the worst headache of his life. More important, a disaster during the rehearsals stirred fears among the Neptune planners that the secrecy surrounding the invasion might have been lost.

CHAPTER FOUR

I KNOW THEM HYMNS

At Slapton Sands in Start Bay and Tor Bay in Devon there was an unspoiled beach of coarse gravel that resembled Utah Beach and a shallow lagoon backed by steep bluffs that resembled Omaha Beach. After the people in the nearby village were evacuated, it was an almost perfect place to simulate the Normandy landings in a series of full-scale rehearsals in late March, April, and early May 1944.

In a practice by the Fourth Division in March, Collins was especially interested in the testing of thirty-two-ton Sherman medium tanks fitted with detachable canvas collars to make them amphibious. With a dual drive system that powered propellers in water and their tracks on land, they were known as "DDs" and were to be carried close to the beaches by landing craft and released to "swim" ashore.

To observe their operation during one of the Seventh Corps exercises at Slapton Sands, Collins left Admiral Moon's flagship *Bayfield* and climbed into a small boat to take him to a line of landing craft tank (LCT) carrying DDs of the Seventieth Tank Battalion. With waves pitching the LCTs about as they lowered their forward ramps, Collins watched the tanks drive off into the water. Noting that their canvas collars "barely avoided gulping water as they plunged overboard," he observed, "once the DDs settled down, they rode very well."

Collins headed back to the *Bayfield* in waves that were much higher and rougher. When his LCVP (landing craft vehicle and personnel) drew alongside, a boom swung out to lift the craft onto the ship by means of a cable with a large hook at the end. This would be connected to three steel cables fastened to the framework of the LCVP that were joined by a heavy steel ring.

"The tricky task now," Collins noted, "was for two seamen, balancing themselves on the pitching deck, to catch the ring on the hook as it swung back and forth like a pendulum. I could foresee that when they did catch the ring, the three cables would pull dangerously taut. I cautioned everyone to flatten himself against the deckhouse."

The men caught the hook just as a large wave pitched the boat sharply to one side. As the full weight of the boat was thrown suddenly on the bales, they snapped taut, catching Collins's head between the deckhouse and one of the cables. Fortunately, his steel helmet protected his left eye as the cable drew across his forehead and cheek. When the boat lurched to level itself, his feet slipped from under him and he skidded across the deck. With blood spouting from his forehead, he wondered for a moment if the top of his head was in place.

After getting a few stitches in his forehead and an overnight stay in a British hospital, he was fixed up in time to conduct a critique of the exercise the next day. His story of the incident in his autobiography lightly dismissed the incident by saying he felt like a battered prizefighter, but if he had been more seriously hurt or killed, Eisenhower and Bradley would have lost a general who was both a brilliant tactician and an experienced combat commander who had participated in the detailed planning of the Utah Beach landings. They would have had to scramble to find a new commander for the Seventh Corps with very little time to do so before D-day.

A month after Collins had his close call, Operation Neptune planners had to deal with a calamity that cost scores of lives and raised the frightening possibility that Germany had discovered the imminence of the invasion. During the night of April 26–27, troops and equipment embarked on the same ships and for the most part from the same ports from which they would later leave for France. Six of the days in an exercise named Tiger were taken up by marshaling of the troops and the embarkation of the landing craft. On April 28, the main force proceeded through Lyme Bay with minesweepers ahead of them, as if they were crossing the English Channel.

Because high-speed German E-boats sometimes patrolled the channel at night, the British navy's commander in chief at Plymouth, who was responsible for the protection of the rehearsal, ordered patrolling across the mouth of Lyme Bay. The ships consisted of two destroyers, three motor torpedo boats, and two motor gunboats. Another motor torpedo patrol was sent to watch for movements of E-boats at their bases at Cherbourg.

Following a simulated bombardment on Slapton Sands, the exercise landings began with the unloading and continued during that day and the next, when a follow-up convoy was expected to arrive. Called Convoy T-4, it consisted of two sections from two ports. The Plymouth section, LST Group 32, was composed of five LSTs (landing ship, tank) and the Brixham section had three LSTs. The convoy joined with HMS *Azalea* as escort and proceeded at six knots in one column. When the convoy maneuvered in Lyme Bay in the early hours of April 28, nine German E-boats out of their Cherbourg base evaded the Allied patrols, discovered the ships in Lyme Bay, and attacked. Torpedoed at 0240, LST 507 burst into flames. Survivors abandoned ship. Several minutes later, LST 531 was hit and sank in six minutes. When LST 289 fired at the E-boats, it was torpedoed but was able to reach port.

The other LSTs plus two British destroyers fired at the Germans as they laid smoke and sped away into the darkness.

When Collins reported the attack to General Bradley, he was asked if there had been any losses. Collins replied that there had been some but no one yet knew how many and that not until the troops were re-formed could a thorough count be made. Of immediate concern to everyone was that in stumbling upon the rehearsal, the German High Command might deduce that the invasion was imminent. Intelligence officers (G-2) worried that if the German boats had plucked survivors from the sea, the men might be coerced into telling what they knew, or have invasion documents on them. If so, the G-2 men worried that an elaborate and intricate deception plan that had been created to trick the Germans into believing the invasion would come in mid-July at the Pas de Calais would be dispelled. In this deception plan, a fake force under General Patton had been fashioned in Scotland, with not-very-well-hidden phony tanks made of rubber and other equipment and buildings, complete with false radio traffic and messages, to deceive German reconnaissance planes and possible German spies.

Bradley assured G-2 that the troops had not yet been briefed and the secret of where the invasion would come, and when, was "presumably" still safe. But in his memoirs, he admitted that with the misfortune of the Slapton Sands attack, the enemy might learn *when* the Allies planned to strike. He wrote, "I now shared G-2's worries."

According to the navy, the attack resulted in 198 navy killed and missing and 441 army dead and missing. A later army accounting gave 551 as the total number of dead and missing soldiers.

Although Eisenhower imposed secrecy on the disaster, invasion planners continued to fear that the Germans might have picked up survivors. Casualty information on Exercise Tiger was not released until after the invasion, but the Slapton Sands losses were made part of the overall D-day statistics. Recording the tragedy in his autobiography, published in 1979, Collins wrote, "Two LSTs were sunk and one damaged, costing over seven hundred casualties, most of whom drowned. The loss was heavier than that suffered by the VII Corps on D-day."

As a result of the German attack on Exercise Tiger, Slapton Sands was closed as a practice area while bodies were being recovered and an investigation made. This meant that an alternate area had to be found for further rehearsals for D-day. In Exercise Eagle, the 101st Airborne Division under Major General Maxwell Taylor practiced a night drop in an area in Berkshire that resembled the planned zone behind Utah Beach. Because there had never been a comparable night training exercise, Collins observed it with what he admitted was "some trepidation," but the drop went well with a minimum of injuries and none of the paratroopers killed, although some of them drifted over villages and crashed through roofs of houses near the drop zone.

In the early-morning darkness of D-day, prior to the infantry storming Utah Beach, the 101st Airborne would have to parachute inland to seize the exits of four causeways over a flooded area south of the town of Sainte-Mère-Église, while Major General Matthew Ridgway's 82nd Airborne Division dropped astride the Merderet River west of the town to seize a road and block any German reinforcements.

What the Seventh Corps would find at Utah Beach had been outlined in a top secret analysis provided to Collins and others by G-2. It described a beach 9,565 yards long that was low lying, without distinctive terrain features, and consisting of compact gray sand between high- and low-water marks. The report continued, "The beach is backed for its entire length by a masonry seawall, with the exception of a stretch of piling 210 yards in length. Behind the wall, from approximately the center of the beach and extending southward, sand dunes approximately 10 to 25 feet high extend inland nearly 150 yards. Inland of the entire beach area are inundated lowlands."

Exits in the form of ramps led off the beach through gaps in the seawall, but all of these were blocked. While normally a good network of roads led into the interior, they had been flooded, leaving only three roads open.

Behind Utah Beach stood the army that had marched out of Germany in 1940 and through France to the shores of the English Channel to build, under the direction of Field Marshal Erwin Rommel, a system of fortifications and obstacles known as the Atlantic Wall, which was designed to stop the Allied invasion on the beaches. Under General Field Marshal Gerd von Rundstedt, Supreme Commander West, were Rommel's Army Group B, General Friedrich Dollman's Seventh Army, and General der Artillerie Erich Marcks's Eighty-fourth Corps. Ready for an invasion were panzer tanks, airborne troops, various grenadier regiments, five divisions, and an array of coastal defenses. Built over four years, they were arranged to sweep beaches with interlocking fields of fire. Approaches to the shore were studded with steel obstacles above and under the water, and the beach itself had been densely land-mined.

Fixed infantry defenses were more sparsely located at Utah Beach than at Omaha, possibly because of the natural obstacles provided by the inundated areas. At and near roads leading off the beach, the defense was in a linear series of infantry strongpoints armed chiefly with automatic weapons. Roughly two miles inland were several coastal and field artillery batteries, with the most formidable located at the towns of Crisbecq and Saint-Martin-de-Varreville. Heavy- and medium-caliber guns were housed in a series of concrete forts to cover both sea approaches and the beach area.

Three weeks before the Exercise Tiger rehearsals, Collins participated in what Bradley in his memoirs called "a full dress rehearsal for air, ground, and naval commanders on the invasion plan." It was convened by the second figure in the Overlord/Neptune chain of command, General Sir Bernard Law Montgomery. As supervisor of the joint planning for the invasion and commander of the British and Canadian Twenty-first Army Group, he held the review at his headquarters in St. Paul's School in Kensington, London, on April 7, 1944. Among those attending were Britain's King George VI and Churchill.

Seated with Eisenhower, commanders in chief of the Allied naval and air forces and distinguished visitors sat in semicircular tiers of chairs looking down on a huge, multicolored map of Normandy spread on the floor of a large room. Waving a long pointer, Montgomery stood on the map and outlined the plan of the attack by striding across the beaches, hills, and streams to point out salient features of five invasion beaches, Juno, Gold, Sword, Omaha, and Utah, and explaining the overall strategy and objectives of the invasion.

Collins saw Montgomery "clearly relishing his role as impresario." In Omar Bradley's description, the lean figure "tramped about like a giant through Lilliputian France."

Beginning with the commander of the British First Corps, the generals who would carry out the master scheme defined by Montgomery took turns outlining their assault plans. Most read prepared statements while aides pointed to the map. Going last, Collins stood on the map as Monty had done, pointer in hand, and gave an extemporaneous explanation of how the Seventh Corps' Fourth Division would link up with the two airborne elements and drive north to Cherbourg. As he sat down, General Walter Bedell Smith leaned forward from his seat behind Collins and whispered, "Joe, done in the best tradition of Benning."

Sometime prior to his performance with Churchill in the audience, Collins had spent most of a day with the pugnacious prime minister who had given voice to the indomitable spirit of the British when they stood alone against Hitler's onslaught. On one of his frequent odysseys to visit American troops, Churchill had traveled with Ike from London on a special train that the British government had put at Eisenhower's disposal to pay a call on the Ninth Division, part of the Seventh Corps. At a dinner on the train, Collins found himself seated next to Churchill. The party was small and informal. With no reporters present, everyone was in a relaxed mood. Also present were Bradley, Ninth Division CO Manton Eddy, Ike's British aide, Colonel James Gault, Ike's driver, Kay Summersby, and Churchill's daughter, Sarah.

"When I saw him that evening," Collins recalled, "Churchill had had two strenuous days of inspections and had ridden for miles perched on the tonneau of an open command car so that he could better see and be seen by the troops. Despite a recent illness he had insisted on getting out of the car to walk around the honor guards and examine the weapons displayed. That day he had stood through a review of our regiments and delivered a stirring address to the men. In one of the towns through which we passed he had gotten out of the car to walk with General Eisenhower for a couple of blocks through throngs of cheering townspeople, who pressed about him in their enthusiasm, many with tears streaming down their cheeks. Yet that evening he was as fresh as we were, and held forth after dinner until eleven o'clock dominating the conversation, alternately regaling us with stories or stirring us as he spoke feelingly of our common ideals and endeavors. He ended the evening with passages from Kipling and Bret Harte's *The Reveille*, to each verse of which he added extemporaneously, 'The drums! The drums!' which he rolled forth with obvious relish. The evening was a fitting end to a memorable day."

Less than two weeks before the invasion was scheduled to commence, G-2 reported the arrival in the Cotentin area of a new German division, the Ninety-first, consisting of two to three regiments and one battalion of tanks. This resulted in shifting the 243rd Division to the west. Addition of the 91st to strengthen the defense of the peninsula's eastern half came as a surprise. On

May 27, Collins was called to Bradley's HQ at Bristol and informed of the 91st's arrival. At the meeting, changes were made in the disposition of the 82nd but the plan for the 101st was left as it was. Because of thick woods and hedgerows between the Merderet and Douve rivers and the lack of clearings for troop-carrying gliders to land, it was decided that the 82nd's drop would be astride the Merderet, with one parachute regiment landing to the east and two regiments west, then securing the western edge of the bridgehead, capturing Sainte-Mère-Église, and taking control of two main roads for a drive toward Saint-Sauveur-le-Vicomte. The 101st was still to clear the way for the seaborne assault to get off Utah Beach via the four exits, set up defensive arcs on the northern and southern segments of the invasion area, and establish bridgeheads across the Douve at two points for the Seventh Corps to close a gap between the landing areas in a linkup with the Fifth Corps.

The missions of the Fourth, Ninth, and Ninetieth infantry divisions remained the same. As the principal seaborne unit, the Fourth was enhanced by attachment of the Eighty-seventh Chemical Mortar Battalion, the 106th Engineer Combat Group, 101st Tank Destroyer Battalion, and one battery of the 980th Field Artillery Battalion, along with antiaircraft units and the Thirteenth Field Artillery Observation Battalion. The Ninetieth Division would land on D-day plus one to join in the drive on Cherbourg. The Ninth Division was to come ashore on D-day plus four, assemble in corps reserve, and prepare for operations in the northwest. A key provision of the plan was the taking of an island, Iles Saint-Marcouf, to capture any installations capable of hindering the landings. All of this would be preceded by intensive air and naval bombardments.

The mounting of the biggest invasion in history began in the second week of May with assault troops assembling in areas of southern England that on planning maps looked like sausages, and were quickly called that by the GIs. With every road jammed by soldiers in trucks, jeeps, tanks, and other kinds of war machines, and every seaport clogged with landing craft and troopships, Collins was amazed that so much activity was not discovered by the Germans.

Even more astonishing, Collins observed, was that there had not been any leaks in the press, intentional or accidental, as a quarter of a million troops waited, "cooped up in the farms and hedgerows of southern England," for Eisenhower to give the signal to go. With amazing foresight, he wondered if it could ever happen again, and speculated that such a massing of men for war could not go unreported in America.

On the evening of June 2, 1944, Collins and Admiral Moon shifted their command posts to the USS *Bayfield.* Moored in Plymouth Harbor, the ship would serve not only as the Utah Beach landings command ship but as the headquarters for General Barton's Fourth Division and the transport for the Third Battalion, Eighth Infantry. Under joint army-navy regulations, Moon was in command of Task Force U until the Seventh Corps was established on Utah Beach.

As D-day approached, relations between the Seventh Corps' staff and Moon's staff grew closer as they worked out final details and went over loading and landing tables, naval gun support, communications, and all the minute elements of putting soldiers ashore on a hostile beach. During increasingly intense meetings, Collins observed a facet of Moon's character that had marked his naval career. Collins noticed in Moon a reluctance to delegate tasks to his subordinates.

Collins noted, "I became a bit concerned about Don Moon's working overtime and his tendency to do too much himself instead of giving some of his responsibility to his staff. . . . I thought also that I detected a certain lack of firmness and a tendency to be overly cautious, which worried me."

In a letter to Gladys on May 17, Collins wrote, "He is the first Admiral I've ever met who wears rubbers on a mere rainy day, but he is all right. He is certainly pleasant to do business with and is genuinely cooperative in every way."

In the wearing of rain gear in the days leading up to the date that had been chosen for the invasion (June 5, 1944), Moon was not alone. As a North Atlantic storm moved across the British Isles, the invaders found themselves deluged for days, with no sign of the weather letting up. On the morning of Saturday, June 3, Omar Bradley left Bristol under frowning clouds and headed south across the river Avon for Plymouth to meet with Collins. Bradley's chief aide, Lieutenant Colonel Chester Bayard Hansen, rode with an aluminum tube of top secret invasion maps between his knees. Other aides followed in a second sedan. Collins awaited them at a road junction north of Plymouth to accompany them to the quay, where a barge would carry them to Bradley's command ship, the U.S. Navy cruiser *Augusta*. She had taken President Roosevelt to a spot off Newfoundland early in 1941 for a conference with Churchill, where they drafted the Atlantic Charter, outlining not only the alliance between the United States and Britain to defeat the Axis Powers but their idealistic vision of a world of peace following the war.

Aboard the ship, a war room had been constructed on the afterdeck that consisted of a temporary shed. An outer wall had a Michelin touring map of France and a terrain study of the assault beaches. Between them was a George Petty pinup girl. Bradley perused a weather forecast provided by G-2 that read, "Mist from Sunday to Wednesday, with low clouds and reduced visibility in the mornings. Winds not to exceed 17 to 22 knots. Choppy water in the channel with five-foot breakers. A four-foot surf on the beaches."

"It doesn't look good," Bradley muttered.

An aide ventured, "It stinks."

Despite the disheartening forecast, no word had come from Ike at his headquarters in Portsmouth about postponing the invasion. He was to meet at 9:30 p.m. on June 3 to get an update on the weather from meteorologist Captain J. M. Stagg. In the report, he said that June 5 would be overcast, with a cloud base of five hundred feet to zero, accompanied by high winds. After a discussion with the Combined Commanders in Chief, Ike decided to put off a decision until 4:30 the next morning. Meanwhile, elements of Task Force U would get under way because it had the farthest to travel.

At Plymouth, Collins and Moon waited in the damp underground naval headquarters for the decision and were not optimistic. When they stepped outside in the early morning, they saw the moon breaking through scattered clouds. The wind was down and the sea seemed appreciably quieter. Collins went to bed. When the admiral woke him at dawn, he announced that Ike had given the order to go. At 9:30, the convoy that would take Collins to Normandy formed up. As the ships maneuvered away from Plymouth, he went to mass in the main mess hall. When he offered to share his hymnal with a soldier beside him, the GI looked at the two-star general scornfully and said, "I know them hymns."

Later, Collins wrote to Gladys and the children, "I thought of you all keenly, as I do each Sunday. I am sure the thoughts of everyone were more on our families at home than they were on the service, though the seriousness of the project on which we were embarked was to me, for the first time, clearly in the air."

CHAPTER FIVE

UTAH

O n May 28, 1944, Major General J. Lawton Collins had stated in his Field Orders No. 1, "The assault on Utah Beach will be pushed at all costs."

With bad weather having delayed the invasion by a day, Task Force U's twelve convoys headed across the choppy channel to arrive before dawn on Tuesday, June 6, 1944. On a visit to Normandy to inspect its defenses, the mastermind of the strengthening of the Atlantic Wall, Erwin Rommel, had reviewed the barrier of bunkers, guns, steel impediments, and explosives and said to an aide, "The war will be won on the beaches. We will have one chance to stop the enemy and that is while he is in the water struggling to get ashore." In the fight for the precious stretches of sand, he declared, the first twenty-four hours would be decisive. For the Allies, as well as Germany, he predicted, it would be "the longest day."

When the fateful date arrived, Rommel was not in Normandy, but in Germany to present to his wife, Lucie-Maria, a pair of Parisian gray suede shoes for her birthday.

As Task Force U sailed from Plymouth, Brigadier General

Ted Roosevelt of the Fourth Division wrote to his wife, Eleanor, "We are starting out on the great venture of this war, and by the time you get this letter, for better or worse, it will be history. We are attacking in daylight the most heavily fortified shore in history, a shore held by excellent troops. We are throwing against it excellent troops, well-armed and backed by superb air and good naval support."

A veteran of the campaign in North Africa and the conquest of Sicily, Ted was plagued by arthritis that resulted from a knee wound obtained in the First World War. He went on to tell Eleanor he would go onto Utah Beach with the first wave of troops. "I'm doing it," he wrote, "because it's the way I can contribute most. It steadies the young men to know I'm with them, to see me plodding along with my cane."

Reports of the invasion heard on the radio and read in the newspapers would be doubly worrying for Eleanor because their son, Captain Quentin Roosevelt, would be landing on Omaha Beach.

When Collins went out on deck of the *Bayfield* just before one in the morning, the pitch-black sky was filled with twin-engine aircraft. Aboard the C-47 transports, Maxwell Taylor's 101st Airborne troops, their grim, taut faces blackened, were heading for drop zones behind enemy lines to seize the exits of the four causeways that Collins's men would use to get off the beach and drive inland. Matthew Ridgway's 82nd Airborne Division would jump toward the Merderet River to grab a road center west of Sainte-Mère-Église to block possible German reinforcements from reaching the beaches.

An hour after the C-47s flew over, Collins and Moon looked skyward as the first of the empty planes returned. Because of the weather, German navy patrols and Field Marshal Hermann Goering's Luftwaffe had stayed at their bases, allowing the mightiest armada in history to cross the tempestuous English Channel unimpeded and undetected. At two thirty, the *Bayfield* dropped anchor off Utah and men of the Third Battalion, Eighth Infantry, began to disembark. With rifles, machine guns, mortars, ammunition bags, hand grenades dangling from belts, first-aid pouches, and crammed backpacks, they went over the rails and climbed down the rope ladders into landing craft that bucked and bobbed on six-foot waves. Once they cleared the *Bayfield*, the crowded boats would assemble like ducklings on a vast pond and wait for warships to guide them shoreward to begin landing at H hour (6:30 a.m.).

At 0430, Collins was informed that detachments of the Fourth and Twenty-fourth Cavalry Squadron under Colonel E. C. Dunn had landed on the first of the objectives of the Utah phase of D-day, the Iles Saint-Marcouf, to capture what was believed to be a German observation post. Ahead of the landing, four men armed only with knives swam ashore. They found no enemy, but confirmed that the island had been heavily land-mined. By 0530, it was the first piece of France in American hands.

At 0552, Marauder bombers of Major General Hoyt S. Vandenberg's Ninth Air Force roared over the fleet to commence pounding German coastal batteries. When the bombs fell, Collins saw pinpoint flashes like a vast Fourth of July fireworks show. From the direction of Cherbourg he heard the crackle of antiaircraft guns. As the sky lightened, he gazed for the first time at the magnitude of the fleet of battleships, cruisers, destroyers, and transports. Lines of landing craft were crammed with tanks, guns, trucks, other vehicles, and soldiers. Fire support for the frail-looking boats as they moved shoreward would be provided by Rear Admiral Morton L. Deyo's Navy Task Force 125. When the troops approached the beach, the firing would shift to blast inland fortifications.

As the shelling continued, Collins found the scene awesome. There had been no such naval barrages when the Twenty-fifth Division landed at Guadalcanal and no opposition by the enemy. When the Tropic Lightning Division went ashore, the Japanese had been driven back from the coast and into the jungles and hills. Awaiting the Fourth Division at Utah Beach was the most deadly stretch of sand in the world defended by soldiers of an army that had conquered and held on to more of Europe than Napoleon. The Wehrmacht had mastered more of the globe than Alexander the Great. Not since the Roman Empire had an army been so successful as that of Hitler's Third Reich. Now, in bunkers and trenches, the defenders of Normandy had orders to stop the Allied invasion at the waterline.

In 1920, Collins had believed that the war that was supposed to end all wars had done so. Twenty-four years later, he stood on the deck of the *Bayfield* as salvos from giant guns from scores of ships lit up the sky. Rolling billows of black smoke gradually obscured the surrounding armada. The whooshing of hundreds of launchers sent rockets in long arcs toward the coast. As their explosions raised clouds of sand and smoke that enveloped the beach, he peered through field glasses and prayed that none of the rockets fell short and hit his troops. At some point during the day, the son of his brother James would be among them. A native Texan and a graduate of West Point in 1939, James Lawton Collins, Jr., was with the 975th Field Artillery. Curiously, Collins made no mention of him in his autobiography.

About an hour before first light on the troopship *Barnet*, carrying the Fourth Division, Brigadier General Theodore Roosevelt, Jr., appeared on deck with a cane in hand, a Colt .45 pistol in a holster, and a dog-eared copy of the work of the nineteenth-century poet Winthrop Praed in a jacket pocket. He approached the deck railing, went over it, and onto the rope ladder.

Seeing him with a life belt around his waist, a soldier who looked no older than fifteen asked him if he had all his armament.

Ted patted the holster and said, "I've got my pistol, one ammunition clip with six rounds in it, and my walking cane. That's all I expect to need."

The landing craft awaiting him held part of E Company, Second Battalion, Eighth Infantry. To get into it he would have to jump down about five feet to the deck. A soldier reached up to assist and said, "Here, General, let me help you."

Ted smacked him on the arm with his cane and growled, "Get the hell out of my way. I can jump in there by myself. I can take it as well as any of you."

If any of the young men in the boat doubted it, none dared say so. With the short, sinewy, grinning, cane-wielding fifty-six-year-old one-star general on board, the Higgins landing craft moved away from the transport and headed for the beach. In rehearsals for the landing, the procedure was for their boat to trail swimming tanks ashore, but the U.S. Navy coxswain running Ted's craft grew impatient with the slow-moving vehicles and steered ahead of them. Consequently, the men of E Company and their brigadier general found that they were headed for the distinction of being the first Allied infantry outfit to set foot on a Normandy beach.

Not all the approaches to the beach sections named Green and Red went as smoothly. Around 0455 the Green Beach primary and secondary control craft and the Red Beach's primary control boats set off for the shore, but after the Red Beach lead vessel's propeller snagged on a buoy, it could not proceed. A Green Beach boat sank, probably because it had hit a mine. As a result, the Green Beach primary control vessel turned about and signaled that it would lead all the landing craft closer to the beach and also guide the DDs.

In the Utah plan, the first wave of twenty troop landing craft carried a thirty-man assault team of the Eighth Infantry. Ten of these craft were to land on Tare Green Beach opposite the Les Dunes de Varreville strongpoint. The other ten were intended for Uncle Red Beach, a thousand yards to the south. This operation was timed against the first assault wave that was scheduled to occur at 0630. Eight LCTs with four DDs were to land at the same time or as soon thereafter as possible. The second wave consisted of thirty-two craft with troops of two assault battalions, some combat engineers, and eight naval demolition teams to clear underwater obstacles. A third wave at H plus fifteen minutes had eight LCTs with tanks equipped to function as bulldozers. The fourth wave would bring detachments of two engineer combat battalions.

Almost exactly at H hour, the first of the assault craft lowered the ramps. As the men charged out and met no opposition, some of them waved their rifles in relief and one shouted with delight, "Goddamn, we're on French soil."

As the rest of the troops followed, Collins learned that they had landed at the wrong spot. "Because of the smoke, wind and tides," he recorded, "the assault waves of the Fourth Division landed almost two thousand yards farther south than planned, leaving Exit No. 4 over the inundated area uncovered, requiring adjustment of the tasks of the assault troops."

At the spot where E Company had landed, the navy control officer for Utah Beach, Commodore James Arnold, dashed for cover behind a Sherman tank that had just come in. As it lumbered forward, Arnold scampered for a shell crater and dove in. A moment later, an officer with a single star jumped in to duck the blast of a German artillery round. The stocky brigadier general grumbled, "Sonsofbuzzards!"

Introducing himself as Teddy Roosevelt, he said, "You're Arnold of the navy. I remember you at the briefing in Plymouth."

Into the crater came a pair of lieutenant colonels, Conrad Simmons and Carlton MacNeeley. While they and Ted studied a map, the fourth wave was coming in. Wading ashore with them was Colonel James Van Fleet. When he joined the officers in Arnold's hole at 0940, he radioed to Collins aboard the *Bayfield*, "I am ashore with Colonel Simmons and General Roosevelt, advancing steadily."

Ted frowned and said, "Van, we're not where we're supposed to be."

A brief, lively discussion followed on the subject of what to do about the mistake.

As Van Fleet recalled, there were two options. "Should we try to shift our entire landing force more than a mile down the beach, and follow our original plan, or should we proceed across the causeways immediately opposite where we had landed?"

Ted looked around at the increasingly crowded beach and spoke words that would be the most memorable utterance of the historic day: "We'll start the war from right here."

In these first moments of confusion on Utah Beach, Theodore Roosevelt, Jr., became an inspiring figure to all who saw him. Among them was Harper Coleman, a member of Heavy Weapons Company H of the Eighth Infantry Regiment, who recalled, "When we came ashore, we had a greeter. Brigadier General Theodore Roosevelt was standing there waving his cane and giving out instructions, as only he could. If we were afraid of the enemy, we were more afraid of him and could not have stopped on the beach had we wanted."

Although Collins was eager to follow troops ashore, he knew that he would have better communications with the airborne divisions, General Bradley on the *Augusta*, and actions on all the beachheads by remaining on the *Bayfield* until every aspect of the landings was clear. From the ship's command center, he waited anxiously to hear from the paratroops and learn if they had achieved their objectives. Meanwhile, he heard with satisfaction that despite initial confusion in the landings, the units ashore were rapidly attaining the goals in the master plan and the errors in putting the troops ashore had actually proved to be fortunate. The beach where they'd come in was not only less thickly obstructed, it was less formidably defended.

An hour after the first man set foot on Utah, the engineers

had cleared the entire beach and elements of the Thirty-seventh Chemical Mortar Battalion, Third Battalion, of the Eighth Infantry, and the Third Battalion, Twenty-second Infantry, were crossing the beach. When Roosevelt reported the error in the landings, it was decided aboard *Bayfield* that the Fourth Division should proceed inland to achieve its original objective. Facing the First Battalion were fortifications in and around the town of Madeleine, while ahead of the Second Battalion stood a fortification just south of Exit 2. Both were soon taken by forces of company size or less against light opposition. At the same time, houses along a road paralleling the beach were cleared. The Germans manning coastal garrisons had apparently been so demoralized by the preparatory bombardment that they put up little in the way of opposition, and some did not fire at all.

As the division moved off the beach, the First and Second battalions diverged, with the First moving through Exit 3 and the Second moving down the coast to Exit 1. By this time, additional waves of infantrymen were ashore. Seventy-five minutes after H hour, the Third Battalion, Twenty-second Infantry, was on Green Beach and moving north, while the Third Battalion, Eighth Infantry, was on Red Beach and moving inland via Exit 2. With more and more units arriving, a traffic jam quickly developed.

In midafternoon, Collins found himself facing a far more immediate problem than too many men and too much equipment trying to squeeze through narrow beach exits. On board the *Bayfield* the difficulty was with the task force commander.

Two years older than Collins, Don Pardee Moon had been born on April 18, 1894, in Kokomo, Indiana, and followed a career path in the navy that was similar to that of Collins in the army. After graduation in June 1916 from the Naval Academy, Ensign Moon served on the battleship *Arizona* and remained with her for more than four years. During this time he devised a number of instruments to facilitate ships' gunnery. In 1921 and 1922 he attended the navy's postgraduate school at Annapolis and the University of Chicago, then had ordnance assignments ashore. He served aboard the battleships *Colorado* and *Nevada* from mid-1923 until mid-1926 and spent most of the rest of the decade with the Bureau of Ordnance and the Naval Gun Factory in Washington, D.C.

As lieutenant commander, he was a destroyer squadron gunnery officer with the U.S. Fleet in 1929–32, followed by instruction and staff duty at the Naval War College. In 1934 he became commanding officer of the Asiatic Fleet destroyer *John D. Ford*. Promoted to the rank of commander in 1936, he commanded a destroyer division, then returned to the Naval War College to attend the senior course and serve on that institution's staff. In 1940 he was again in command of a destroyer division. After attaining the rank of captain in September 1941, he moved up to command an Atlantic Fleet destroyer squadron. In 1942 he headed a squadron in convoys through the dangerous waters north of Norway. In command of Convoy PQ-17 en route to Russia, he saw most of his ships sunk by German submarines and bombers.

After participating in the invasion of North Africa, Moon served on the staff of Admiral Ernest J. King, the Chief of Naval Operations. At the end of this tour he was promoted to rear admiral and placed in command of an amphibious task group based in Italy and then shifted to England to take command of Task Force U. Still haunted by the slaughter of Convoy PQ-17, he was in command during the disastrous raid by German torpedo boats in Lyme Bay during Exercise Tiger.

Summoned to the flagship of his boss, Rear Admiral Alan Kirk, Moon met with Kirk's chief of staff. When Rear Admiral Arthur Struble observed a British submarine pass by the flagship displaying a broomstick, which meant the sub had made a clean sweep during its patrol, Struble said, "Well, I see somebody did his duty." Turning to Moon with what a Western Naval Task

Force staff officer who was present called the coldest glance he'd ever seen, he said in an unfriendly tone, "All right, Moon, tell me what happened."

Collins knew that Moon was a moody, somber, and solitary figure by nature, with "a certain lack of firmness and a tendency to be overly cautious," but he was shocked when he was called to Moon's office in the afternoon of June 6 to find Moon agitated over the loss of several of his ships and landing craft to mines and gunfire. This gloomy mood grew darker with receipt of a report from shore by Moon's intelligence officer. As Commander Robert H. Thayer reported the mistakes by the landing craft crews in putting troops ashore, Moon suddenly suggested suspension of landing operations until the water had been cleared of mines. There is no record of what Collins replied. In his memoirs, he said only that he had to put his foot down to persuade Moon not to do so. In an account two years later, he said, "I urged that this [delay] not be done and after some discussion Admiral Moon decided to continue with the landing operations."

An obviously tortured figure, Moon was subsequently returned to the Mediterranean theater. While his ship was moored in the harbor of Naples, Italy, he killed himself with a bullet to his head.

By the end of D-day, General Tubby Barton's Fourth Division established a beachhead and expanded it west to Sainte-Mère-Église and the town of Les Forges, but Collins noted that little progress was made to the north and an enemy pocket existed south and west of Sainte-Mère-Église. The next morning, Collins sent his deputy chief of staff, Colonel Howard S. Seale, and several aides to find a spot near the Fourth Division for a command post. Going ashore in a landing craft, Collins heard shell bursts from the direction of Omaha Beach, indicating that General Leonard Gerow's Fifth Corps was having a much rougher time taking its objectives. Greeted by Seale opposite Exit 2, Collins got into an armored car and headed for the CP that had been set up on a farm of the Cotelle family near the hamlet of Audouville-la-Hubert. He found that General Barton had established his command post across the road in a small grove of trees. Entering Barton's tent, he found an officer of the Eighty-second Airborne who had come from Sainte-Mère-Église with a message from Matthew Ridgway.

Expecting a strong counterattack by a column of German armor moving down the road from Sainte-Mère-Église, Ridgway wanted to borrow a tank unit that was attached to the Fourth Division, Company C, of the 746th Tank Battalion. It was parked under the cover of trees close to Barton's CP. When Barton was reluctant to release the armor, Collins directed him to turn the tanks over to Ridgway. With the messenger showing the tanks the way to Ridgway's position, they arrived just in time to stop the counterattack.

Back at his own CP, Collins met with James Van Fleet and the two went to see Ridgway at Sainte-Mère-Église in an armored car. They found him in fine spirits and grateful to have gotten the tanks. After Ridgway briefed Collins on the night jumps and landings by the Eighty-second between the Merderet and Douve rivers, Collins moved south to Maxwell Taylor's CP at Hiesville and located Taylor at a lookout post in an open field that afforded a view of a lock of the Douve River that Taylor's men had seized as part of the plan to move from the beach. They were to take the city of Carentan, drive up the Cotentin Peninsula, and capture the port of Cherbourg. To achieve this, the Seventh Corps was to link up with the Fifth Corps on D-day plus one. Although a meeting of the forces had yet to be achieved, Collins was confident that Taylor's paratroopers would soon close the gap.

As Collins devoted most of his attention to an attack that the Fourth Division was to execute northward from Utah to Carentan, General Bradley sent his deputy commander, Lieutenant General Courtney H. Hodges, to check on Taylor's progress. Assigned the task of confronting the German 6th Parachute Regiment and elements of the 91st Division were the 501st and 506th parachute infantry regiments under the command of Brigadier General Anthony C. McAuliffe. Supported by naval gunfire, artillery, and mortars, the attack began at two in the morning on June 12. After intense fighting, the city was taken and the flanks of the Fifth and Seventh secured. Having completed its mission by extending the beachhead's southern arc, the 101st Division was transferred from the Seventh Corps to the Eighth Corps, which gradually assumed responsibility for protection of the Seventh Corps' southwest flank.

Realizing that Cherbourg was not going to be taken as readily as the invasion master plan called for, Bradley told Collins to give top priority to sealing off the Cotentin Peninsula to prevent the Germans from reinforcing the port. This meant a change in direction of the Seventh Corps from north to west. On the afternoon of June 13, Collins told commanders, "The major effort of the corps is now to cut the peninsula."

To begin this effort, he ordered that an attack begin on June 16 along a line from the Douve to Gourbesville and continuation of drives by the Eighty-second Airborne Division, the Ninth Division, 358th Infantry, and other units on the peninsula. Because of the shifting of units, slight progress had been made by June 14. The next day, Collins shuttled between the CPs of Ridgway and Manton Eddy, leading the Ninth Division. When it appeared that the Germans were adjusting their position from a north-south defense west of the Douve to an east-west line, he ordered Eddy to speed up an attack by sending the 60th Infantry across the Douve to take high ground while other units attacked to the southwest. While these moves were put in motion, the Second Battalion, 60th Infantry, under Lieutenant Colonel Michael E. Kauffman, supported by a company of tanks, made a wide, cross-country sweep to the key objective of Saint Colombe, then crossed the Douve at three points and held their ground until the arrival of reinforcements. Collins described the maneuver as one of the most brilliant actions that he knew of in the entire war. By the night of June 17–18, 1944, he was confident that in all of these actions in cutting the Cotentin Peninsula, the fate of Cherbourg was sealed.

In a rare expression of approval of an American action, General Montgomery sent Collins a message congratulating the Seventh Corps for "roping off" the Cotentin Peninsula.

For the drive on the port city, Collins had in his command the Fourth, Ninth, and Seventy-ninth divisions. His plan contained in Field Orders No. 2 called for a coordinated attack to begin on June 19. Planning had begun with an analysis of the terrain and what was known of the enemy's objectives and potential. A relief map of the Cotentin Peninsula prepared by Seventh Corps engineer Mason Young showed that the Divette River and the upper reaches of the Douve divided the northern half of the peninsula into two broad compartments. The eastern, in which the Fourth Division had been fighting, contained two small cities, Montebourg and Valognes. Their stone houses provided strong enemy positions. The compartment west of the Douve was more open country, with fewer natural obstacles, and was not held in strength. The ground rose steadily in the compartments to form a ring to protect Cherbourg. The region was broken only by the narrow Trotebec and Divette streams that flowed into Cherbourg harbor. Aerial photographs showed that the Germans had organized the hills for defense.

Cresting four to five miles from the city, they had a formidable series of mutually supporting strongpoints consisting of concrete machine-gun, antitank, and 88mm gun emplacements and tank barriers. Colonel Leslie D. Carter of G-2 had estimated that the Germans would fight stubborn delaying actions until they withdrew within the ring defenses. This was confirmed by the capture of the orders of the German Eighty-fourth Corps and the

Seventy-seventh Division. The total enemy force, including coastal defense, antiaircraft, naval personnel, and organized labor battalions, was estimated to be twenty-five to forty thousand.

Collins decided to hit the Germans with three divisions abreast. In order from the east they were the Fourth, Seventy-ninth, and Ninth. The major effort of the corps would be in the form of a double-pronged attack by the Fourth and Ninth, moving against the Cherbourg defenses from east and west, with the Seventy-ninth Division and Fourth Cavalry Squadron serving as a link between the two prongs.

The Seventh Corps attack was begun by the Fourth Division under cover of darkness at three a.m., June 19, without artillery preparation. With Barton's men having made little progress in taking the strongly defended city of Montebourg by daylight, James Van Fleet's Eighth Infantry made a double envelopment that forced evacuation of the city, and by June 20 the forces under General Karl von Schlieben had been pulled back to Cherbourg's outer-ring defense. The other components of Collins's forces encountered little or no opposition, and the recently arrived Seventy-ninth Division in its first combat discovered an uncompleted launching base for V rockets.

While the Seventh Corps was moving against Cherbourg, the urgent need to capture the huge port was dramatized by the battering of the Normandy beachhead by the worst storm to hit the coast of France in recent memory. Blowing in from the English Channel on June 19, it raged for four days and either sank transport ships and supply barges or drove them onto the beaches. A series of artificial harbors that were built in England and floated to Normandy were ripped from their moorings. Unloading of ammunition and other supplies had to be suspended.

After a period of saturation bombing on the night of June 21, with the Seventh Corps arrayed in front of Cherbourg and no way for the Germans to escape, Collins sent an ultimatum by radio and by messenger to General von Schlieben to surrender. So that the radio message would be understood not only by the Germans in the city but by the Polish, Russian, and French troops who had joined the German army, it was also broadcast in those languages. The ultimatum gave von Schlieben until 0900 on June 22 to order his forces to give up or be annihilated.

What Collins and others up the Allied chain of command did not know was that Hitler had personally ordered von Schlieben not to surrender, saying that he had a duty to defend the city to the last bunker and to destroy all of its facilities for receiving and unloading ships so the Allies would find "not a harbor but a field of ruins." Hitler also told von Schlieben that all the German people and the world were watching the fight for Cherbourg, and on it depended not only the honor of the German army but von Schlieben's name.

Receiving no reply to the ultimatum, Collins had all three Seventh Corps divisions, with close support by fighter-bombers, penetrate the perimeter defenses on June 22. Two days later, they closed in on Cherbourg. When Bradley visited Collins on June 25, he said that he had arranged with Admiral Deyo to send Task Force 129 to cover seaward approaches with three battleships and four cruisers. Bradley also said with a chuckle, "Joe, you will love this. Monty has just announced, 'Caen is the key to Cherbourg.'"

The generals smiled at the irony of the situation. In the Overlord plan, Montgomery's force was expected to immediately drive in from its beachhead and take the city of Caen, yet nearly three weeks after D-day, he had failed to do so.

"Brad," Collins replied, "let's wire him to send us the key."

Expecting that the Seventh Corps would be in Cherbourg on the morning of Sunday, June 25, Collins went to a nine o'clock mass in a stable that had been used by German artillery. After a meeting with Bradley that took most of the morning, he had lunch and set out in an armored car that served as a rolling command post to visit all the divisions in the company and a correspondent for the *Chicago Daily News.* Arriving at the Fourth Division, they were taken by Ted Roosevelt to see a captured German position overlooking the city from the east. A short distance away, GIs were rounding up hundreds of German prisoners who had decided not to obey Hitler's order to fight to the last man.

That night, the Fourth Division flooded into Cherbourg while the Germans worked frantically to carry out Hitler's command that the Allies must find the port in ruins.

On June 26, Collins wrote to Gladys, "Yesterday was one of our great days."

Before Monday was over, he would relish the capture of General von Schlieben and the commander of the Cherbourg naval arsenal, as well as the fall of the last enemy bastion in the city, Fort du Roule. It was the highest point in the city and dominated the harbor.

While elements of the Seventh Corps eliminated the last vestiges of four years of Germany's occupation of France and its largest seaport, Collins chose not to wait until the campaign was over to turn over the government of the city from the U.S. Army to the French. On the afternoon of June 27, he assembled all his divisional commanders on the steps of the city hall to witness him presenting the French flag to the mayor of Cherbourg, Paul Reynaud. Speaking in halting French, Collins said that he was proud on behalf of the United States of America to return to a sister republic the first French city to be liberated by the Allies.

Even before the fall of Cherbourg, General Bradley, who had said to Eisenhower that Collins spoke their language, stopped at Collins's CP to discuss the next phase of operations—the breakout from Normandy.

CHAPTER SIX

COBRA

The confidence Eisenhower and Bradley placed in Joseph Lawton Collins when they met him in London had been justified in the Utah landings and by his Seventh Corps' masterful sweep to take Cherbourg. Now they would rely on Collins to lead the breakout from Normandy. To set the operation in motion, Ike left the London headquarters of SHAEF the day before Cherbourg fell to the Seventh Corps. Eager to see how the war was going, Ike went with Bradley to the center sector of the line held by the Seventy-ninth Division. Picking up the division commander, they drove to a regimental bivouac. When they got out of their vehicle, they found a captain stripped to his undershirt and bending over a helmet being used as a bucket for shaving. With a towel around his neck, the captain looked up with eyes wide in surprise at finding three generals. He snapped to attention, saluted, and fell in behind them as Ike strode among troops who were not only just as astonished at being reviewed by three generals but amazed that one of them was their Supreme Commander.

In his fresh summer worsteds and smart overseas cap, recalled

Bradley, Eisenhower stood out crisply in the monotonous parade of sweaty GIs in their olive drab field uniforms and helmets. The bolder ones shouted, "Hey, Ike."

Eisenhower turned to Bradley and said, "Wish I didn't have to go back. I'll be mighty glad when I get to move over here with you."

Fondly recalling visiting the front, Eisenhower wrote in *Crusade in Europe*, "I spent much time in France, conferring frequently with General Bradley and General Montgomery concerning timing and strength of projected battle operations. Such visits with Bradley were always enjoyable because he shared my liking for roaming through the forward areas to talk to the men actually bearing the burden of battle."

After the success of Operation Overlord/Neptune, Ike faced the daunting challenge of breaking out of the Normandy beachhead and carrying out the simple order given to him as commander of SHAEF: destroy Germany's war machine and give the Allies victory in Europe.

For the men in Collins's Seventh Corps who captured Cherbourg, bearing the burden of battle had resulted in an unexpected and delightful dividend. Anticipating a prolonged holdout against the Americans, General von Schlieben's forces had stocked underground shelters with thousands of bottles of the finest French wine, champagne, and brandy. "As a result," Bradley recorded, "we fell heir not only to a transatlantic port but to a massive underground wine cellar."

As word of the prize spread through the ranks even before fighting ended, GIs scurried to be in a position to reap an intoxicating reward. Collins and Bradley tossed the dilemma of potentially having a mass of drunken soldiers on their hands to a higher authority, along with a recommendation that the wine trove be padlocked until it could be "equitably distributed" among all divisions. Ike agreed. When the distribution began, Collins sent some to Ike and gave Bradley half a case of champagne, which he saved and took home after the war to celebrate the christening of his grandson.

While the U.S. Army school system introduced middle-rank officers who would go on to be future generals to strategy, tactics, logistics, supply, and all the military arts that evolved over centuries of warfare, none of the classes during the Roaring Twenties and in the decade of the Great Depression anticipated that on some future date Eisenhower, Bradley, and Collins would be in France in command of more than a million men. In the twenty-five days since June 6, they had been ferried across the English Channel by the U.S. Navy to join the initial invasion force, along with more than half a million tons of equipment and supplies. This mighty host now stood poised behind a forty-mile front that started with a forward bulge in the marshy land at Caumont, fell back to behind the town of Saint-Lô in an arc that ran through the Carentan swamps, turned across the Cotentin, and went on to the west channel coast. Greater than the combined strength of all the forces under Montgomery and George Patton in the Sicilian campaign, the Americans in France were in eleven divisions and ready to break out of Normandy for a sweep across the French heartland and into Germany.

Under Monty, sixteen divisions on a forty-mile front had been stymied by fierce German resistance west of the city of Caen. According to the Overlord master plan, the attack out of the lodgment would pivot at Caen and the entire Allied line would wheel eastward. Collins and the Seventh Corps were to sweep south from the Cotentin Peninsula as part of this great cartwheel that had the goal of taking Paris and then rapidly driving onward to smash Hitler's Third Reich.

"Only a *breakout*," Bradley emphasized in his book, *A Soldier's Story*, "would enable us to crash into the enemy's rear where we could fight a war of movement on our own best terms. As long as the enemy confined us to the bocage [thick, high, and almost impenetrable hedgerows] of Normandy where we were forced to match him man to man, he could exact a prohibitive price for the few miserable yards we might gain."

With no desire to become bogged down in a repeat of the trench warfare of World War I, Eisenhower and Bradley needed a breakthrough in which they could unleash their armor as the spearhead of a rapid movement into the center of France. In the plan that emerged, Collins was to take over part of General Troy Middleton's Eighth Corps front across the Cotentin marshes and nudge the Germans out through the neck of the peninsula while Middleton drove to the crucial objective of Coutances.

Informed of this design during the battle for Cherbourg, Collins was told he would have five days for the turnaround of his troops. Bradley appreciated that this was a tall order, even for Lightning Joe Collins, and a taller one yet for his troops. They consisted of the Fourth, Ninth, and Eighty-third divisions. Positioned to drive across the Cotentin toward Coutances, they would be opposed by German troops whose command in France after the reverses inflicted at Normandy had been ruthlessly shaken up by Hitler.

Replacing Field Marshal Karl Gerd von Rundstedt as commander in chief, Field Marshal Gunther von Kluge had commanded a corps on the Russian front. The Seventh Army was now commanded by General Paul Hausser. The ever-reliable Erwin Rommel remained in command of Army Group B. Immediately opposing Collins's Seventh Corps and Troy Middleton's Eighth Corps was the Eighty-fourth Corps under Lieutenant General Dietrich von Choltitz. Brought in from Italy, he had the Seventeenth SS Panzer Grenadier Division and Sixth Parachute Division, both understrength.

In the fight to meet the objective of taking Cherbourg, the Seventh Corps had suffered more than twenty-two thousand casualties, with twenty-eight hundred killed, fifty-seven hundred missing, and the rest wounded. In choosing an interim military governor for the city, Eisenhower and his subordinates agreed that no one in the European Theater of Operations was better suited than the man who had been governor general of Puerto Rico and then had held the same post in the Philippines. With headquarters set in a cellar lit by a single lamp, Theodore Roosevelt, Jr., governed until Collins handed over the city to the French. Returning to the Fourth Division, Roosevelt wrote to his wife on July 10 that after being out in the rain, he was a "pretty sick rabbit," but after a physical checkup the doctor said that his troubles were primarily from having put an inhuman strain on a body that was not exactly new.

The day after writing to Eleanor, he was visited by his son Quentin and confessed that he had been having small heart attacks, but kept them secret. When Quentin returned to the First Division, he was told that his father was dead. At that moment on Eisenhower's desk ready to be signed was a set of orders dated July 14, 1944, appointing Ted Roosevelt commander of the Ninetieth Division in the rank of major general. Also pending at SHAEF headquarters was a recommendation by General Tubby Barton, endorsed by Collins, that Ted be awarded the only Congressional Medal of Honor issued for action on Utah Beach. Presenting it to Eleanor on September 22, 1944, President Franklin D. Roosevelt said, "His father would have been proud." Bradley wrote that Ted "braved death with an indifference that destroyed its terror for thousands upon thousands of younger men. I have never known a braver man nor a more devoted soldier."

Eleven days before learning of Roosevelt's death, Collins had moved his CP to Bloisville, north of Carentan, and on the following day (July 2) took over the Eighty-third Division, commanded by Major General Robert C. Macon, a veteran of North Africa. Studying maps of the terrain on the corps front, Collins recognized that his troops were in for "tough sledding." On July 4, the Eighty-third with regiments abreast commenced a movement to take the city of Saintency and immediately ran into trouble as its tanks bogged down in spongy ground in the face of a powerful

German force. Among those killed was a regimental commander, Colonel Martin Barndollar. By the end of the day, the division had lost almost fourteen hundred men and failed to reach its objective.

Convinced that the Eighty-third Division could not break the enemy front alone, Collins brought in the Fourth Division, but it also made little headway. In an attack on July 7, rain prevented the use of supporting dive-bombers. Confronting the Fourth, and all the American units as they planned to move away from the beachhead, was the bocage region's hedgerows with walls that were as formidable as the stone fortresses of medieval castles. Separating farmland plots of varying sizes, they were not only barriers but perfect for concealment of machine guns or small combat teams. To the frustration of American commanders, these hedgerows even thwarted the armor. Eisenhower wrote, "Our tanks could help but little. Each, attempting to penetrate a hedgerow, was forced to climb almost vertically, thus exposing the unprotected belly of the tank and rendering it easy prey to any type of armor-piercing bullet. Equally exasperating was the fact that with the tank snout thrust skyward it was impossible to bring guns to bear upon the enemy; crews were helpless to defend themselves or to destroy the Germans."

Having heard of the hedgerow problem, Ike saw it for himself on a visit to the front. At a forward observation tower on a hill that rose about a hundred feet above the surrounding hedgerows, he found his view of the area so limited that he called on the air force to fly him over it in a fighter plane. When it landed, Ike expressed concern to Bradley that word of the flight might reach newsmen and they would send stories to newspapers at home. "General Marshall," Ike explained to Bradley, "would give me hell."

Bradley did not doubt it.

"While Collins was hoisting his VII Corps flag over Cherbourg," Bradley recorded in his memoirs, "Montgomery was spending his reputation in a bitter siege against the old university city of Caen. For three weeks he had rammed his troops against panzer tanks he had deliberately drawn toward that city as part of our Allied strategy of diversion from the Normandy campaign. Although Caen contained an important road junction that Montgomery would eventually need, for the moment the capture of that city was only incidental to his mission."

Monty's primary task was to attract German troops to the British so that the Americans might more easily secure Cherbourg and get into position for the breakout.

While planning the strategic and tactical aspects of mounting a breakout, Eisenhower was also looking farther ahead. "It became necessary," he recorded in *Crusade in Europe*, "to specify a date on which the whole ground situation should take its final form."

In this grand design, he planned to send into the fighting in France the most controversial commander of the war to lead a brand-new unit. To take command of the Third Army, Eisenhower's choice was Lieutenant General George S. Patton, Jr. Having planned and carried out the invasion of French Morocco in 1942 as part of Operation Torch, Patton had been hastily shifted to Algeria to take over the Second Corps and rally it after it suffered a humiliating defeat in the first exposure of American troops to combat in a battle at the Kasserine Pass. With a carefully self-cultivated, swashbuckling demeanor that he enhanced with a pair of ivory-grip pistols on his hips, blunt language sprinkled with obscenities, enameled helmet, and cavalry breeches with riding boots, he had achieved famous victories in North Africa and Sicily, only to be relieved of command by Ike after the war correspondents, whose attention he had courted, reported that he had slapped a shell-shocked soldier and accused him of cowardice. Stripped of command, he was brought to England and made "commander" of a phony army supposedly based in Scotland for the purpose of misleading the Germans into believing the invasion would occur at the Pas de Calais, with Patton in command.

Eisenhower envisioned activating Patton's Third Army on August 1, 1944, creating the Twelfth Army Group, with Bradley in command, and turning Bradley's First Army over to his deputy, Lieutenant General Courtney H. Hodges. What he could not have foreseen was the time required to effect the breakout from Normandy. The July battling all along the front, Ike noted, involved some of the fiercest and most bloody fighting of the war in swamps and streams and over ground that was unusually advantageous to the Germans.

For Bradley, pressures to launch a breakout were exacerbated by Montgomery's request that Bradley relinquish the U.S. Third Armored Division and send it to Caen to bolster British forces in the face of an expected German onslaught. Feeling more in need of the tank division, and believing, as General Black Jack Pershing did in World War I, that Americans should never be put under foreign command, Bradley also recalled that in the Tunisia battle "extra-national" assignments of U.S. forces had "calamitous" results. Determined to oppose Monty's request, he had a meeting with him and proposed that Americans take over part of the British front. Monty said that he would send a brigade of tanks to "keep an eye" on German armor on the Fifth Corps' flank. At the same time, Bradley provided the Fifth Corps with a division of inflatable "rubber tanks," which had so successfully deceived the Germans into believing that Patton was amassing a mighty army in Scotland to attack the Pas de Calais. Eventually, none of this mattered. Several days after Bradley's visit, Montgomery launched an all-out attack, with strong air support by heavy Royal Air Force bombers. By July 10, Monty had eliminated German resistance. Instead of achieving this on D-day as the Overlord plan anticipated, he did so thirty-six days late.

Frustrated by difficulties in launching the breakout from the Cotentin Peninsula, Bradley studied maps for another springboard that promised to be less costly in casualties. He found that there was no alternative but to "club our way" through marshland at Carentan. The operation he devised was given the code name Cobra. Unveiled at a conference with corps commanders at his CP in back of Omaha Beach on July 12, it called for saturation bombing as the prelude to Collins's Seventh Corps spearheading the breakout west of Saint-Lô. The plan also provided for the rearrangement of corps boundaries and division assignments that gave Collins firmer ground on which to advance. During the conference, Collins persuaded Bradley to give him the Fourth Division to bolster his forces in the breakthrough and for later exploitation by the Ninth and Thirtieth divisions.

Explaining this complex plan in his autobiography, Collins wrote that it divided Cobra into three phases: breakout, exploitation, and consolidation. The operation plan made important changes in the scheme for maneuvering during the phases. With selection of the Marigny–St. Gilles front for the breakthrough, Bradley decided to make the principal effort using the redoubtable First Infantry Division, and the motorized and reinforced combat command, CC "B," of the Third Armored to drive on Coutances. Known as the Big Red One because of its unit insignia, the First Division was a veteran of the North Africa and Sicily campaigns and was commanded by Major General Clarence R. Huebner, in whom Bradley had great confidence. The Third Armored, less CC "B," would follow a roundabout route from Marigny to Coutances. The First Infantry and Third Armored would join in the destruction of any enemy troops between the Eighth and Seventh corps.

The Second Armored Division, under Major General Edward H. Brooks, with the motorized Twenty-second Infantry Regiment attached, would follow the Thirtieth Division and seize the area of Le Mesnil-Herman–St. Sampson to cover movement of the First Division and Third Armored through the Marigny–St. Gilles gap. The Second Armored would push a combat team to the southwest via the St. Gilles–Canisy road, prepared, on Bradley's orders, either to seize points along the Brehal-Hambye road between Cerences and St. Denis-le-Gast in order to prevent any reinforcements moving through this area, move on Coutances in support of the Third Armored, or move to the southeast to reinforce the main body of the Second Armored in its mission.

This scheme of maneuver was developed during the week following publication of the First Army's Outline Plan on July 13, issued after several informal discussions with Bradley and the division commanders, with almost continuous collaboration between the staff of the First Army and the Seventh Corps. As approved by Bradley the plan was embodied in the Seventh Corps Field Orders No. 6 on July 20.

Bradley stated in *A Soldier's Story* that he picked Collins as the corps commander for Cobra because he was "nervy and ambitious."

While Collins worked on the ground plan, the air element was in the hands of Major General Elwood R. Quesada, chief of the Ninth Tactical Air Command, whose planes had softened up Cherbourg and operated in direct support of the First Army. Nicknamed "Pete" and described as flamboyant and handsome, he was born in 1904 in Washington, D.C., and had attended the Wyoming Seminary in Wilkes-Barre, Pennsylvania, the University of Maryland, and Georgetown University. Enlisting in the army in September 1924 as a flying cadet, he received his wings and commission in the Air Reserve a year later. Inactive for one and a half years, he returned to duty as an engineering officer at Bolling Field, Washington, D.C., and served until June 1928, then was an aide to the chief of the Air Corps, Major General James Fechet. From October 1930 until April 1932, he was in Cuba as assistant military attaché.

He also served as personal pilot for Colonel George C. Marshall at Fort Benning. In 1929 he joined Carl Spaatz and Ira Eaker on a daring, record-setting flight over San Diego. Following a stint on Hap Arnold's staff, he was named commander of an air defense group on Long Island in July 1941. As a brigadier general, he led an air group in North Africa in 1943. Named the deputy commander of the Coastal Air Force, he was responsible for defending the Allied ports against Luftwaffe attacks and interdicting enemy shipping in the Mediterranean. After a bit of difficulty with a British superior, he performed well. As a result, in late 1943 he was sent to England as head of the Ninth Fighter Command in preparation for the Normandy invasion. In the three months prior to D-day his aircraft flew escort missions for heavy bombers of the Eighth Air Force and bombed bridges, rail yards, and enemy fortifications in western France. When the Allies landed, his fighter-bombers had worked closely with the ground forces.

Bradley wrote admiringly of Quesada that although he could have passed for a prototype of the hot pilot with his shiny green trousers, broad easy smile, and crumpled jaunty hat, he was a brilliant, hard, and daring air-support commander on the ground who had come into the war as a young and imaginative man unencumbered by the prejudices and theories held by many of his seniors on the use of tactical air. Of the plan for the use of Quesada's planes in the breakout Bradley wrote, "Just as soon as Collins's tank and motorized columns broke through, they were to highball toward Brittany while disregarding both their flanks and rear. To protect these columns from the danger of ambush and to assist them in breaking through the enemy's strongpoints, the air arm was to put up a dawn-to-dusk fighter-bomber umbrella over the head of each column. Thus [they] could reconnoiter for the column commander and attack any barrier to his advance. Air and ground were to communicate through an air-support party to be attached to the head of each column."

Meeting with Quesada, Bradley asked, "You can keep them in radio contact with each other?"

"Sure we can," said Quesada, "but it may be tough on my boys supporting your columns. They'll be riding in open radio jeeps while yours are riding in tanks."

"Well," said Bradley, "why not put your air-support parties in tanks?"

"Do you mean it, General?" replied Quesada excitedly. "By golly, that would do it! But we'll have to check on the radios and see if they can get through from the inside of a tank."

"Fine, Pete," said Bradley. "I'll have a couple of Shermans delivered to your CP by noon."

Quesada left and Bradley directed ordnance to send two medium tanks at once to the Ninth Tac. The officer in ordnance looked at the note he had scribbled and said, "Ninth Tac? Why, that's the air force. What in hell would they be doing with tanks? The Old Man's screwy. He must mean Ninth Infantry Division."

When the two Shermans clanked into Manton Eddy's CP, an officer said, "Not us. Must be some mistake. We don't need any replacements."

When ordnance called back to Bradley, he was asked, "About those tanks, General?"

"Oh, those two for Pete Quesada," said Bradley. "Yes, did he get them?"

"You mean General Quesada—the Ninth Air Force Quesada? Well, I'll be damned."

When the tanks sallied into Quesada's CP, Bradley wrote, an officer there hurried out to turn them away. It was not until late afternoon that the tanks were finally delivered for testing, but the radio worked and Quesada acquired an armored force of his own. In the planning for the use of Quesada's planes, the only question Collins asked was about the size of the bombs. Quesada had proposed that because the British had complained about their armor having to deal with cratering from heavy bombs, his force would use 250-pounders. Collins replied that he'd take the gamble of getting around craters in favor of the greater blast effect of 500-pound bombs armed with instantaneous fuses.

At this time, Collins learned that the solution to the problem of getting through hedgerows had been solved by an ingeniously inventive sergeant named Curtis G. Culin, Jr., of the 102nd Cavalry Reconnaissance Squadron. Fashioning tusklike prongs made from pieces of a German roadblock, he had fitted them onto the front of a Sherman and demonstrated that they not only plowed through the thick foliage and earth of hedgerows but that the scooped-out clumps served to both hold down the fronts of the tanks and camouflage them. Culin named the devices Rhinos. Seeing a demonstration, Bradley ordered all Operation Cobra tanks equipped with them. The sweet irony of Culin's invention was that they were made from steel barriers that Rommel had installed on the invasion beaches.

When Bradley set July 19 as the tentative date for the start of the breakout, it became clear to Collins that the date was too early, because four days of laborious fighting by the Ninth and Thirtieth divisions were required before the Périers–St. Lô road was reached on July 20. Furthermore, Collins noted, the Nineteenth Corps' Twenty-ninth Division did not enter the battered city of Saint-Lô until the nineteenth. On that date, Bradley flew to England to arrange details of the saturation bombing with British Air Chief Marshal Trafford Leigh-Mallory, commander of Allied Air Forces. Also present at the conference were Marshal Arthur Tedder, Eisenhower's deputy; General Carl "Tooey" Spaatz, commander of the U.S. Strategic Air Europe; Lieutenant General Lewis H. Brereton, commanding the American Ninth Air Force, who was to arrange bombing; and General Quesada. Leigh-Mallory approved the plan and promised to use 2,246 heavy and medium bombers with fighter-bombers. These were many more than Bradley hoped for. He and Collins agreed that the area to be bombed would be a rectangle seven thousand yards wide and five thousand yards deep south of the Périers–St. Lô road. In this plan, troops were to pull back about a mile just before the bombing.

On July 24, the mightiest air armada ever planned took off. The weather over the target area was miserable. Although Leigh-Mallory decided to postpone the attack, planes were already in the air. The word reached six fighter-bombers to turn back, and others found the weather too bad to drop their loads, but more than three hundred heavy bombers went ahead with the attack. Instead of flying perpendicular to the road according to the plan, they came in parallel and rained some of their bombs on the Americans, killing 25 men of the Thirtieth Division and leaving 131 wounded. In hard fighting to regain the territory from which the troops had pulled back, the Thirty-ninth Infantry suffered 77 casualties and the unit commander, Colonel Paddy Flint, was killed. In a second air attack on July 25, bombs fell short again, killing 61 and wounding 374 men of the Thirtieth Division. The Forty-seventh Infantry Regiment of the Ninth Division had 14 dead and 33 wounded, bringing total Seventh Corps casualties to friendly fire to 601, with 111 killed. Among the dead was Lieutenant General Leslie J. McNair. Unknown to Collins, the former commander of Army Ground Forces, who had also been the acting commander of the phantom Army Group that Adolf Hitler still expected to attack at the Pas de Calais, had joined an assault battalion to see the bombing firsthand.

When Collins reported McNair's death to Bradley, Eisenhower was in France to be present during the breakout. Fearing that McNair's death might be found out by reporters, and that their stories might undermine the cover plan that the invasion was to come at the Pas de Calais, Ike and Bradley arranged for McNair to be buried secretly. Any reports of his demise were to be suppressed by censors until a successor to McNair could be found to command the fictional Army Group.

As to the errant bombing, Ike vowed that he would never again okay the use of heavy bombers against tactical targets.

"That's the job for artillery," he explained to Captain Joseph J. Ryan en route to an airstrip for a return to England. "I gave them the green light this time, but I promise you it's the last."

Although the bombing mistakes temporarily set back the Seventh Corps attack, the large air assault also had the effect of raising havoc among the enemy. Collins received G-2 reports that the German defensive positions were churned into mounds of earth and buried Germans in tons of debris. Dazed prisoners babbled about the hell that the bombs had made of a key road and a command post. Despite the intelligence, the ground attack by the Fourth, Ninth, and Thirtieth divisions met dogged resistance from the infantry of the Panzer Lehr Division and troops of the Fifth Parachute Division. Having already been hit by friendly bombs, the Thirtieth Division found itself strafed by British fighter-bombers and checked by Mark V tanks, but managed to take part of its objective.

While fighting raged in and around the town of Marigny for two days, the Second Armored, the Thirtieth Division, and General Maurice Rose's Combat Team A reached Saint-Gilles in the middle of the afternoon, rolled through it, and opened the exploitation phase of Cobra. After a fight that Collins termed "some of the wildest melees" of the war, the Seventh Corps was directed in Bradley's Field Orders No. 2 to "continue present operations to isolate enemy forces north of Coutances and at the same time continue to push rapidly to the south." Because the advance of the Seventh Corps would be made while the Eighth Corps was also moving south, Collins anticipated that the two might cross paths, with a resultant horrific traffic jam. Arriving at Coutances on July 28, he found the wild confusion he'd expected. He wrote, "Both divisions were trying to get on the Gavray Road, which was originally in the VII Corps sector."

Hooking up his portable phone, he called First Army HQ. When he described the mess to Bradley, he was told that the Eighth Corps Fourth Armored should have the right-of-way. By the end of the day, Bradley straightened out the tangle by shifting the boundary between the two corps, and Collins turned his attention to reorienting the Seventh Corps to the south and getting on with Cobra by pushing an attack on July 31, but with General Leroy Watson relieved as the CO of the Third Armored and replaced by Maurice Rose. Forty-three years old, Rose had lied about his age and enlisted in the National Guard at age sixteen with a desire to join General Black Jack Pershing's Punitive Expedition in Mexico, but was discharged when his true age was found out. Undaunted, he signed up for Officers Training School at Fort Riley, Kansas, in 1917, and was commissioned second lieutenant in the infantry. He sailed with the 333rd Infantry for duty in France and was wounded in the Saint-Mihiel Offensive. Returning to the States in January 1920, he gave civilian life a brief try but returned to the army and served at various posts in the United States and in the Panama Canal Zone. Following the Japanese attack on Pearl Harbor, he became chief of staff, Second Armored Division, in January 1942. In North Africa, he was the first officer to take the surrender of a large German unit and was promoted to brigadier general on June 2, 1943.

Satisfied that the Third Armored was in capable hands with Rose, Collins found himself having a reunion with an officer he hadn't seen since 1941 at Fort Benning. Called to a meeting with Bradley at his CP in an apple orchard near Colombiers, fifteen miles northeast of Saint-Lô, he found George Patton waiting to see Bradley.

As they chatted, Patton said, "You know, Collins, you and I are the only people around here who seem to be enjoying this goddamned war!"

At that point, Collins recalled, Patton's face clouded.

Referring to the slapping incident in Sicily that got him relieved of command, Patton said, "But I'm in the doghouse. I'm in the doghouse! I've got to do something spectacular!"

CHAPTER SEVEN

KILLING GROUNDS

"As Collins struggled toward the bomb-pitted carpet at Saint-Lô on that jittery afternoon of July 25," wrote Omar Bradley, "he broke path for an army now grown to 21 U.S. divisions. It was as large a force as we dared hitch to a single army command."

On July 20, Eisenhower pinned Distinguished Service Medals on Collins and Gerow and added an oak-leaf cluster to a DSM Bradley had already earned. The decorations came as a change was being made in the structure of the Allied command. Earlier in July, Eisenhower had given Bradley authority to split the U.S. forces into two field armies whenever Bradley thought it was desirable. The change would give Bradley full-time command of the Twelfth U.S. Army Group and place Courtney Hodges at the helm of the First Army. Montgomery would relinquish command of Allied ground forces and revert to head of British armies. At a meeting on July 20 in Bradley's CP, Eisenhower asked Bradley if he had a date in mind for the changes. Bradley suggested August 1, 1944. Ike assented, with the understanding that at some point he would establish SHAEF headquarters in France. Restructuring of the Allied forces remained a secret until August 12, when a reporter for the Associated Press evaded censorship and broke the news. When word of the shift reached the British people, they saw a humiliating demotion of Montgomery and an affront to Britain. The flap was somewhat assuaged when Montgomery was promoted to field marshal to coincide with the reshuffle, but Bradley felt that British resentment never completely healed.

What very few British knew as the Montgomery flap raged on was that the American general who had beaten Montgomery in a race to capture the Sicilian port city of Messina in 1943 had been smuggled out of Great Britain to France. Crossing the channel on July 6 with the vanguard of the newly constituted Third Army, George Patton was hidden in a bivouac in the Cotentin Peninsula until Bradley was ready to see him and define his and the Third Army's role as part of Bradley's Twelfth Army Group. Having served under Patton in North Africa and Sicily, Bradley was apprehensive about how Patton would accept the reversal in roles. He said in *A Soldier's Story* that his main concern was that he might have to spend too much time curbing Patton's impetuous habits, although he had no worries that he would have to goad Patton to keep the Third Army on the move. Bradley wrote, "We had only to keep him pointed in the right direction."

Returning to Seventh Corps headquarters after encountering Patton at Bradley's command post, Collins had more on his mind than Patton's future in Operation Cobra. By August 1, one week after its start, the Seventh Corps had advanced more than thirty miles south of Saint-Lô. Unknown to him, the German Seventh Army commander, Paul Hausser, was preparing to counterattack.

On August 1, Patton's Third Army became operational. Bradley relinquished command of the First Army to Hodges and assumed command of the Twelfth Army Group. At this point, the Allied ground forces consisted of two American armies under Bradley, plus a Canadian and a British army, both under Montgomery's Twenty-first Army Group. Until Eisenhower took personal direction of the ground campaign, Montgomery would function as the commander of the land forces executing Overlord, with the initial objective of taking and holding the portion of France between the Seine and the Loire rivers. Preinvasion plans had envisioned the Allies gaining a lodgment by sending Patton's Third Army west from Avranches to take the Brittany area and its vital ports. Hodges's First Army was to protect Patton's forces, swing to the right of the British and Canadian armies to the southeast and east, and move eastward to the Seine. This scheme had to be revised because of a paucity of enemy in Brittany, the disorganization of the German left flank forces near Avranches, and the reality that in driving to Avranches the U.S. forces had outflanked the German defensive line in Normandy.

Issuing Field Orders No. 7 on August 1, 1944, Collins sketched a plan to envelop the German west flank and exploit the breakthrough south of Villedieu. The First Division was to turn east to take high ground west of Mortain, while the Fourth Division seized the St. Pois–Cherence-le-Roussel line and the Ninth Division seized high ground and road centers on the Fourth Division's left. Crucial to First Division success was the capture of a hill designated 317. When Collins contacted First Division commander General Ralph Huebner to remind him to take the hill, Huebner replied, "Joe, I've already got it."

On August 7, the Germans began a counterattack that was not a surprise to the Allies. Because of the capture in 1940 of the German High Command's complex coding machine and success in figuring out how it worked in a supersecret program called Ultra, the Allied field commanders had been receiving German operational orders from Hitler and his top officers often before they were received by the German field officers. Having taken direct charge of the war in the west, Hitler on August 2 had ordered General von Kluge to close the gap between Mortain and Avranches with a counterattack. What did surprise the

Allies, Collins recorded, was the strength and exact timing of the attack. It came as Collins was shifting the First Division from Mortain and replacing it with the Thirtieth Division. The attack began without artillery preparation shortly after midnight of August 6–7.

In Montgomery's analysis of the situation created by the breakout, the only hope the Germans had of saving their armies would be by a staged withdrawal to the Seine. By swinging the Allied right flank toward Paris, Monty hoped to speed up and disrupt the German pullout. With the German counterattack, he felt that if he acted quickly enough and drove south from Caen to Falaise, he would leave the Germans in what he envisioned as an "awkward situation." This would be the beginning of a wide encirclement. Consequently, he wanted a wide swing past Germans west of the Seine by the U.S. Fifteenth Corps while the Canadian First Army attacked toward Falaise no later than August 8.

On August 3, it had been decided to clear Brittany with one corps, while the remainder of the force turned eastward with its sights on the Seine. The intention was to swing the right flank in order to push the Germans back against the lower part of the river. With the bridges having been taken out by air bombardment, the Germans would be encircled. The Fifteenth Corps, commanded by Major General Wade H. Haislip and under Patton's Third Army control, was committed to action near Avranches between the Eighth Corps of the Third Army and Collins's Seventh Corps. Because the Fifteenth Corps was already around the Germans' left, Haislip's assignment was initiating a sweep toward the objectives of Laval and Le Mans. Expecting the Germans to try to escape the breakout by pivoting on the Caen area as they fell back, he planned to block this with Lieutenant General Henry Crerar's First Canadian Army driving southward to Falaise from positions near Caen, then swinging northeast from Falaise to the Seine near Rouen. Lieutenant General Miles C. Dempsey's Second British Army, which had been attacking near

Caumont, was to continue eastward through Argentan on its way to the Seine. On the Allied right, Bradley's Twelfth Army Group was to launch its main effort by driving rapidly toward the Seine.

In an analysis of this situation, the historian Martin Blumenson wrote that Montgomery's intentions were postulated on the belief that the Germans had no alternative but to withdraw to and across the Seine, and that the Allies could disorganize, harass, and pursue them, turning their retreat into a rout and destroying their forces while they were west of the Seine.

What Montgomery did not anticipate, Blumenson noted, was that the Germans would upset his logic and counterattack. When they did so from an area east of Mortain in an attempt to retake Avranches and establish a new and continuous defensive line, they hoped to halt the Allied war of movement and a drive to the Seine by imposing static conditions that had made it possible to successfully contain the Allies during June and much of July.

Reviewing the position of the Seventh Corps as the Germans attacked, Collins felt satisfied that they would be unable to break through the Fourth and Ninth divisions. With five infantry and two armored divisions, he was confident the Seventh Corps was prepared to fight the battle of Mortain with a combination of offense and defense. Critical in this fight was a struggle for Hill 317. Surrounded by the Seventeenth SS Panzer Grenadier Division, the Twenty-second Battalion, 120th Infantry, had to be supplied with food and ammunition by airdrop, while the 230th Field Artillery crammed smoke-shell casings with bandages, morphine, and other medical supplies and lobbed them onto the hill. French farmers on the broad hilltop helped with food by sharing chickens and vegetables. Flying to aid the defenders, General Quesada's fighter-bombers and Royal Air Force squadrons pounded the German armor. After four days of what Collins saw as one of the most outstanding small-unit actions of the European war, the

Thirty-fifth Division beat off the Germans southwest of Mortain and the Thirtieth Division stormed the south slopes of the hill like a scene in a Hollywood war movie. In the battling, the Second Battalion of the 120th Infantry counted three hundred out of its seven-hundred-man strength killed or wounded. On August 12, the panzers clanked away with nearly a hundred tanks abandoned.

Four days earlier, the American commanders, with Ike present, discussed the possibility of trapping the Germans. Bradley telephoned Montgomery and secured approval for a change in plan. Bradley's proposal was based on the fact that the Fifteenth Corps had rounded the Germans' left flank and was attacking through lightly defended territory. By turning the Fifteenth Corps north from Le Mans toward Alençon, Bradley reasoned, it would threaten the counterattacking Germans from the south while the First Canadian Army was already launching an attack from positions near Caen toward Falaise that threatened the Germans from the north. Bradley realized that by attacking toward Avranches, the Germans in Normandy had actually stuck their heads into a noose, and now he saw an opportunity to surround them. Possession of Falaise and Alençon would not only threaten Germans with encirclement but make it possible to deprive them of two of the three main east-west roads that they controlled. With the Canadians attacking from the north and the Fifteenth Corps moving from the south, the pincers could close a possible escape route.

This meant suspending the drive to the Seine, but a snag developed when the Canadian attack bogged down in the Caen-Falaise corridor eight miles north of Falaise. The Fifteenth Corps took Le Mans, and the following day jumped off to the north. As the gap between Canadians and Americans narrowed, Montgomery estimated that the Germans would bring up additional divisions from the east, or move their armored and mobile forces eastward out of the pocket toward supplies of ammunition and gasoline. If the Germans chose the latter course, Monty reasoned, they would probably operate in the Argentan-Alençon area to have the benefit of the difficult bocage country. The intent of this would be to hold off the Americans while using the advantageous hedgerow terrain to help their withdrawal. Expecting the Germans to mass stronger forces in defense of Alençon than of Falaise, Montgomery ordered the Canadians to continue their efforts to capture Falaise and proceed from there to Argentan. Meanwhile, the Fifteenth Corps was to advance through Alençon to just south of Argentan.

Drawing a line to separate the zones of operation of the American Twelfth Army Group and the British-Canadian forces of the Twenty-first Army Group, Monty envisioned a meeting of Canadian and American forces south of Argentan, encircling the enemy. Moving westward, the British Second Army and U.S. First Army were to corral the Germans into a Canadian-American pen and assist in their destruction.

As the Canadians resumed their attack toward Falaise, the Fifteenth Corps drove north from Le Mans on August 10 and secured Alençon on August 12. Meanwhile, George Patton had as his objective the army group boundary north of Alençon and south of Argentan so that Haislip's forces could go on with their attack. While the Fifteenth Corps attacked toward Argentan, Haislip told Patton that he was about to capture its last objective and suggested additional troops be placed under his command in order to block all the east-west roads under his control north of Alençon. Because the Canadians had made no further progress toward Falaise while the Fifteenth Corps moved rapidly, Patton told Haislip to go beyond Argentan and to "push on slowly in the direction of Falaise." After reaching it, Haislip was to continue until contact was made with the Canadians. Attacking toward Argentan on the morning of August 13, the Fifteenth Corps hit strong resistance that temporarily halted the advance. As the corps was preparing to launch a renewed effort to get to and through Argentan, Patton received a message from Bradley forbidding him to move any farther northward. This forced Patton to order Haislip to halt and remain in place.

In the face of this stop order, which has fueled heated debate among scores of World War II historians and armchair generals since Bradley issued it, the Germans were presented with an avenue of escape in the opening created between the Canadians and Americans. Both Bradley and Eisenhower later explained that they feared that the dual advance by Canadians and Americans would result in a dangerous and uncontrollable maneuver. In Ike's words, it might have caused a "calamitous battle between friends." Bradley said that he had preferred "a solid shoulder at Argentan to a broken neck at Falaise."

The result of the order was a failure to seize an opportunity to capture or kill the main German army in France. This allowed much of it to slip through the gap to fight again and to continue the war for nine months. Blumenson's World War II histories attributed blame to the Supreme Commander. "Eisenhower," he wrote, "who was in France and following the combat developments, might have resolved the situation had he thought it necessary. Yet General Eisenhower did not intervene. Interfering with a tactical decision made by a commander in closer contact with the situation was not Eisenhower's method of exercising command."

On the day after the German counterattack, Bradley checked with Courtney Hodges to find out how the First Army was doing. He found it holding. Hodges reported that the German attack failed to deepen and appeared to have lost momentum. When Montgomery dropped his plan to drive to the Seine and committed his forces to ending the crisis at Mortain, Bradley told Patton to go only as far as Argentan to avoid running into Montgomery's force. But five days after the German onslaught, the force had pushed only halfway to Falaise. Patton said in his sarcastic style that if he were allowed to go to Falaise, he would not only beat the

Germans but drive the British back into the sea for a repeat of their defeat in 1940 at Dunkirk.

"Nothing doing," snapped Bradley. "Just stop where you are."

In the twenty-twenty perspective of hindsight, it is clear that Bradley blundered, Montgomery failed to come through, and Patton was left to watch helplessly as Germans escaped through the gap in Allied lines.

Bradley would write later, "Although Patton might have spun a line across that narrow neck, I doubted his ability to hold it."

Eisenhower backed him.

Meanwhile, nineteen German divisions escaped the trap.

Ike wrote in *Crusade in Europe*, "In the face of complete disaster the enemy fought desperately to hold open the mouth of the closing pocket so as to save as much as he could from the debacle."

The battlefield of Falaise, he said, became one of the greatest "killing grounds" of any of the war areas.

Collins looked back at the episode and wrote in his autobiography, "Falaise marked the end of the Normandy phase of the war, during which the VII Corps had borne a major share of the fighting of the First Army, including the Cherbourg campaign, the Cobra breakout from the Normandy bridgeheads and the subsequent pursuit, and the great decisive battle of Mortain." Conceding that historians would debate for years the failure of the Allies to destroy the German Seventh Army in the Falaise pocket, and that the failure resulted from slowness of the Allies in losing the open eastern end of the pocket, he put as good a face on the failure as possible.

"Though the Allied victory was not quite as great as Eisenhower had hoped," he wrote, "it resulted in German evacuation of France. Elements of the Seventh Army and the Fifth Panzer Army that had escaped were harassed by the British Second Army and the American First Army as they retreated to the north. And the VII Corps was destined to have another hard crack at them as we surged into Belgium, after crossing the Seine, following the fall of Paris."

This was true, but the questions remain: What would have happened if the Allies had not let so many Germans wriggle out of the Falaise pocket, and how many American lives would have been spared if the war had been ended in France instead of nine months later after the bitterest battles of the war in Germany?

CHAPTER EIGHT

DEADLY FOREST

Seven months after Joseph Lawton Collins was surprised to be invited to a stag dinner at Washington's exclusive Alibi Club by General George C. Marshall, he had behind him the detailed planning for the Seventh Corps D-day landing on Utah Beach, capture of the key port of Cherbourg, a crucial part in the breakout from the Normandy lodgment, and a bitter battle that culminated in a slaughter of German troops trying to escape an Allied juggernaut that went into the history books as the Falaise Pocket. Ahead of him and the Allied forces lay an open route to the Seine and the city of Paris.

On the southern coast of France, with fabulous Mediterranean beaches and resorts that were playgrounds for the rich and famous before the war, Allied forces had landed in August in Operation Dragoon. The invasion force's commander was Collins's colleague in the wrap-up of Guadalcanal, Lieutenant General Alexander Patch. The ground forces were under Lieutenant General Lucian K. Truscott, Jr., who had been Patton's deputy in Operation Torch and in Sicily. Recently in command of the Sixth Corps at Anzio in Italy, he led a breakout from the beachhead and a march to take Rome two days before the landings in Normandy. Encountering little German opposition, and assisted by French resistance forces, the Dragoon operation quickly took the large port of Marseille, adding it to Cherbourg and Brest on Ike's list of assets in supplying the Allied armies. But because the Allies had so quickly moved deeply into France, these facilities were so far removed from the action that supply lines were perilously long. To overcome this, Ike looked to the nearer Belgian port of Antwerp. "With thirty-six divisions in action," Ike recalled, "we were faced with the problem of delivering from beaches and ports to the front lines some 20,000 tons of supplies every day. Our spearheads, moreover, were moving swiftly, frequently seventy-five miles per day. The supply service had to catch these with loaded trucks. Every mile of advance doubled the difficulty because the supply trucks had always to make a two-way run to the beaches and back, in order to deliver another load to the marching troops."

Although the Allies grew to fifty-four divisions by October 1, in numerical strength the Germans still had the advantage. Counting all types of divisions, arrayed from Belgium to the Swiss border, the Allies could, on average, deploy less than one division to each ten miles of front. In view of these conditions, and with winter about to descend on the huge battlefield, the accepted wisdom in U.S. Army command schools was that a force such as Eisenhower's should go into a defensive posture to conserve strength and build up the logistic system. With all the main combat commanders agreeing, Ike chose to push an offensive.

On August 24, 1944, the U.S. First Army, consisting of the Nineteenth, Fifth, and Collins's Seventh Corps, had begun a march to the Seine between Melun and the City of Lights, which four years before had surrendered to Hitler's goose-stepping army without resistance. With the U.S. Fourth Cavalry in the fore to screen the Seventh Corps advance, the Seventh Corps found no opposition, but Collins was told that the honor of entering Paris had been given to the Free French and that infantry and armor of Major General Jacques-Philippe Leclerc must be ceded priority on the roads. This proved to be not as easy an advance as the high command in London anticipated. In colorful terms, Collins recorded that Leclerc's men, moving in small groups, "were having too gay a time receiving the plaudits of the French villagers" to be greatly concerned about pressing on to Paris. "They stopped in each town en route," he noted, "while the demoiselles climbed on their tanks, decking them with flowers and plying the men with vin rouge. We had trouble getting by the halted vehicles in the narrow streets, and by the time we reached Chartres we were well behind schedule. At the western entrance to this city we ran into a company of Leclerc's tanks, laden with troops and girls, going round and round a large traffic circle, the riders waving gaily to the cheering crowds while blocking all traffic."

Finding an American MP, Collins ordered him to let each group go around the circle twice and then direct them on their way.

Collins and his men reached Paris on August 25, the day the German commander surrendered the city to Leclerc. The next day, the Seventh Corps' First and Ninth divisions crossed the Seine via a bridge taken by Maurice Rose's Third Armored Division. On August 26, Collins climbed into a small Piper Cub airplane to visit each division and give verbal orders for the next day's advance. As the light airplane neared Paris on the way back to Collins's CP near Melun, the pilot proposed a detour over the city. Coming in at a thousand feet, they reached the Eiffel Tower and were tempted to dash through its supporting arch, but decided not to risk the life of a corps commander. They circled the landmark, then zoomed above the Champs-Élysées from the Louvre to the Arc de Triomphe as a parade flowed down the grand boulevard with Charles de Gaulle in the lead. After circling the Arc de Triomphe, they flew on to Melun.

In a letter to his wife, Collins described the aerial excursion, lamenting that he had not been able to see if the bookstalls along the Seine that they had browsed in their youth were still operating. But he assured Gladys that the Notre Dame cathedral was intact "in all its glory."

By the end of August, the Seventh Corps was near the Belgian border. On the evening of the last day of the month, Collins took a phone call from General Hodges. The commander of the First Army said urgently, "Joe, you've got to change direction at once toward Mons to help cut off the German Seventh Army."

Collins replied, "But who will fill the gap that will develop between my right and the Third Army?"

Hodges answered, "Joe, that's your problem."

After improvising a special task force under Colonel Joseph M. Tully to handle the objective, Collins notified his three divisions and Rose's armored division to move out. By the evening of September 2 elements of Rose's force entered Mons, only to be forced to halt by a shortage of gasoline. Driving to Rose's CO south of the city on September 3, Collins was concerned by reports of small groups of Germans on the Third Armored's left. Rose stated that he had reports of enemy to his left rear. Collins told Rose to sit tight while he went to the Ninth Division near Charleroi to ready it for movement to the east. While en route, he was told that Rose's division was engaged in "a wild melee." In a battle that lasted to September 5, the Americans took twenty-two thousand prisoners and dealt a crippling blow to the German Seventh Army.

When the Seventh Corps reached the Meuse River, which had been fought over again and again in World War I, retreating Germans had blown up the main bridge and held the opposite bank. In driving to the river, Collins's troops were impeded by throngs of Belgian civilians. Cheering the liberating Americans, they were oblivious to the fact that they were in range of German guns. During the next two days, Rose's Third Armored crossed the river and captured the important city of Liège and found all the bridges destroyed. As the Seventh Corps prepared to cross from Belgium into Germany, Collins noted in a letter to Gladys that the Seventh Corps advance from Mons had been so swift that the Germans had no time to destroy public utilities, leaving Collins and his men to enter communities and find streetcars still running. Ahead of the Seventh Corps as it prepared to cross the frontier into Germany lay the ancient city of Aachen. On maps as Aix-la-Chappelle, it had been fought over since the time of Charlemagne and venerated by Adolf Hitler, who saw himself as a modern Charles the Great. In front of the Seventh Corps lay the Siegfried Line. Also called the West Wall, it was a defensive barrier.

Construction had started on the wall at Hitler's order in May 1938. By September, more than half a million men were working on it at a cost of approximately one-third of Germany's total annual production of cement. It was to extend from a point north of Aachen along the border south and southeast to the Rhine River, then along the German bank to the Swiss border. More than three thousand concrete pillboxes, bunkers, and observation posts were built.

"As much because of propaganda as anything else," wrote Charles B. MacDonald in his volumes on the U.S. Army in World War II, "the West Wall came to be considered impregnable. It contributed to Hitler's success in bluffing France and England at Munich. In 1939, when Hitler's designs on Danzig strained German-Polish relations, Hitler ordered a film of the West Wall to be shown in all German cinemas to bolster home-front conviction that Germany was inviolate from the west."

While additional work was done between 1938 and 1940, Germany's quick victory over France and a need to shift the defenses to the Atlantic and English Channel brought work on the wall almost to a halt. Not until August 1944 was any new effort made to strengthen the line. When U.S. patrols probed the border, Allied intelligence was skimpy. Most reports on it dated back to 1940. Because four years of neglect had given the wall a realistic camouflage, aerial reconnaissance failed to pick up many of the positions. Its value as a fortress had been vastly exaggerated by Hitler's propagandists, and by the time of the Allied invasion the wall was nothing like its depiction. In the early fall of 1944 no strong troop reserves existed and there was a lack of soldiers either to man the line or to counterattack effectively.

On the American side, a shortage of gasoline forced General Hodges to order a pause in the advance to let supplies of fuel and ammunition catch up. Eager to keep going and not lose the momentum built up by the Seventh Corps, Collins asked Hodges to authorize a reconnaissance in force on the Seventh Corps front. Hodges gave permission to Collins and to Gerow's Fifth Corps. Analyzing the situation, Collins saw two major obstacles in the Seventh Corps zone in addition to the West Wall. One was Aachen on the north. The other, ten miles south, was the dense Hurtgen Forest. He felt that he had two choices: seize Aachen and clear it in order to get room to maneuver to the wall, or try a quick, sharp break through the Stolberg corridor (named after the nearby industrial town) between the city and the forest.

Because the capture of Aachen would be the exclusive task of the First Division, Collins discussed with General Huebner how best to handle it. The city lay in a bowl and was partly surrounded by hills. Though not a walled city, nor organized as a fortress, it was a jumble of solid stone houses that would be a tough proposition if the Germans decided to defend it. In no mood to get involved in what could be a costly street battle, Huebner posited that if Collins were to seize and hold the bordering hills on the south side, he could dominate the city and prevent passage of any German reinforcements, yet have some of the First Division available to assist breaking through the corridor between Aachen and the town of Hurtgen.

The Ninth Division was given the task of clearing the northern section of the Hurtgen Forest to prevent its use by the enemy as a base to counterattack or a place to fire against the south flank of the Third Armored as it drove head-on against the West Wall. This decision by Collins and Hodges would prove to be momentous, with ghastly results.

Known to Germans as Hurtgenwald, the Hurtgen Forest was thick with fir trees rising from seventy-five to a hundred feet, packed so densely that they blocked the sunlight. "Any green soldier with any feeling for war drilled into him during basic training would recognize that this woods was perfect for concealment of machine gun nests and snipers," said one historian, "and any officer with a modicum of savvy would choose to go around it." But the Lightning Joe Collins of Guadalcanal jungles who had brought the Seventh Corps off of Utah Beach to the German frontier wanted the Hurtgenwald cleared, and every GI also knew that in the army you did not ask why, you saluted, said, "Yes, sir," and did it. Consequently, Major General Louis Craig, the commander of the Ninth Division, led his men into the Hurtgen on September 19.

Although barely mentioned by Bradley and Collins in their war memoirs, and covered by Eisenhower with one line ("The weather was abominable and the German garrison was particularly stubborn, but Yankee doggedness finally won"), Ike conceded in the sentence following that thereafter whenever veterans of the American Fourth, Ninth, and Twenty-eighth divisions referred to hard fighting they did so in terms of comparison with the Hurtgen Forest, "which they put at the top of the list."

In *The Battle of the Hurtgen Forest*, Charles B. MacDonald described the forest of the men who fought in it in the autumn of 1944 as full of gloom, misery, and physical and moral abrasion. "Like some amorphous leech," he wrote, "the forest sucked at the lifeblood of a man's body and spirit."

Craig's soldiers were to attack southeast to a field called Deadman's Moor, take it, and move northeast to the town of Germeter by six p.m. In this endeavor they were to pass by a woodchopper's hut called Jaegerhaus and proceed to a highway juncture. Before they could do this, a German machine gun opened fire, followed by blasts from a camouflaged pillbox. The ensuing battle took the rest of the afternoon. When it was over, a company commander and all of his men were killed or wounded. Only when a platoon of tank destroyers arrived on the third day (September 22) to attack a series of pillboxes was substantial progress achieved.

When the Germans launched a counterattack, it was driven back on the third day after close combat with hand grenades as shells blasted treetops and rained shrapnel on the Americans in foxholes. In one German night attack, forty-nine GIs were captured, including a company CO, leaving only thirty to fight on. An operation in the forest that Collins expected to be wrapped up dragged on with increasing casualties into October and November.

Writing the official U.S. Army history of the Hurtgen Forest fighting, MacDonald found that clearing the forest was a costly, frustrating procession of attack and counterattack in which a weary, plodding battle pitted individual against individual with little opportunity for utilizing American superiority in artillery, air, and armor. Enemy patrols constantly infiltrated supply lines. Although U.S. units at night adopted a perimeter defense common to warfare in jungles, the perimeter still might have to be cleared of Germans before the new day's attack could begin. So heavy a toll did the fighting take that at the end of the month the Sixtieth Infantry and an attached battalion from the Thirty-ninth Infantry were in no condition to resume the attack toward the town of Hurtgen.

Germans effectively utilized terrain and persistent small-unit maneuvers to thwart the limited objective of the widespread Ninth Division. As others discovered all along the First Army front, General Craig found his frontage too great, his units too spent and depleted, and a combination of enemy and terrain too effective to enable the division to reach its objectives.

Many months after the Hurtgen fighting ended, *Time* featured the harrowing story of Private William H. Edwards of the Fourth Infantry Division. From Hayti, Missouri, he was on a night patrol in the Hurtgen Forest when a mine blew off a foot.

"He lay where he had fallen," the article said, "keeping his mouth shut so as not to betray his comrades to German infantrymen nearby. Artillery shells whistled overhead in a constant barrage."

A shell fragment struck his good leg. The next night, three Germans found him. When he asked for water, they refused. Instead, they took his field jacket, rifled through his pockets for cigarettes, then methodically went to work rigging him as a booby trap. When they departed, they left him lying on an explosive charge and too weak to move.

All through that night, and all the next day, Edwards fought to stay conscious, knowing that unless he did, anyone who attempted to move him before he could warn them would be blown to pieces. He smoked a few cigarettes that the Germans had overlooked and waited. Hours past midnight, American corpsmen discovered him. Edwards had just enough strength left to warn them. They gingerly cut the wires and, after seventy excruciating hours, got him out of the forest to safety.

On November 19, Hodges directed commitment of the Fifth Corps to the fight at a time when a regiment of the 104th Division on the Seventh Corps' north wing was having a tough fight to capture dominating heights of the Donnerberg and the Eschweiler woods east and northeast of Stolberg. At the same time a neighboring attack for a limited objective by a combat command of the Third Armored Division had proved as costly. In the First Division sector, which was making the corps' main effort, getting a toehold on the Hamich ridge and carving out a segment of the Hurtgen Forest near Schevenhuette had been laborious. On the corps' south wing between the First Division at Schevenhuette and the Fifth Corps near Hurtgen, the Fourth Division still was ensnared in the forest's coils.

The Fourth Division stood to benefit most directly from Hodges's order to the Fifth Corps to join the offensive. General Barton would gain both additional troops and a narrowed sector. The Twelfth Infantry, which had fought long and futilely on the bloody plateau near Germeter, at last was able to join its parent division, and the shift northward of the intercorps boundary removed both Hurtgen and Kleinhau from Fourth Division responsibility.

After-action reports and official army and unit histories record that no lengthy wait was necessary before measuring the effects of the Fifth Corps' commitment upon the Fourth Division's fight. Having paused to consolidate the limited gains of the first four days, General Barton had ordered renewal of the attack on November 22, the day after the start of the Fifth Corps offensive. Despite alarming casualties, neither assault regiment of the Fourth Division before November 22 had penetrated much more than a mile beyond a north-south road designated "W" that followed the Weisser Weh Creek at the approximate center of the Hurtgen Forest. On the north wing, the Eighth Infantry was a thousand yards short of its first objective of forested high ground around a ruined monastery at Gut Schwarzenbroich.

Troubled by a right flank dangling naked in the forest, the Twenty-second Infantry was still more than a mile away from taking its objective of Grosshau.

On the more positive side, the army account stated, a day or so of consolidation had temporarily eased two of the more serious problems the Fourth Division faced. Two regiments now had vehicular supply routes reaching within a few hundred yards of the front. A gap more than a mile wide between the two regiments had been closed. Had General Barton believed that these problems would not recur, and had he been fighting an enemy force that was incapable of reinforcements or other countermeasures, he might even have entertained genuine optimism. As it was, mud, mines, enemy infiltration, and shelling might compound the supply situation; and so long as the Twenty-second Infantry drove on Grosshau while the Eighth Infantry moved northeast more directly toward Düren, a gap between the two regiments would reappear and expand dangerously.

As for the enemy, the 275th Division had incurred crippling losses, as had the 16th Panzer Division's 156th Panzer Grenadier Regiment. But by November 21, the eve of renewal of the American attack, the last contingents of the German 344th Infantry Division that had been brought up from the south were arriving. As this division took over, the 116th Panzer Division was pulled out for refitting, and the new division began absorbing survivors of the 275th. This meant the Americans faced a completely new German unit.

The closeness of opposing lines and the density of the forest having denied unqualified use of air, armor, and artillery support, commanders of the Fourth Division assault regiments in their attacks of November 22 turned to deception. One battalion was directed to make a feint to the east with every weapon available, including smoke. At the same time, another battalion of each regiment was to make a genuine attack through woods off a flank of each demonstrating battalion. The Germans reacted exactly as desired. Upon the demonstrators, who were relatively secure in foxholes topped by logs and sod, they poured round after round of artillery and mortar fire. Against the battalions that were slipping through the woods, they fired hardly a shot.

On the north wing, the official accounts noted, a flanking battalion of the Eighth Infantry swept through a thousand yards of forest to reach Gut Schwarzenbroich. Only there, in a cluster of ruins of a monastery, did the Germans resist in strength. While this fight went on, a reserve battalion poured in behind the main enemy positions opposite the demonstrating battalion. Although the Germans soon deciphered this maneuver and opposed later stages of the advance, the fact that they had been lured from their prepared positions meant that the ruse had succeeded. As night came, a reserve battalion dug in securely around a triangle of roads at a key intersection.

In one respect, a battle history noted, the fruits of deception in the sector of the Twenty-second Infantry west of Grosshau were even more rewarding. While a lone battalion on the regiment's north wing staged a demonstration, the battalion stealing around the enemy's flank met no opposition. Alongside a creek and then along firebreaks, the battalion slipped like a phantom through the thick forest. For more than a mile, the men marched without encountering a German, and at nightfall dug in to cover at a road junction near the edge of the forest no more than seven hundred yards west of Grosshau. Colonel Charles Lanham's reluctance to order this battalion alone and unsupported out of the woods into Grosshau, the army history noted, may have stemmed from his knowledge of experiences elsewhere in his sector. The enemy remained in strength astride the Twenty-second Infantry's communications, as Colonel Lanham's right-wing battalion found while trying to protect the regimental southern flank.

Only after incurring the kind of casualties that had come to be associated with fighting in the forest did this battalion succeed in gaining nine hundred yards to reach a junction of firebreaks between roads designated X and Y, still a thousand yards short of the eastern fringe of the forest. The battalion was so understrength and so disorganized from its losses among officers and noncommissioned officers that at one point Lanham had to plug a gap in the front line with a composite company of one hundred replacements.

The problems to be solved before Grosshau might be attacked were serious. Though the Twelfth Infantry had left a wooded plateau near Germeter on November 22 to begin an attack to secure the Twenty-second Infantry's right flank, this depleted regiment would require several days to do the job. It took, in fact, four days, until November 26. In the meantime, the Twenty-second Infantry was open to a punishing blow from the Germans who still held Hurtgen and Kleinhau. Neither was there a quick solution to eliminating the enemy that had been bypassed or to the sweeping of mines so an attack on Grosshau might be supported.

On November 25, the day before the Twelfth Infantry reached the woods line to provide the Twenty-second Infantry a secure flank, Lanham saw a chance to capitalize on the commitment that day of the Fifth Armored Division against Hurtgen. In conjunction with that attack, he ordered an immediate attempt to capture Grosshau. Seeking surprise, he maneuvered one of his battalions through the woods to hit the village from the northwest while another converged on it from the southwest. Delayed four hours while tanks and tank destroyers picked their way over the muddy trails and firebreaks, the attack lost every vestige of surprise. When the jump-off actually came at noon, coordination with the armor failed. Only three tanks and a tank destroyer emerged from the woods with the infantry. Antitank gunners in Grosshau quickly picked off the tanks. At the same time violent concentrations of artillery fire drove the infantry back. The results of this attack prompted the division commander, General Barton, to approve another pause in the Twenty-second Infantry's operations. Lanham was told to consolidate his positions, bring up replacements, and make detailed plans for taking Grosshau. In particular, the regiment was to make maximum use of nine battalions of artillery that were either organic or attached to the division. Here on the edge of the forest the artillery for the first time might provide close-in fire capable of influencing the fighting directly and decisively.

In the meantime, on the division's north wing, the Eighth Infantry drove northeast for more than a mile. Although subjected to shelling, a battalion encountered only disorganized infantry resistance. On November 24, it was sent northward to fill out a line between Road U and the division's north boundary and at the same time cut behind those Germans who still were making a fight of it at Gut Schwarzenbroich. During the same two days, another battalion moved slowly against more determined resistance southeast and on November 25 surged to the regiment's south boundary. The total advance was more than a mile.

As a result, the Eighth Infantry stood on the brink of a breakthrough that could prove decisive. In four days, the regiment had more than doubled the distance gained during the first six days of the November offensive. Just over a mile of forest remained to be conquered. But the troops were exhausted. Because their leaders had to move about to encourage and look after their men, they had been among the first to fall. A constant stream of replacements had kept the battalions at a reasonable strength, but the new men did not have the ability of those they replaced. For all the tireless efforts of engineers and minesweepers, great stretches of the roads and trails were still infested with mines. Even routes declared clear might cause trouble. Along a reputedly cleared route, Company K on November 23 lost its Thanksgiving dinner when a kitchen jeep struck a mine.

Every day since November 20 had brought some measure of sleet or rain to augment the mud on the forest floor. To get supplies forward and casualties rearward, men trudged at least a mile under constant threat from shells that burst unannounced in the treetops and from bypassed enemy troops, who might materialize at any moment from the depths of the woods. A gap had grown between the Eighth Infantry and the Twenty-second Infantry that was a mile and a quarter wide.

With the failure of the Twenty-second Infantry at Grosshau on November 25, General Barton had an all-too-vivid reminder of the condition of his units. Much of the hope that entry of the Fifth Corps into the fight might alter the situation had faded with unrewarding early efforts of that corps to capture Hurtgen. The successes of the Eighth and Twenty-second infantry regiments in renewing the attack on November 22 appeared attributable more to local maneuver than to any general pattern of enemy disintegration. Barton reluctantly ordered both regiments to suspend major attacks and take two or three days to reorganize and consolidate.

Unable to strengthen the regiments other than with individual replacements, he decreased zones of action. Having reached the high ground about Gut Schwarzenbroich, the Eighth Infantry now would derive some benefit from a boundary change made earlier by the Seventh Corps, which had transferred a belt of forest northeast of Gut Schwarzenbroich to the adjacent First Division. For four days, the division paused.

Having cleared the Twenty-second Infantry's right flank by nightfall of November 26, the Twelfth Infantry relinquished its positions to a battalion from the Fifth Corps. Dropping off one of its battalions as a division reserve, a luxury General Barton had not enjoyed since the start of the November offensive, the Twelfth Infantry on November 28 attacked to sweep the gap between the Eighth and Twenty-second infantry regiments, but this task was not completed until the next day. In the meantime, most men of the Twenty-second Infantry were scarcely aware that the division had paused. For two of the three days, the regiment made limited attacks with first one company then another, in order to straighten the line and get all of its units into position for a climactic attack on Grosshau. One of these attacks inspired an intrepid performance from an acting squad leader, Private First Class Marcario Garcia. Although painfully wounded, he persistently refused evacuation until he had knocked out three machine-gun emplacements and another enemy position to lead his company on to its objective. For this, he earned the Medal of Honor.

Undoubtedly aware that an attack on Grosshau was impending, the Germans concentrated their mortar and artillery fire against the Twenty-second Infantry. In two days of its limited operations, the Twenty-second suffered more than 250 casualties.

Despite a smattering of replacements, two companies had less than fifty men each in the line.

During the month of November the Fourth Division received as replacements 170 officers and 4,754 enlisted men. Most commanders agreed that the caliber of replacements was good. "They had to be good quick," said one platoon leader. "They sometimes would take more chances than some of the older men, yet their presence often stimulated the veterans to take chances they otherwise would not have attempted."

Integrating these new men into organizations riddled by losses among squad and platoon leaders was a trying proposition.

"When I get new men in the heat of battle," said one sergeant, "all I have time to do is impress them that they have to remember their platoon number, and tell them to get into the nearest hole and to move out when the rest of us move out."

"That heavy casualties would strike men entering combat under conditions like these hardly could have been unexpected," wrote an army historian. "Indeed, so unusual was it to get a packet of replacements into the line without incurring losses that companies noted with pride when they accomplished it. So short was the frontline stay of some men that when evacuated to aid stations they did not know what platoon, company, or even battalion and sometimes regiment they were in. Others might find themselves starting their first attack as riflemen and reaching the objective as acting squad leaders." Most of the newcomers were reclassified cooks, clerks, drivers, and others combed from rear-echelon units both in the European theater and in the United States. Typical was Private Morris Sussman. From a cook and baker's school in the United States, he had been transferred for basic infantry training. He arrived in Scotland in early November and soon found himself in the Hurtgen Forest. At the Service Company of the Twenty-second Infantry, he recorded, someone took away much of what was called "excess equipment." From there Sussman and several other men walked about a mile to some dugouts and received company assignments and their names and serial numbers were taken down. A guide then led them toward the front lines. On the way they were shelled and saw a number of German and American dead scattered through the forest. Private Sussman said he was horrified at the sight, but everything appeared as if it were in a dream.

At a frontline company, Sussman's company commander asked if he knew how to operate a radio. Sussman said no. Handing him a radio, the captain told him: "You're going to learn." Training consisted of carrying the radio on his back and calling the captain whenever he heard the captain's name mentioned over the radio. For all his ignorance of radios, Sussman felt good. Being a radio operator meant he would stay with the captain, and back in the States he had heard that captains stayed "in the rear."

Subsequently, Private Sussman said, he "found out different." In the kind of slugging match that the Siegfried Line Campaign had become, little opportunity existed, once all units were committed, for division commanders to influence the battle in any grand and decisive manner. That was the situation General Barton had faced through much of the Hurtgen Forest fighting. But as of November 28, matters were somewhat different. Having narrowed his regimental zones of action, he had managed for the first time to achieve a compact formation within a zone of reasonable width. Looking at only this facet of the situation, one might have anticipated an early breakout from the forest. Unfortunately, he could not ignore another factor. By this time his three regiments were, in effect, masqueraders operating under the assumed names of the three veteran regiments that had come into the forest in early November.

In thirteen days some companies had run through three and four company COs. Staff sergeants and sergeants commanded most of the rifle platoons. The few officers still running their platoons usually were either replacements or heavy-weapons platoon leaders displaced forward. Most squad leaders were inexperienced privates or privates first class. One company had only twenty-five men, including replacements. Under such circumstances command organization hardly could be effective. Men and leaders made needless mistakes leading to more losses and thereby compounded the problem. One man summed up the campaign by saying, "Soon there is only a handful of the old men left."

Barton knew that the critical action was at Grosshau. It presented the ripest opportunity to break out of the forest and at last bring an end to seemingly interminable platoon-sized actions. If Colonel Lanham's Twenty-second Infantry could capture Grosshau, the division would be in a position to turn its full force northeastward on Düren along a road net that was adequate for a divisional attack. Already commanders at the corps and army level were making plans to strengthen the division for a final push.

Lanham intended to attack early on November 29 at the same time the Fifth Corps was striking the neighboring village of Kleinhau. For all their proximity, Grosshau and Kleinhau were different types of objectives. Kleinhau was on high ground, while Grosshau nestled on the forward slope of a hill whose crest rose five hundred yards northeast of the village.

Appreciating this difference and aware of the carnage that had resulted on November 25 when the whole regiment had tried to move directly from the woods, Lanham planned a wide flanking maneuver through the forest to the north in order to seize the dominating ridge in the hope that the enemy in Grosshau might be induced to surrender without the necessity of another direct assault across open fields.

German shelling interrupted attack preparations early on November 29. By sundown, in the face of persistent resistance, Lanham's flanking battalion finally cut the Grosshau-Gey road in the woods north of Grosshau, and as night came one battalion emerged onto the open ridge northeast of Grosshau, virtually in the rear of the Germans in the village. Coincidentally, tanks and tank destroyers took advantage of the gathering darkness to reach embattled infantry along the road into Grosshau from the west. Firing constantly, the armor moved on toward the village and the infantry followed.

In a matter of minutes, resistance collapsed. By the light of the burning buildings and a moon that shone for the first time since the Fourth Division had entered the Hurtgen Forest, infantry methodically mopped up the objective. More than a hundred Germans surrendered. In a larger setting, Grosshau was only a clearing in the Hurtgen Forest, the point at which the Twenty-second Infantry at last might turn northeastward with the rest of the Fourth Division to advance more directly toward the division objective of Düren.

During the night of November 29, General Barton directed a sweep to occupy a narrow, irregular stretch of woods lying between Grosshau and Gey. This accomplished, a unit of the Fifth Armored Division would be committed to assist the final drive across the plain from Gey to Düren and the Roer River.

To help prepare the way, Barton attached the combat command's Forty-sixth Armored Infantry Battalion to the Twenty-second Infantry. Lanham in turn directed the armored infantry to move the next day, November 30, to Hill 401. From there the armored infantry was to attack into the woods east of the clearing in order to block the right flank of the Twenty-second Infantry when that regiment turned northeast. Lanham held one battalion of his infantry in reserve, directed another to attack alongside the Grosshau highway to gain the woods line overlooking the town of Gey, and ordered the Second Battalion to cross eight hundred yards of open ground east of Grosshau, enter the woods, and then turn northeastward along the right flank of the battalion that was moving on Gey. The direct move through the narrow stretch of woods to Gey was blessed with success. Behind a bank of cross fire laid down by fourteen tanks and tank destroyers advancing on

either flank of the infantry, a battalion of the Twenty-second Infantry by nightfall was at the edge of the woods overlooking the
village.

Records show that things did not go as well for the rest of the
regiment and the attached armored infantry. As men of the Forty-
sixth Armored Infantry Battalion moved up Hill 401, German
fire poured down the open slopes. All day long the armored infantry fought for the hill, and when night came they finally succeeded
through sheer determination. Yet in one day this fresh battalion
lost half its strength.

Fire from this same hill and from the edge of the woods east
of Grosshau made the attempted advance of the Second Battalion, Twenty-second Infantry, just as difficult. The edge of the
woods was to have been a line of departure. In reality, the battalion fought all day to get to this line. Upon gaining it, the two
companies that made the attack had between them less than a
hundred men. That this little force could continue northeast
through the woods to come abreast of the battalion that had
gained the woods line overlooking Gey was impossible.

Early the next day, December 1, Lanham reluctantly relinquished his reserve to perform this task. Now that Hill 401 was
in American hands, the job was easier. A favorable wind that
blew a smoke screen across open ground leading from Grosshau to the woods also helped. By nightfall the reserve battalion
had reached the woods line overlooking Gey and dug in. At long
last, sixteen days after the start of the November offensive, the
Twenty-second Infantry—or what was left of it—was all the way
through the Hurtgen Forest.

On December 2, the Germans counterattacked. In estimated
company strength, they struck to the southeast from Gey, quickly
penetrated the U.S. line, surrounded a battalion command post,
and gave every indication of rolling up the front. Only quick artillery support and rapid commitment of the composite reserve
saved the day.

Since November 16, the Fourth Division had fought in the Hurtgen Forest and made a maximum advance of a little over three miles. Some 432 men were known dead and another 255 were missing. The division had suffered a total of 4,053 battle casualties, while another 2,000 men had suffered trench foot, respiratory diseases, and combat exhaustion.

Late on December 1, General Barton spoke in detail to Collins about the deplorable state of the division. The Twenty-second Infantry, in particular, he reported, had been milked of all offensive ability. Replacements were courageous, but they did not know how to fight. Since all junior leadership had fallen by the way, no one remained to show the replacements how to deport themselves.

General Collins promptly ordered Barton to halt his attack. As early as November 28, both the Seventh Corps and the First Army had noted the Fourth Division's condition and had laid plans for relief. On December 3, a regiment of the Eighty-third Division, brought north from the Eighth Corps sector in Luxembourg, was to begin relief of the Twenty-second Infantry.

In the course of the next eight days, the entire Fourth Division was to move from the Hurtgen Forest to Luxembourg for rest, refitting, and force replenishment. For all the damage inflicted on the enemy, the First Division had paid dearly. With 3,993 battle casualties, the Big Red One would go down as one of the more severely hurt participants in the Hurtgen Forest fighting. The Twenty-sixth Infantry, which fought fully within the forest, lost more than any other regiment, 1,479 men, including 163 killed and 261 missing. These did not include nonbattle losses attributable to combat exhaustion and the weather.

When the Hurtgen Forest fight was over, the Eighty-third Division, which had relieved the Fourth Division, and parts of the Fifth Armored Division still would have to drive through a narrow belt of woodland before reaching the Roer, but the bulk of the forest was clear.

Since September 14, when part of the Ninth Division first entered fringes of the forest near Roetgen, the records showed, some American units had been engaged continuously in the forest. A total of five American divisions, a combat command of armor, an additional armored infantry battalion, and the Second Ranger Battalion had fought there. One division, the Ninth, had engaged in two separate fights in the forest, one in September, another in October, and one of its regiments, the Forty-seventh Infantry, had been involved a third time. The Twenty-eighth Division in early November had lost more men in the forest than any other U.S. unit.

The Hurtgen Forest battle was recorded as the longest fight by the U.S. Army in the Second World War.

In the course of the struggle, five U.S. divisions became enmeshed: the Big Red One, the Fourth, Eighth, Ninth, and Twenty-eighth. Americans counted more then twenty-four thousand killed, wounded, captured and missing. Another nine thousand were victims of respiratory disease, trench foot, and fatigue. In a war in which the American command considered losses of 10 percent high, the rate in the Hurtgen Forest was more than 25 percent.

Just as devastating as these statistics was a belated judgment by military and civilian historians that the Hurtgen Forest fight had not been needed. The consensus was that the battle had been unnecessary because the forest could have—and should have—been bypassed.

In 1983, Collins defended the Hurtgen operation in a seminar at the Fort Leavenworth Command and General Staff School, where he had been a student and instructor before the war. Asked why he'd kept pushing divisions into the forest in what seemed to be a stalemate, he answered, "Well, I complied with the orders of the First Army. It was an area that had to be covered by somebody, and we happened to draw the area. I didn't have any choice in it. I would never pick it as the place to be."

While the Hurtgen Forest tragedy unfolded, Collins had primarily kept his sights on taking Aachen, piercing the West Wall, and advancing to and crossing the Roer River. As in Cherbourg, Hitler decreed that the forces of Colonel Gerhard Wilck "hold this venerable city to the last man," and that if necessary Wilck allow himself "to be buried in its ruins." Complying, the German garrison moved into cellars and sewers and made fortresses of stone houses lining narrow, winding streets. The American assault commenced on October 7 with the occupation of a northern suburb, Alsdorf, by the First Division and the First Army's Thirtieth Division of the Nineteenth Corps. Tough resistance, including a counterattack by the First Panzer Corps, staved off the breakthrough for more than a week. By October 19, Collins's forces held the high ground of a city park. When a task force of the Third Armored Division surrounded the bunker occupied by Wilck and opened fire with a 155mm gun, Wilck chose to defy Hitler and surrendered.

Touring the city a few days after it fell, Collins found more destruction than in any city he'd seen in the drive from Utah Beach. But while he saw scarcely any building with its roof intact, the American attack left the city's ancient Gothic cathedral mostly unscathed. A small chamber purportedly containing the throne of Charlemagne that had been protected by a brick encasing was intact.

In addition to criticisms by latter-day historians and military analysts of the bloodbath in the Hurtgen Forest, the U.S. commanders of the drive toward the Roer through Aachen have been faulted for not directing their efforts to capturing a pair of dams that, if opened by the retreating Germans, would have flooded the downriver areas and broadened the already wide river. Built years before, they were meant to control flooding in the Roer Valley and provide hydroelectric power. In the perfect rearview perspective of historians, the faultfinding on the topic of the dams certainly appeared justified, but Collins defended himself and his superiors by pointing a finger of blame to a failure of battlefield intelligence.

In his memoirs and during questioning in the Command and Staff School seminar in 1983, he explained that the dams were not targeted in the autumn of 1944 because he and other commanders were not alerted to the potential threat they posed, and therefore the dams had not been given priority.

While the fighting in the forest raged on October 18, Eisenhower met with Bradley and Montgomery in Brussels. The result was a decision to continue the push to the Rhine through the fall and, if necessary, in the winter. The First Army was directed to attack in early November with the object of establishing a bridgehead beyond the Rhine south of Cologne. In this effort, Collins was directed to submit a plan for the Seventh Corps to execute the main thrust. Asked if he would like to add the 104th Division of Major General Terry de la Mesa Allen to his command, he agreed. Although Allen had a reputation for being hard to handle, and had been relieved of command of the First Division by Bradley at the end of the Sicilian campaign, Collins had known Allen at the Infantry School and respected his record as a commander.

Fifty-six years old, Allen was a third-generation soldier, but when he failed a gunnery course in his second year at West Point, he'd quit and finished his college education at the Catholic University in Washington, D.C. Evidently missing the army in 1912, he passed a competitive exam to get back into uniform. Commissioned second lieutenant, he served in France, attended army schools, rose in rank, and in 1942 was given command of the First Division. With the nickname "Terrible Terry," and with Ted Roosevelt as his deputy, he led the Big Red One through North Africa and Sicily. Because of what General Omar Bradley deemed to be markedly unsoldierly manners and methods, he and Roosevelt were relieved of command after the fall of Sicily. While Roosevelt wound up in the Fourth Division, Allen found himself commanding the 104th "Timberwolf" Division. It entered

France on September 7, 1944, and had its first combat engagement in Belgium clearing a German stronghold at Antwerp. After it was committed to the Hurtgen Forest, the division captured the city of Hurtgen on November 28. Knowing that Allen vowed to make the 104th equal in reputation to the proud First Division, Collins decided it would be "stimulating" to position the Timberwolves in the line adjacent to Allen's former command. Addition of the 104th raised the Seventh Corps to four divisions deployed on a twenty-mile front. For the attack into the Roer plain, Bradley planned to unleash a massive air bombardment ahead of the November 5 attack, but bad weather forced postponement to the sixteenth. By then, the Germans were well dug in with support by additional artillery and their front had been thoroughly mined.

When Allen was slow in his first action under the Seventh Corps, Collins read him the riot act, but it still took the Timberwolves four days in heavy fighting to capture the high ground east of the town of Stolberg. At the same time, the First Division was fighting through and around the north tip of the Hurtgen Forest and Barton's Fourth Division struggled south of the deadly wood. By the night of December 16, these actions and others culminated in Seventh Corps control of the entire west bank of the Roer. To reach that point, the corps had endured its toughest and costliest operations. But Collins also knew the battles had taken their toll on the enemy and had forced Field Marshal von Rundstedt to engage divisions, tanks, ammunition, gasoline, and troops that weakened the defenses of the western barrier to Germany's heartland, the mighty Rhine River. But to get to the Rhine, the Allies had to cross the Roer.

CHAPTER NINE

WE CAN STILL LOSE THIS WAR

I n mid-September 1944, the Allies sniffed the sweet scent of victory.

Dazzling successes since D-day and heartening reports of German defeats on the Eastern Front by Soviet armies combined to foster a conviction that the Third Reich was tottering. While the Allied commanders had been chastened by surprisingly revitalized German armies standing their ground in defense of the West Wall, and the awful bloodletting in the Hurtgen Forest, they remained upbeat. When the Allied attack began rolling again in late November and in the early days of December, the optimism increased. It was bolstered on December 12 by an intelligence summary that stated it was certain that attrition was steadily sapping German strength on the Western Front and that the crust of its defenses was thinner, more brittle, and more vulnerable than it appeared on maps.

This sense of imminent victory was tempered by the reality that attacks in November with the objective of a decisive defeat of the enemy west of the Rhine River and the seizure of a foothold on its east bank had not been fully achieved. By the end of the month, the U.S. First and Ninth armies, charged with the main effort, had made some gains in the direction of Bonn and Cologne, the Twenty-first Army Group in the north had crossed the left arm of the lower Rhine, and Patton's Third Army had put troops on the Saar River. Farther to the south the U.S. Seventh Army had captured Strasbourg and reached the Rhine. The First French Army, on the extreme south flank, had liberated Belfort and trapped sizable German forces at Colmar.

Although Allied losses had been high, those inflicted on the enemy had been even greater. But the Allies still had failed to achieve main strategic goals. They had not decisively defeated the German armies west of the Rhine, and they had not crossed the river.

The Americans also faced a crisis of manpower.

By December, Bradley was so alarmed that he asked Eisenhower for permission to send a man to the Pentagon to try to straighten out the problem. "Not only had Washington juggled our quotas to shortchange us on infantrymen," Bradley noted, "but in November at a time our requirements increased, the War Department cut back our monthly allotment of replacements from 80,000 to 67,000 men. At the very moment we needed them most, too many men were being diverted to the Pacific."

He complained to Ike, "Don't they realize that we can still lose the war in Europe? There will be plenty of time left after we're finished here to clean up in the Pacific."

Although Eisenhower knew better than Bradley that General Douglas MacArthur was pressuring the Pentagon for speedier buildup of the Pacific forces, Bradley observed, Ike held his annoyance in check. "Indeed MacArthur and the Pacific were so remote from our daily problems," he wrote, "we became aware of the other war only when shortages reminded us that it was competing for resources."

In December, Bradley wrote to Patton, "I would suppose that everybody in Washington had made a wrong guess as to the date on when this war will be over."

At the same time, Bradley cautioned Ike that if no remedy were forthcoming on the issue of replacements, "we would soon have exhausted the assault strength of our infantry divisions." During the middle of November, he recorded, G-2 reported that the Sixth SS Panzer Army had been moved from its assembly point in Westphalia to an area nearer Cologne. Another panzer army, the Fifth, was reported to have massed its tanks a little farther north. So conspicuous were these telltale signs of von Rundstedt's apparent intent to catch Americans astride the Roer that Bradley later felt they should have sifted them for evidence of a German deception. But if anyone on the Western Front detected in the German preparations an intent to mislead the Allies on a German offensive elsewhere, he did not share his suspicions with Bradley. "In estimating von Rundstedt's capabilities," Bradley wrote, "we reasoned that any counteroffensive must necessarily be directed against a limited objective where it could best blunt our threatening advance to the Rhine."

Any more ambitious an effort, the Allies estimated, would greatly exceed enemy resources. As much as the Allies had been hurt in the November offensive, the enemy had been bled more severely. Intelligence put German casualties, exclusive of prisoners of war, at upward of 100,000 for the five-week campaign. Patton's Third Army alone had picked up 35,000 prisoners in its Saar offensive, while other units had another 22,000.

In its G-2 estimate of the enemy situation on December 10, the First Army said, "It is apparent that von Rundstedt, who obviously is conducting military operations without the benefit of intuition, has skillfully defended and husbanded his forces and is preparing for his part in the all-out application of every weapon at the focal point and the correct time to achieve defense of the

Reich west of the Rhine by inflicting as great a defeat on the Allies as possible. Indications to date point to the location of this focal point as being between the cities of Roermond and Schleiden, and within this bracket this concentrated force will be applied to the Allied force judged by the German High Command to be the greatest threat to successful defense of the Reich."

The "bracket" to which G-2 referred, noted Bradley, described a forty-five-mile sector that extended from the Roer dams north of the Ardennes to where the Roer flowed into the Meuse high up in Montgomery's sector. In estimating the enemy's capabilities against the First Army front, General Hodges came to four possible conclusions:

1. The enemy could hold where he was on the line of the Roer and southward along the Siegfried Line.
2. He could counterattack with air, armor, infantry, and secret weapons at a selected focal point at a time of his own choosing.
3. He could fall back to a narrow river line between the Roer and the Rhine and thereafter retire behind the Rhine, the most formidable defensive position in western Europe.
4. He could collapse or surrender.

Of these possibilities, Bradley noted, the First Army found its weight of evidence pointing to the second. It was expected that when major ground forces crossed the Roer River, and if the dams were not controlled, a maximum effort would be made by the Germans to flood the Roer valley. Bradley accepted the First Army's conclusions and anticipated a knock-down-and-drag-out battle just as soon as the Americans bridged the Roer.

On December 7, 1944, Eisenhower, Bradley, and Montgomery met at Ike's HQ in the city of Maastricht to lay plans for future operations. There was general agreement on an all-out offensive on the Western Front early in 1945, but Ike and Monty held differing views as to the future scheme of maneuver and disposition of forces. Montgomery wanted a single strong thrust across the Rhine north of the Ruhr and restriction of all other operations to containing actions by limited forces. Eisenhower agreed with a Montgomery proposal for a main attack north by Montgomery's Twenty-first Army Group and was prepared to give Montgomery the U.S. Ninth Army, but Ike was unwilling to abandon his concept of Patton's Third Army swinging a secondary blow toward Frankfurt.

Following the meeting, Eisenhower set plans in motion to continue exerting pressure on the enemy and chew up as many German divisions as possible before the main offensive in the north. To accomplish this he gave permission for the Third Army to mount an offensive along the Saar front on December 19 and directed Lieutenant General Jacob L. Devers, the Sixth Army Group commander, to support the drive with elements of the Seventh Army. In the meantime these two armies continued heavy local attacks, with Patton driving on to the city of Saarlautern, while Patch's Seventh Army turned north into the Saverne region. At the opposite end of the long Allied line, Montgomery gave orders for the British Second Army to "tidy up" the Twenty-first Army Group position on the Meuse with an attack calculated to erase a salient at Heinsberg. On December 16 advance parties were moving north as the first step in a major shift to the left preparatory to an attack toward Krefeld and the Ruhr that had been tentatively scheduled for the second week in January. South of the Twenty-first Army Group Lieutenant General William H. Simpson's U.S. Ninth Army had closed along the Roer River. On the Ninth's right, Hodges's First Army was also at the Roer, but after the Hurtgen battle he could not risk a crossing attack while Germans held the dams. A series of air attacks was launched early in December to breach them and remove the threat of enemy-controlled floods, but the bombs had so little success that the goal passed to the First Army. Bradley ordered Hodges to seize the key points in the system of dams, and in December Hodges sent the Fifth Corps into an attack toward the dams. Collins's Seventh Corps to the north was assigned a support role in this attack. But the start of this grand design had been unnecessarily delayed by the fight in the Hurtgen Forest.

While the Americans had battered at least six German divisions, they had little in the way of positive advantages in order to deny Germans use of the forest as a base for thwarting the drive to the Rhine. In the process, the fight had failed to carry on to the critical objective, securing the Roer River dams.

Eisenhower's view of the situation encompassed not only the matter of getting across the Roer without the Germans opening the dams and flooding the valley below them, but the state of the entire front, from the German frontier to the Swiss border, and going on offense at a time when he had an acute shortage of manpower. Through late November and early in December, the badly stretched troop strength required concentrating available forces in the vicinity of the Roer dams in the north and bordering the Saar region of Germany in the south. This weakened a protective force in the Ardennes Forest region of Belgium. While only four divisions guarded a seventy-five-mile front between Treir and Monschau, Ike and Bradley agreed that it would be a mistake to suspend attacks all along the front to protect an area that seemed to be an unlikely place for a German offensive. Should one occur, Bradley was sure that it would prove abortive.

In early December, Patton was making preparations to renew the attack against the Saar, with the assault to begin on the nineteenth. He was hopeful of a decisive result, but determined to avoid involvement in a long, inconclusive, and costly offensive. Bradley and Ike agreed that the Third Army attack would have to show tremendous gains within a week or be suspended.

"We knew of course that if it was successful in gaining great advantages the enemy would have to concentrate from other sectors to meet it," Eisenhower wrote, "and therefore Patton's success would tend to increase our safety elsewhere."

On the other hand, if a considerable number of divisions were embroiled in costly and slow advances, they not only would be accomplishing little, they would be in no position to react quickly at any other place along the front.

In the meantime, Hodges's First Army's attack against the Roer dams had gotten off as scheduled on December 13, but with relatively few divisions engaged. Early in the month the weather, which had been intermittently bad, took a turn for the worse. Fog and thick clouds prohibited aerial reconnaissance and snow began to appear in the uplands. Temperatures fell.

It was a situation that favored von Rundstedt's plan to carry out an order that had come directly from Adolf Hitler. The World War I corporal, who by willpower, deceit, and treachery had taken over the German government, cast a bewitching spell over the German people, bluffed the French and the English into appeasement, rearmed his nation, launched the Second World War, and survived an attempt on his life by army officers, had conceived an audacious plan.

On September 16, with his right arm crippled by an assassination attempt in July, Hitler told the officers at his daily briefing, "I have just made a momentous decision. I shall go over to the counterattack." Sweeping a hand over a situational map, he said, "That is to say, here, out of the Ardennes, with the objective of Antwerp."

Told of the plan, code-named *Wacht am Rhein* (Watch on the Rhine), von Rundstedt wrote, "I was staggered. It was obvious to me that the available forces were too small for such an extremely ambitious plan."

But he knew that it was useless to protest to Hitler about the possibility of anything.

On December 2, 1944, Field Marshal Walter Model said to his general staff, "If it succeeds, it will be a miracle."

The plan the generals devised was based on Germany's offensive in 1918 and the successful attack through the Ardennes of 1940 that carried them all the way to Paris. In the first two weeks of December, 1,500 trains carrying troops, armor, and artillery unloaded in secrecy in rail yards east of the Ardennes. In the last three nights before the offensive was to start, a quarter of a million men, 717 tanks and assault guns, and 2,623 heavy artillery pieces were in position less than four miles from understrength American divisions.

The generals of the gathering force were told by their führer, "This battle will determine whether we live or die. I want all my soldiers to fight hard and without pity. The battle must be fought with brutality and all resistance must be broken by a wave of terror. The enemy must be broken. Now or never! Thus lives our Germany."

Without the troops having been told their purpose, von Rundstedt sought to rally them with the exhortation, "Soldiers of the Western Front! Your great hour has arrived." Every one of them, he said, bore "a holy obligation to give everything to achieve things beyond human possibilities for our Fatherland and our Führer!"

On June 6, 1944, Eisenhower had told the D-day troops that they were about to begin "a great crusade" and that the eyes of the world were upon them. For a year and a half the GIs had fought and marched to the doorstep of Germany and few doubted that victory was near. In that time, thousands of them had been killed or wounded. From September to December 1944, the First, Third, and Ninth armies counted 134,000 casualties. Since D-day, the Americans lost five hundred tanks and one hundred artillery pieces. Hundreds of planes had been shot down. Every day they were consuming twenty thousand tons of provisions, 6 million gallons of gas, and two thousand tons of ammunition.

Officers who were unknown before the war—Ike, Patton, Bradley—were now famous, but only the serious follower of the war had heard about Terrible Terry Allen, Ted Roosevelt, and Lightning Joe Collins. It would be a good bet if a GI wagered that nobody but Brigadier General Anthony McAuliffe's family and friends knew he was commander of the garrison at the Belgian town of Bastogne, and that hardly anyone in the U.S.A. could point to it on a map.

At Seventh Corps headquarters, Collins had reports of a concentration of German armor somewhere south of Cologne. He and Courtney Hodges at First Army HQ feared that it threatened the right flank of the Seventh Corps once it crossed the Roer. Neither general expected that a far greater German force would strike against the American Fifth and Eighth out of the Ardennes. They focused their attention on the challenge presented by the Roer River and its problematic dams.

On December 16, Bradley hitched a ride with Brigadier General Joseph James O'Hare, who was beginning a trip to the Pentagon to hash out the issue of a lack of manpower. While O'Hare would go on to Paris, Bradley's destination was Ike's HQ at Versailles. After a night in the Alfa Hotel in Luxembourg, Bradley was told that weather had grounded his plane and that he'd have to go by road, a four-hour drive. Seated in the rear of a Cadillac sedan, with four bottles of Coca-Cola, he presently looked up in alarm as a Renault sedan skidded out of a side street and almost forced his car into a ditch. Unscathed, he arrived in a rainy Paris and had lunch with O'Hare at the Ritz. When he arrived at Eisenhower's HQ, he learned that Ike had been promoted to five-star general.

That afternoon, a colonel from SHAEF G-2 entered the conference and handed a note to Ike's intelligence chief. The British major general Kenneth Strong read it and interrupted the conversation to announce that at five o'clock that morning the Germans had counterattacked at five points across the First Army sector in Belgium.

General Walter Bedell Smith put a hand on Bradley's shoulder and said, "Well, Brad, you've been wishing for a counterattack. Now it looks as though you've got it."

"A counterattack, yes," said Bradley, "but I'll be damned if I wanted one this big."

As the Germans attacked, the Allies had sixty-three divisions deployed along a 400-mile front. Of these, forty were American. Thirty-one were assigned to the Twelfth Army Group on a 230-mile front, with Hodges's First Army holding 115 miles, and two-thirds arrayed across the Ardennes sector. On the north of this area were seventeen divisions of Simpson's Ninth Army. Four divisions of Middleton's Eighth Corps faced the Ardennes. Seventeen divisions were under General Devers. Montgomery's two armies comprised fifteen divisions. Together, these forces made up about half of the Allied strength in the west. South of the Ardennes, Patton's Third Army stood on a 100-mile front that ran from the Moselle, forming the Luxembourg border, halfway to the Rhine. In Patton's control were a quarter of a million men.

As Bradley contemplated the reports of the German counterattack, he supposed that it was meant as a maneuver to force a halt to Patton's advance to the Siegfried Line and a quick breakthrough into the Saar region of Germany. "If by coming through the Ardennes," Bradley speculated, "he [von Rundstedt] can force us to pull Patton's troops out of the Saar and throw them against his counteroffensive, he can get what he's after. And that's just a little more time."

What Allied intelligence missed, and Bradley therefore did not know, was that on the day that counterattack began the Germans had amassed thirty-six divisions in four armies, not with the goal of diverting Patton, but of crashing westward to the

English Channel, splitting Allied forces, and perhaps attaining a negotiated settlement of the war. Spearheading the attack were four SS panzer divisions of General Joseph "Sepp" Dietrich's Sixth Army. To their left were three panzer divisions and four of infantry. The force totaled six hundred tanks.

Americans were not alone in misjudging German potential. Montgomery had stated, "The enemy is at present fighting a defensive campaign on all fronts; his situation is such that he cannot stage major offensive operations."

Recognizing that something major was afoot in the Ardennes on December 16, Bradley phoned Patton in Nancy and said, "George, get the Tenth Armored on the road to Luxembourg, and have [Tenth Armored commander Major General William H. H.] Morris report immediately to Middleton for orders."

"But that's no major threat up there," Patton replied. "Hell, it's probably nothing more than a spoiling attack to throw us off balance down here and make us stop this offensive."

"I hate like hell to do it, George," said Bradley, "but I've got to have that division. Even if it's only a spoiling attack as you say, Middleton must have help."

Orders also went from Bradley to have General Simpson turn his Seventh Armored over to Hodges to hit the German attack on its flank. On the Fourth Division front, General Barton filled ranks that had been badly depleted in the Hurtgen Forest with cooks, bakers, and clerks, then reported, "But we're not stopping them. If the Tenth Armored doesn't get up here soon, Army Group had better get set to barrel out."

At Eisenhower's villa at St.-Germain-en-Laye on Sunday morning, December 17, Bradley awoke to foul weather that grounded his plane, forcing him to head for his command post in Luxembourg. When G-2 told him the size of the enemy forces, he exclaimed, "Just where in hell has this son of a bitch gotten all this strength?"

By the next morning, the Germans had crushed the center of

the American front, but the U.S. Seventh Armored had beaten off a panzer assault at Saint-Vith. Barton's Fourth Division, bolstered by the timely arrival of the Tenth Armored, held on to its position on a shoulder of what was now a bulge in the lines. There, the Twenty-eighth Division and Middleton's reserves had been overrun by General Hasso-Eccard von Manteuffel's panzers. This left the Germans free to head for the crucial crossroads town of Bastogne. Determined to hold it "at all costs," Bradley summoned the "Screaming Eagles" of the 101st Airborne Division.

Because its commander, Maxwell Taylor, was in Washington, D.C., for a conference, the paratroopers had been taken over by Brigadier General Anthony Clement McAuliffe. Forty-six years old, he was a native of the nation's capital. After studying for two years at West Virginia University (1916–17), he entered West Point and graduated in 1918. On D-day, he parachuted behind enemy lines. A few months before the German Ardennes counterattack, he was carried by glider into an ill-fated Allied attack in Holland known as Operation Market Garden.

Deciding to go to Bastogne on the evening of December 18, Bradley discovered it was not so easy a journey. In *A Soldier's Story*, he noted that because Germans who dressed in GI uniforms had gotten behind U.S. lines, half a million wary Americans "played cat and mouse with each other" when they met on the road, and neither rank nor credentials spared a traveler an inquisition. The result was that Bradley was stopped three times and questioned by suspicious sentries on his knowledge of Americana. He recalled, "The first time by identifying Springfield as the capital of Illinois (my questioner held out for Chicago); the second time by locating the guard between the center and tackle on a line of scrimmage; the third time by naming the current spouse of a blonde named Betty Grable. Grable stopped me but the sentry did not. Pleased at having stumped me, he nevertheless passed me on."

Within two days of the German surge through the Ardennes, Bradley no longer believed that it was a spoiling attack.

He went to see Patton and told him to call off the Saar attack and to thrust north into the German underbelly.

Unhappy to be giving up a toehold on the Siegfried Line, Patton said, "But what the hell, we'll still be killing Krauts."

"We won't commit any more of your stuff than we have to," replied Bradley. "I want to save it for a whale of a blow when we hit back—and we're going to hit this bastard hard."

At a hastily convened conference at Verdun on December 19, with Eisenhower presiding in a drafty room with only a potbellied stove to provide warmth, Ike's generals agreed on an overall plan to squeeze the bulge from its flanks. Of immediate concern was the plight of the defenders of Bastogne. Confident that McAuliffe's paratroops could hold on until aid reached them, Bradley appreciated that it could only come from Patton.

Turning to the general who had been his senior in North Africa and Sicily, he asked, "How soon will you be able to go, George?"

Patton startled everyone by replying that his Third Army could be in Bastogne in forty-eight hours. With the confidence of knowing that he'd had his staff working on this challenge since he'd heard of the attack, he said, "I can attack on December 21 with three divisions, the Fourth Armored, the Twenty-sixth and the Eightieth."

Ike responded, "Don't be fatuous, George. If you try to go that early, you won't have all three divisions ready and you'll go in piecemeal. You will start on the twenty-second and I want your initial blow to be a strong one. I'd even settle for the twenty-third if it takes that long to get three full divisions."

Patton agreed and left to give the orders. When he returned, he and Ike talked alone. "Funny thing, George," said the new five-star commander, "every time I get another star I get attacked."

"And every time you get attacked," said Patton, remembering being called to turn around the American whipping at Kasserine Pass, "I have to bail you out."

Later, lighting a cigar and pointing to the bulge on a map, he said to Bradley, "Brad, this time the Kraut's stuck his head in a meatgrinder. And this time I've got hold of the handle."

To close the bulge from flanks that were commonly referred to as its "shoulders," Ike chose to put the U.S. forces in the northern shoulder under Montgomery (over Bradley's strong objections). Word that the Seventh Corps would be changing its objective from the Roer to the bulge reached Joseph Lawton Collins on December 20.

CHAPTER TEN

CHANGE OF PLANS

W hen Lightning Joe Collins learned that he was to turn the Seventh Corps away from the Roer River, which had been its goal to assist in repulsing a German counterattack, Allied jaws were gaping at hearing of the counterattack everywhere from Ike's HQ at Versailles to Churchill's warlords in a London underground command post. They were also sagging in Alibi Club armchairs, where members contemplated the news while quietly sipping Scotch whiskies, among MacArthur's combat chiefs in the far reaches of the Pacific Ocean, and in the Pentagon. But for George C. Marshall, there was no doubt that the counterattack was a major offensive. When Colonel George Lincoln of the Operations Division came to him with suggestions concerning units that could be moved to reinforce the beleaguered Ardennes forces, Marshall said, "We can't help Eisenhower in any way other than not bothering him."

In cities and towns across America, citizens in the midst of their best Christmas-shopping spree in three years suddenly had hopes of seeing an early end to the war in Europe dashed by alarming newspaper headlines and radio reports. To stem a tide of bad news, Ike had imposed even tighter censorship, but a handful of reporters close to the action were more immediately concerned with not being killed than in getting out stories. Huddled and shivering in a farmhouse south of Bastogne were Walter Cronkite of the International News Service, John Driscoll of the *New York Herald Tribune*, Norman Clark of the *London News Chronicle*, and Cornelius Ryan of the *London Daily Telegraph*. When General Maxwell Taylor showed up, still wearing his dress uniform after a hasty return from Washington, D.C., and offered rides in his jeep to Bastogne, none accepted, and all pleaded with him not to risk a perilous journey on a road that the Germans had in their sights. A correspondent who reached the front lines with Tubby Barton's Fourth Division was Ernest Hemingway. Though suffering from a severe cold and told by his doctor to stay in bed in his suite at the Ritz in Paris, the forty-six-year-old author who had been at Normandy and in the Hurtgen Forest fighting, where he killed several Germans with a Thompson submachine gun, rushed to join the Fourth on December 19.

As sketchy reports of the fighting filtered out, the name Bastogne was suddenly rolling off Americans' tongues as if everyone had known where it was all their lives.

In the White House, President Roosevelt's delight in his landslide victory over New York's Republican governor Thomas Dewey in November, giving FDR a historic fourth term, diminished with every alarming report from the battlefront.

Readers of *Time*'s Christmas Day issue found the headline "Explosion." The article began, "On a 60-mile front, from gloomy, blood-soaked Hurtgen Forest to the eastern bulge of Luxembourg opposite Trier, the Germans finally smashed back. They struck with more weight and fury than they had mustered at any time since their ill-fated attempt to break the Allied line at Mortain, in Normandy. On the Roer River, north and south of Düren, an explosive situation had been built up. It was like a gas-filled room waiting for someone to light a match. General Bradley's First and Ninth Armies occupied 27 miles of the river's west bank."

Stating that General Hodges of the First Army struck the match by attacking Monschau and readying to cross the Roer headwaters in the hills, the writer speculated that Field Marshal Gerd von Rundstedt acted to take off the Allies' pressure by a full-out attack. "After a short spell of bad weather which grounded Allied reconnaissance and attack planes," the article went on, "Rundstedt struck." Crack German armored and infantry divisions drove in behind massive artillery barrages, said the article, noting that German paratroops landed behind the U.S. lines with the heaviest German thrust delivered in the heart of the Ardennes, east of Malmédy, where they overran the U.S. forward positions, massacred prisoners, and drove five miles into Belgium.

On December 18, Eisenhower's headquarters lifted censorship so that Americans would know that in a field at Malmédy the Germans obeyed Hitler's order to be ruthless and inhumane by murdering American captives and executing the wounded.

The *Time* report on the German counterattack concluded, "While SHAEF clamped a blackout on the exact locations of the fighting, Berlin claimed major breakthroughs and progress in Luxembourg and Belgium. Disconcerting, at least. Generals Bradley and Hodges had been surprised and caught off balance. They now seemed to expect more blows before the feverish explosion of enemy strength petered out. Until it did, they would probably yield in one place, try to hold in another, to make the push as costly for Rundstedt as they could. But U.S. casualties would rise as the drive was broken down."

For Collins, the shifting of his corps required him to travel almost constantly between the units. Like Bradley, he was frequently stopped by U.S. sentries and required to prove he was an American. By noon of December 22, the Seventh Corps was fighting an entirely different sort of battle. The original intention was for its divisions to assemble out of contact with the enemy and to prepare to counterattack and seal off the enemy penetration. Second Armored and the Seventy-fifth infantry divisions and corps artillery, cavalry, engineers, and service troops were still arriving in their assembly areas, but the Eighty-fourth Division at Marche was in contact with the leading elements of German columns and quickly went on defense to repel several small attacks. Instead of being assembled in reserve, the Seventh Corps was to hold a front between the U.S. Eighteenth Airborne Corps and the British Thirtieth Corps. With the German attack in its seventh day, noted situation reports, the enemy's intentions and order of battle began to crystallize. Saint-Vith had fallen, but Stavelot and Bastogne were still in American hands. Units of three panzer corps, including four SS panzer divisions and four others, had been identified in the thirty-five-mile penetration. It became apparent that the German High Command had mustered some of its best troops in their bid to cut the supply lines behind the American and British forces on the northern half of the Western Front. The attack was an all-out effort.

While all of this was transpiring, the encircled Screaming Eagles Airborne at Bastogne had been holding on by their fingernails. At eleven thirty in the morning on December 22, men of the 327th Glider Infantry Regiment spotted four Germans approaching and carrying a white flag.

One of them announced in halting English, "We are parliamentaries."

Probably intending to say that they'd come to "parlay," he went on, "We want to talk to your commanding general."

Blindfolded, they were escorted to a cellar under a military barracks in Bastogne that was the headquarters of Brigadier General Anthony McAuliffe. Because he wasn't present, they met with the 327th's CO, Colonel Joseph H. Harper, and his acting chief of staff, Colonel Ned Moore.

Handed a German ultimatum demanding that the Americans

give up Bastogne, they hurried to locate McAuliffe and inform him of the arrival of German emissaries.

Interrupted while congratulating his men on having repulsed a German attack, McAuliffe impatiently asked, "What do they want?"

"They want us to surrender," Moore said.

McAuliffe muttered, "Aw, nuts."

The ultimatum warned that if surrender was not forthcoming after two hours, an artillery corps and six heavy antiaircraft battalions would annihilate U.S. troops in and near Bastogne.

McAuliffe wondered aloud how to word his rejection of the surrender demand.

An aide, Lieutenant Colonel Harry O. W. Kinnard, said, "That first remark of yours would be hard to beat."

McAuliffe asked, "What was that?"

"You said 'nuts.'"

McAuliffe's face lit up. He said, "That's it."

On the bottom of the German ultimatum, he wrote:

22 December 1944

To The German Commander:

NUTS!

The American Commander

When Harper delivered the surrender demand with its answer at the bottom, the German who spoke English looked puzzled and asked, "Is the reply affirmative or negative?"

"It is decidedly negative," said Harper, adding, "If you continue this foolish attack, your losses will be tremendous."

Before the Germans headed back to the commander who'd issued the surrender demand, Harper told them, "If you don't understand what 'nuts' means, in plain English it is the same as 'Go to Hell.' And I will tell you this, if you continue to attack, we will kill every goddamned German who tries to break into this city."

During its second day in its new area, the Seventh Corps formed a defensive line by setting up roadblocks and outposts east and west of Marche. Engineers, cavalry, artillery, tank destroyers, tanks, and service troops manned defenses behind the frontline divisions in the event of an enemy infiltration or breakthrough. Numerous small enemy armored thrusts from the southeast and southwest were either repulsed or destroyed. The lineup to stop the German offensive drive consisted now of the Third Armored, the Eighty-fourth Infantry and Second Armored divisions, with the Seventy-fifth Infantry Division in reserve. The enemy continued to build up his forces in the Marche-Hotton area with the intention of launching a new drive for the Meuse River, and his reconnaissance and probing of the lines resulted in numerous pitched battles with small groups of infantry and tanks.

The day before Christmas, Collins welcomed Maurice Rose's Third Armored back into the Seventh Corps. On the same day, Collins received instructions releasing the Seventh Corps from all offensive missions and giving it the job of stabilizing the right flank of the first U.S. Army sector. While these instructions released the corps from the responsibility of carrying on the offensive to the enemy and stressed defense of the area, they did not prohibit attacking.

Collins gave an order directing an "active defense," including several limited attacks to improve his positions and stop the enemy drive where it was, both east and south of the Meuse River. U.S. and enemy lines were fluid during the early days of the fighting, and a few Seventh Corps units were temporarily cut off by German columns.

Task forces of the Third Armored Division were isolated in two different spots with too little gasoline and ammunition to return. In the little town of Marcouray, a defense was set up and units waited for reinforcements and supplies. Attempts were made to drop gasoline and ammunition by plane, but unsuccessfully. Eventually, the forces disabled their equipment to prevent it from being used by Germans and made their way back to Seventh Corps lines on foot. Third Battalion, 335th Infantry, was guarding an area south and west of Rochefort when it was cut off by advancing enemy tanks. Finding all the roads north to their division sector blocked, they withdrew by circuitous routes, moving west of the Meuse, and then north, to rejoin their regiment several days later.

Because several more German tank attacks were repulsed on Christmas, heavy losses were inflicted on the enemy, both in prisoners taken and in tanks and other equipment destroyed. An attack of the Second Panzer Division south of Ciney was checked by the Second Armored Division, and in an ensuing three-day battle, the German tank outfit was badly mauled by Seventh Corps armor.

On Christmas night, Collins was able to relax for the first time in several days and did so with his staff by sitting down to a turkey dinner. A year earlier, when he'd had his Christmas dinner with Gladys, the two girls, and son Jerry at West Point, the army he was now battling had stood in readiness behind Erwin Rommel's Atlantic Wall to stop an Allied landing in Normandy at the water's edge. For six months the Germans had been defeated in battle after battle and driven relentlessly back to the frontier of their fatherland, yet somehow the army had managed to rally and strike westward out of a Belgian forest where the American lines were weakest and threaten to break out from the bulge they created and undo all that had happened since D-day. Instead of commanding the Seventh Corps in crossing the Roer and pushing on to the Rhine, Collins had to spend December 26 devoting attention to the east wing of the corps front between the Belgian towns of Hotten and Manhay, where Rose's Third Armored Division, supported by the Seventy-fifth Division, in conjunction with Matthew Ridgway's Eighteenth Airborne Corps, was in a battle to checkmate Sepp Dietrich's Sixth Panzer Army. Spearheading the main German effort of the Ardennes offensive, the tanks were stopped at Saint-Vith, but now they were trying to turn north at Liège through the Third Armored Division and the Eighty-second Airborne.

"Fortunately, Ridgway and I knew one another well," Collins noted. They were able to make the complicated adjustment of troops and boundaries to thwart Dietrich's drive. In a three-day fight, the Second Armored Division under Major General Ernest Harmon stopped it and left more than eighty panzers in flames. Harmon gleefully notified Bradley that his tanks had also "polished off" 405 trucks and 81 artillery pieces while killing or wounding twenty-five hundred Germans and taking twelve hundred prisoners. Bradley called it the high-water mark of von Rundstedt's attack. Harmon said it was a "great slaughter."

At four in the afternoon of the twenty-sixth, Patton called Bradley to report that the Fourth Armored Division had broken through to relieve Bastogne. In resisting three German divisions, McAuliffe's paratroopers suffered 482 killed and 2,449 wounded and had named themselves "the battling bastards of Bastogne." When the American public learned of Anthony McAuliffe's reply to the surrender demand, "Nuts" was welded into the memories of the World War II generation with "Let's Remember Pearl Harbor," the song "Praise the Lord and Pass the Ammunition," and the warning not to talk idly about military topics, "Loose lips sink ships."

With the German offensive blunted, Collins and Ridgway fretted about what they saw as an unnecessary delay by Montgomery in launching the Seventh Corps in a counterattack. During every-other-day visits by Monty at Collins's CP, they urged action. Collins argued that the Seventh Corps ought to be positioned farther east, opposite Saint-Vith, and that a counterattack would force the enemy out of the bulge and into a position like that of the Falaise Pocket. Ridgway agreed. But Montgomery contended that a northern front had not been sufficiently stabilized. He expressed concerns that the Sixth Panzer Army might break through the U.S. First Army's northern front.

Referring to Collins's plan to use a highway from Liège to Saint-Vith, Montgomery said, "Joe, you can't supply a corps over a single road."

In exasperation, Collins retorted, "Well, Monty, maybe you British can't, but we can."

Recalling that he had submitted three plans to the First Army for the Seventh Corps to attack with the aim of a junction in the vicinity of Bastogne with Patton's Third Corps driving up from the south, Collins wrote, "After some delay, during which Hodges, Ridgway, and I continued to press Montgomery to launch the First Army's attack as soon as possible, and from as far east as possible. Bradley was as anxious as we were to get an attack going and had suggested to General Eisenhower on December 27 that the corresponding attack of the Third Army be direct from Bastogne toward St. Vith. Ike approved and the Third Army drive began on December 30, with Middleton's VIII Corps' objective the high ground south of Houffalize, northeast of Bastogne."

Montgomery finally decided on December 31, with Hodges's concurrence, to direct the Seventh Corps on Houffalize and the Eighteenth on Saint-Vith, but they were not to jump off until the third of January. The Seventh Corps, to consist of the Seventy-fifth, Eighty-third, and Eighty-fourth infantry divisions and the Second and Third armored divisions, with twelve corps artillery battalions and other supporting troops, totaling close to 100,000 men, was to attack east of the Ourthe River toward Houffalize. Ridgway was to protect the left flank of the Seventh Corps and on Hodges's order was to drive toward Saint-Vith.

Monty fixed the time of attack at 8:30 a.m.

CHAPTER ELEVEN

COUNTERATTACK

B ack in Germany, the Seventh Corps took over much the same sector it had held in December before the Battle of the Bulge. Its two frontline divisions, the Eighth and the 104th infantry divisions, held sectors along the west bank of the Roer River with little enemy contact. Corps records noted that enemy forces opposing them were generally inactive, but were being reinforced as troops shifted north from the Ardennes sector to bolster the Roer defenses against the inevitable attack across the Cologne plain.

Reflecting on the Battle of the Bulge in his autobiography, Collins stated that he had felt from the start of the German assault that it was doomed. He wrote, "A dangerous break in the front had been opened, which would have made it difficult if not impossible for Bradley to have controlled operations north of the Bulge from his headquarters in Luxembourg. Eisenhower was right, in my judgment, in placing Montgomery temporarily in command of all troops on the north side. But I never doubted as soon as we could reinforce the flanks of the Bulge with experienced troops we would stop the German drive east of the Meuse."

With Russians threatening on the Eastern Front, he felt, the Germans would draw many more troops from the east, and they did not have sufficient reserves in the west to initiate a second offensive north of Aachen, or in the Saar region, to pin down units of the Ninth or Third armies that might be moved against the Bulge.

While the Seventh Corps continued its inactivity after the Ardennes battle, the Eighteenth Airborne Corps on its right attacked to seize the Roer dams, to force the enemy's hand with respect to this continued threat of several million gallons of water. Efforts made to capture the dams had so far been unsuccessful, and aerial bombardment of the largest dam by British commando units had only pocked the huge earth-and-concrete structure.

"Now the barriers must either be captured or be blown up," a Seventh Corps historian noted.

Against strong resistance, the Americans closed in. On February 11, Germans destroyed the outlet gates on the largest dam, releasing the water, but not fast enough to cause the flood that had been feared.

Records note that during this quiet period in the Seventh Corps sector, troops were being regrouped and plans completed for the river crossing and the drive to the east. The Third Armored Division and the Fourth Cavalry Group moved back into Germany from Belgian rest areas, and the Ninety-ninth Infantry Division joined the Seventh forces.

On February 22, 1945, six thousand Allied air units began a series of mass attacks on German transportation, bombing and strafing railways, roads, and canals. German units had been moving from one threatened area to another as Allied and Red Army pressure increased or lessened. To prevent this shuffling of troops it was necessary to paralyze German transportation. In two days of the operation, planes of the Ninth Tactical Air Command carried out hundreds of sorties in front of the First Army sector, destroying 481 railway cars, damaging 556 others, exploding 52 locomotives, and cutting rail lines in more than one hundred locations.

Before daylight on February 23, the Ninth U.S. Army opened its drive to the Rhine and the Ruhr industrial area, and at three thirty a.m. on that date the Seventh Corps attacked across the Roer River to protect its right flank. In the Timberwolf Division's zone downstream, the bridgehead was established quickly and bridges soon carried supporting weapons and supplies east of the stream, but Brigadier General Bryant Moore's Eighth Division had trouble bridging the swifter current. Several attempts to build crossings failed when enemy artillery and the fast-moving water combined to prevent their completion. However, by February 25 all units held their initial bridgeheads and crossings. The Eighth quickly occupied Düren, and both divisions attacked across the plain against an enemy defending the villages with intense fire from self-propelled guns, dug-in tanks, and artillery.

As the advance pressed forward with a minimum of losses, the Fourth Cavalry joined the attack east of the river, and on the twenty-sixth the armor was committed to spearhead the drive to the northeast, gaining five miles that day in spite of poor roads and heavy mud. Air assistance, both in close support of the attackers and on armed reconnaissance in the zone of the corps' advance, continued whenever the weather permitted.

Commencing in the morning of February 5, Americans attacked into the Hurtgen Forest for the final time. The area fell on February 7, opening the way for an advance to secure the Roer dam. Although the flooding delayed Simpson's attack until February 23, at 0230, the first of the assault forces slipped across the flooded river, surprising the Germans. By the end of the day, twenty-eight battalions crossed, firmly establishing a Ninth Army bridgehead.

In the first four days of the attack, the Seventh Corps advanced fifteen kilometers, cleared the city of Düren and twenty-five other towns and villages, and took thirty-five hundred prisoners. Although forced to withdraw east of the Erft River, German troops defended every foot of the way to the maximum extent of their ability and used their available forces west of the Rhine in a desperate final defense of the approaches to Cologne.

CHAPTER TWELVE

FLAG RAISING ON THE RHINE

I n January 1945 Eisenhower had seventy-one divisions available and anticipated having eighty-five by the spring, consisting of sixty-one American, sixteen British, and eight French. He envisioned using them in a three-phased operation. First, the Allies would destroy remaining German forces west of the Rhine and close along the river that was legendary to Germans throughout its length. Next, they would seize bridgeheads over the river from Emmerich and Wesel in the north to Mainz and Karlsruhe in the south. In the final phase, they would advance from the lower Rhine into plains of northern Germany and from the Mainz-Karlsruhe area to Frankfurt and Kassel.

In addition to capturing the Ruhr, noted the official army history, Ike's plan would yield the prize of the industrialized Saar basin and major airfields around Frankfurt and Giessen. Not at all pleased with this approach, the British felt it would dissipate Montgomery's main attack in the north. But on February 2, the Combined Chiefs of Staff approved SHAEF's plan with Ike's assurance that the principal effort would remain in the north and that the crossing of the Rhine in the north was not contingent on clearing an entire area west of the river.

Early in the morning of February 8, more than one thousand guns unleashed a barrage of more than 500,000 shells at Germans opposite Crerar's Canadian First Army in an operation called Veritable. It called for Crerar to attack southeast from Nijmegen and the Reichswald Forest to destroy German forces west of the Rhine in the northern portion of the Twenty-first Army Group sector. On February 9, the offensive had pushed into Cleves, but rain, floods, and tough German resistance slowed the attack. By February 23, Crerar had moved past enemy positions near Goch to attack toward the enemy defenses that extended from Geldern to Rees.

To Montgomery's south, Simpson's Ninth Army, under the operational control of the Twenty-first Army Group, prepared to launch Operation Grenade. Simpson's forces would drive northeastward to link up with the attacking Canadians on the Rhine on February 10.

The U.S. Fifth Corps was now under the command of Huebner because Gerow had left in January to command a newly organized Fifteenth Army, designed for occupation duty. The corps got the mission of taking the key Schwammenauel Dam. The Seventy-eighth Infantry Division was responsible for the main attack, while elements of the Eighty-second Airborne Division and the Seventh Armored Division made supporting efforts. Simpson unleashed his armored forces on February 27, and rapidly advanced east toward the key city of Düsseldorf and northward toward Geldern and Wesel. They linked with elements of the Canadian First Army at Geldern. By March 5, the Ninth had driven fifty miles and stood at the Rhine from Düsseldorf to Moers. They had killed or captured thirty-six thousand Germans at a cost of less than seventy-three hundred American casualties. Together, Crerar and Simpson attacked the last bastion west of the Rhine in their sector at the bridgehead at Wesel, forcing the enemy across the Rhine by the tenth. Unfortunately for the Allies, noted the army historian Ted Ballard, the Germans succeeded in destroying bridges across the Rhine wherever the Allies retreated.

South of Simpson, the Twelfth Army Group had been attacking since January 18. In a belief the Germans were off balance in the aftermath of their failed Ardennes offensive, Ike urged Bradley to attack with "all possible vigor" as long as he had a chance of decisive results. By the end of January, the Twelfth Army Group had forced the Germans in its sector back to the West Wall, but the drive lost momentum. Although Bradley wanted to continue to the Rhine River, Eisenhower halted the advance on February 1 in preparation for both Veritable and Grenade. With the start of the main Allied effort in the north, Bradley's army group took only a secondary role. In the First Army sector, aside from the mission of capturing Roer River dams, elements of Collins's Seventh Corps advanced, protecting Simpson's flank.

As the rest of the First Army went on the defensive, in the Third Army area, Patton made limited advances north of the Moselle River. By the end of February, his army punched through the Siegfried Line below Saarburg, taking the Saar-Moselle triangle and Trier. To the far south, the Sixth Army Group made elimination of Germans in a pocket at Colmar its priority. For this, Eisenhower had given Devers five U.S. divisions and twelve thousand service troops from the SHAEF reserve to assist. While the Seventh Army held in the Saar Valley and made small advances in the region flooded by the Moder River, the First French Army also attacked the Colmar pocket. Ultimately, the Twenty-first U.S. Corps attacked south toward Colmar. By February 9, the Allies had eliminated the problem, driving the surviving Germans back across the Rhine.

With the west side of the river secure, Devers gave General Alexander Patch the go-ahead to commence a limited drive. On February 17, the Seventh Army attacked, straightening its lines and, by the end of the month, had established a foothold south of Saarbruecken. With the Twenty-first Army Group firmly established along the Rhine, Bradley's Twelfth Army Group prepared to carry out Operation Lumberjack. The plan called for the First Army to attack southeastward toward the juncture of the Ahr and Rhine rivers and swing south to meet Patton's Third Army coming north. If Lumberjack succeeded, the Twelfth Army Group would move to the Rhine in the entire area north of the Moselle River. Bradley launched Lumberjack on March 1. In the north, the First Army would rapidly exploit bridgeheads over the Erft River, entering Euskirchen on March 4 and Cologne on the fifth. At the same time, Patton's Third Army would sweep to the Rhine River.

By February 26, a Seventh Corps bridgehead around Düren was linked up with a Nineteenth Corps front east of Jülich. Collins directed Maurice Rose's Third Armored to the bridgehead on the night of the twenty-fifth, prepared to attack on the twenty-sixth in the first phase of the Seventh Corps' drive on Cologne.

"The checkerboard pattern of towns on the Cologne plain, most of them organized for defense by the Germans," wrote Collins, "suited perfectly organization and tactics employed by General Rose in spearheading the attack of the Corps. By now I made a standard practice of attaching an infantry regiment from one of our infantry divisions to the Third Armored Division. This enabled Rose to form six task forces, each consisting of a battalion of tanks and a battalion of infantry, each task usually reinforced with artillery, engineers, and tank destroyers. The Division Reconnaissance Battalion, reinforced, was often used as a seventh task force. Rose normally attacked in four columns, pitting two task forces against each town in turn, permitting variation to maneuver and providing some rest for those not actively engaged."

The city of Cologne was guarded on the west by a low, flat ridge that provided excellent observation over the flat land west of the city. This area was dotted with open-pit lignite mines, intermingled with flooded areas, slag piles, factories, and small towns. To the northwest, the region was flat and pastoral with no major obstacles. Collins decided to pass the Third Armored around the north end of the ridge and attack Cologne from the northwest, with the 99th Division on its left flank, while the 104th and Eighth divisions moved on the city from the west and the southwest. The Third Armored attacked before dawn on March 2 and made progress, but the Ninth Panzer Division, fighting stubbornly behind a series of antitank ditches and fortifications, prevented a breakthrough. The next morning, in another predawn attack, a combat command caught the Germans by surprise and cut the main road north of the city, while the 104th cleared the crest of the hills on the Düren-Cologne highway. It was now only a question of time before Germans in the city would be squeezed by the Americans to the east and the Rhine on the west.

"I got quite a thrill," Collins recalled, "as I saw the great city, fourth largest in Germany, spread out before us. Smoke hung over the city from the factories, many of which were still operating. The great cathedral towered above the smoke, seemingly undamaged despite its nearness to the main railway station, which was an empty shell from the many bombings, and to the Hohenzollern Bridge over the Rhine, two spans of which had been blown by the Germans a day or so before. As we drove into the outskirts in search of Rose's CP, I was relieved to find that, while sporadic fighting was still going on, no effort was being made to turn Cologne into a Stalingrad. Rose was confident that in a couple of days he would have the city cleared."

A city that dated to Roman times and gave its name to perfumes, Cologne had been left in ruins by Allied bombers. From the first raid of a thousand RAF planes in May 1942 to the most recent on March 2, 1945, the city had been hit 262 times. Although bombardiers had been told to take care to avoid its magnificent Gothic cathedral, errant bombs struck it fourteen times.

Because it was unsafe to approach the cathedral until the city was fully secured, Collins visited it a few days after he was told it was safe to proceed. Entering the church with General Walter Bedell Smith and British Air Marshal Tedder, he encountered a priest who had stayed in the church throughout the war. With him as a guide, they found the floor of the nave littered with rubble from the interior ceiling, which the priest said had finally collapsed only a few days before. Even in this condition, Collins found the nave awe-inspiring in its soaring height. The north tower had been hit by a stray bomb, which caused no structural damage.

"The escape was almost miraculous," Collins wrote, "for the cathedral was circled with ruins. But none of this could take away the majesty of the magnificent twin spires, which towered above the surrounding destruction."

Cologne marked another major phase of Seventh Corps operations since D-day. It had come more than six hundred miles from Utah Beach, and on the day before Collins paid a visit to the cathedral it had captured its 140,000th prisoner. This was more than the POW tally of the entire First Army.

In the middle of all this action, Collins noted, General Eisenhower had been on a quick swing around the front. He stopped at Collins's CP in Cologne long enough to say hello and to express his pleasure at how well things were going. Before leaving, he asked to talk to Collins privately. He said he thought Collins should know his work as corps commander since D-day had greatly impressed himself, Bradley, Hodges, and Montgomery. He then said that if he saw an opportunity to give Collins an army command, he would not hesitate to do so.

"I had given no thought to an army command," Collins wrote, "and would have hated to give up the VII Corps at the time the war in Europe was nearing its end."

Having commanded it since D-day, he wanted to have the privilege of leading it all the way to Berlin or wherever the corps met the Russians, who were closing in on Hitler's lair.

Taking over from Marines in the battle for Guadalcanal, troops of Major General J. (Joseph) Lawton Collins's 25th "Tropical Lighting" Division march to the front for their first taste of combat on January 10, 1943.

Right: Collins points out strategic ridges held by the 25th Division on Guadalcanal in a briefing for Secretary of the Navy Frank Knox (*hands on hips*), Pacific Fleet Commander Chester Nimitz (*without a helmet*), and Major General Alexander (Sandy) Patch (*next to Collins*) on January 21, 1943.

Below: Captain Cecil Bayless, commander of M Company, Third Battalion, 27th Infantry, updates rifle-toting Collins on the mortar situation along the Zeta Trail on the island of New Georgia, August 14, 1943.

All photos: Courtesy National Archives

Collins shows his prowess as a fisherman while heading back to the 25th Division command post by boat after inspecting the front on Bariroko Island in New Georgia.

In fierce fighting for a strategic ridge on Guadalcanal, Captain Charles W. Davis dodged Japanese fire over open ground to locate a concealed enemy strong point and direct a mortar barrage that knocked it out. For gallantry and intrepidity at the risk of his life beyond the call of duty, Davis was awarded the Medal of Honor and promoted to lieutenant colonel.

After addressing his troops at a rest area in New Zealand, Collins returned to the U.S. on leave and found himself ordered to England to command VII Corps at Utah Beach on D-Day.

Collins (*right*) waits for an interpreter (*back to camera*) to translate a statement by German army commander Lieutenant General Dietrick von Schleiben after the surrender of the port of Cherbourg. On the far left is the German naval operations commander, Rear Admiral Walter Hennecke.

At a ceremony on the steps of Cherbourg's city hall, Collins returns the liberated port city to the control of its prewar mayor, Dr. Paul Renaud.

Ignoring Hitler's order to fight to the death to keep Cherbourg out of Allied hands, thousands of German troops surrendered to the U.S. Army's VII Corps.

Above: Alert to possible German or French snipers or artillery spotters, a U.S. patrol picks its way through ruins of the city of St. Lo toward its Notre Dame Cathedral on July 25, 1944.

Left: A bazooka team of the 39th Infantry Regiment spots a German halftrack lurking in a forest at Andaine, France, August 15, 1944.

An exultant Lieutenant General George S. Patton was the first U.S. commander to cross the Seine River in the drive to liberate Paris, but the honor was afforded to the Free French forces. General Collins took a tour of the city by flying over the huge victory parade down the Champs-Élysées at low altitude and buzzed the Eiffel Tower, the Louvre, and the Arc de Triomphe.

Fourth Cavalry Group Commander, Colonel Joseph Tully of San Antonio, Texas, greets Collins at Butgenbach, Belgium, on September 29, 1944, for a ceremony awarding medals to men of Tully's outfit.

Army Chief of Staff George C. Marshall is briefed by Collins (*left*) and Eisenhower's chief aide, Lieutenant General Walter Bedell Smith (*right*), about the U.S. attack on the city of Aachen as the Allies rapidly advanced toward the heart of Germany.

Chief of Staff Marshall, General Smith, and Collins tour the Siegfried Line front in Collins's armored car, with Marshall's four stars attached to the fender.

A U.S. tank destroyer opens up on a target in street-to-street fighting to take Aachen.

Collins welcomes American Red Cross "Clubmobile" volunteers, who handed out coffee and doughnuts to VII Corps enlisted men and officers at Kernelmunster, Germany.

Left: An M-10 tank destroyer of the 893 Tank Destroyer Battalion rolls through the Huertgen Forest in the bloodiest battle of the European Theater of Operations.

Right: Third Armored Division commander Major General Maurice Rose. His division drove more than one hundred miles in a single day, a record march for modern warfare, and played a key role in several campaigns. On March 31, 1945, Rose turned a corner in his jeep and found himself surrounded by German tanks. As he drew his pistol to surrender, a young German commander, apparently misunderstanding Rose's intentions, shot and killed him.

Below: Private Wallace C. Carrington (*right*) of Portland, Oregon, and Private Ernest R. Gross of Middletown, Ohio, fire at a German sniper position from their foxhole built in the side of a dike in Holland.

General Dwight D. Eisenhower and Fourth Infantry Division Commander Major General Raymond O. ("Tubby") Barton.

First Army infantrymen move warily through snowy Krinkelter woods in Belgium. Two weeks later, the Germans counterattacked and began the Battle of the Bulge.

Thirty-fifth Division machine gunners guard against enemy infiltrators east of Bastogne, Belgium, January 1, 1945.

Rooftop snipers of the 290th Infantry, 75th Division of Collins's VII Corps stop to reload in Beffe, Belgium.

Winter-camouflaged American riflemen on patrol in a Luxembourg field on December 20, 1944.

Left: General "Fighting Joe" Collins and British Field Marshal Sir Bernard Law Montgomery outside VII Corps headquarters at Mean, Belgium.

Below: Montgomery awards Collins the British honor of "Companion of the Order of the Bath."

A U.S. First Army tank rumbles from the east end of the Remagen Bridge. Failure of the retreating troops to destroy the bridge, allowing the Allies to get forces across the Rhine River, was one of the costliest German mistakes of the war.

Medics stand by to aid injured troops trapped in the wreckage of the Remagen Bridge after it collapsed due to both Germany artillery hits and weakening caused by the weight and rumbling of Allied vehicles rushing to cross the Rhine.

Liberated by VII Corps troops, a Polish inmate of the Nordenhausen concentration camp shows Technical Sergeant Fifth Class John E. Lyndon of Rome, New York, one of the ovens used to dispose of the corpses of victims of the Nazis.

A VII Corps GI stands guard as civilian residents of the city of Nordenhausen dig graves for mass burials of victims of the nearby death camp.

General Collins shares his cigarettes with Russian Major General Baklanov, Major General M. A. Sachanow of the First Ukrainian Army, and a translator at Leipzig, Germany, following the linkup of U.S. and Russian forces at the Elbe River.

Bound for home, on June 5, 1945, Collins says goodbye to his VII Corps staff. They fought their way from Utah Beach on June 6, 1944, to the German surrender on May 8, 1945.

Promoted to Lieutenant General, Collins toured the ETO in August 1945 to confer with U.S. occupation officers, Army public relations officers, and news agency representatives about improving relations between the Army and the press during the demobilization process. In 1949, Collins succeeded General Omar N. Bradley as Army Chief of Staff. He served in that post until 1953, followed by two years as a chief adviser on Vietnam policy to President Eisenhower.

Remembering the stirring sight of the hoisting of the American flag at Coblenz at the end of World War I, Collins decided to have a flag raising in the Cologne city stadium where the Nazis had staged rallies glorifying Hitler. The ceremony on March 11 was brief and simple. A platoon from each major unit of the corps acted as a guard of honor for the massed colors of all units. Collins then presented an American flag to the color bearers and spoke on the significance of the assembly and the symbolic meaning of the raising of the Stars and Stripes on the Rhine.

The massed colors marched to a flagpole that was at one end of the field. Arms were presented, and as a band played "The Star-Spangled Banner" the flag was run up while a flight of fighter-bombers, which had been furnishing cover, wheeled overhead.

Four days before Cologne fell, a task force of the Ninth Armored Division under the command of Lieutenant Colonel Leonard Engeman reached the town of Remagen and to their amazement found that a bridge over the Rhine was intact. Located ten miles south of Bonn, the bridge had been built in World War I because the German army commander, Erich Friedrich Wilhelm Ludendorff, needed a means across the river to guarantee a faster and better connection to the Western Front. In 1916, the firm of Grun and Bilfinger started to build it with two railroad tracks, using Russian POWs as labor. The final result in 1918 was a 4,642-ton bridge that was hailed as among the most beautiful bridges along the Rhine. After its completion, it was named in honor of Ludendorff. The towers resembled fortresses and were equipped with barracks for troops and storage rooms, and their tops provided far-reaching surveillance. The bridge itself was easily and quickly converted for road and pedestrian use, with wooden planks covering the railroad tracks. While intended as a logistics backbone in World War I, it ultimately served as an escape route for the beaten German army in 1918. Later, a pedestrian walkway was added so town residents could walk across it.

On September 4, 1944, Allied planes started to bomb all Rhine bridges. During a raid of thirty-three bombers on October 9, 1944, the Remagen span was damaged and reported as destroyed. Regular railroad and pedestrian traffic resumed on November 9. During a raid on December 29, four bombs damaged it. More air raids followed in January and February of 1945, but each time the bridge was repaired. In the first days of March 1945 it was being equipped with roadway planks as in World War I and preparations were being made to be able to blow it up in the event of an enemy attempt to capture it.

On March 7, 1945, German soldiers on the bridge looked with alarm as troops of the Ninth Armored Division appeared on the Rhine's west bank. They were no more surprised than Brigadier General William Hoge. Commander of Combat Team B of the Ninth Armored Division, he could hardly believe his eyes. Like everyone in the U.S. Army from Eisenhower down the chain of command to the lowly GI, he did not expect to find a bridge anywhere on the Rhine still standing. Yet here was a bridge that appeared his for the taking. An engineer officer by training whom the fortunes of war had turned into an armored force general, he gave an order at 1630 that would send Omar Nelson Bradley and all the brass up the line into near ecstasy when they heard of the intact bridge at Remagen. With an outward composure that masked his excitement, and certain that the Germans had rigged the bridge with explosives, Hoge said, "Block the demolitions, cross the bridge and capture it for our use."

Springing into action, First Lieutenant Karl H. Timmerman, the commander of Company A, Twenty-seventh Armored Infantry Battalion, crouched on the west end of the bridge and cautiously moved onto it. At that moment the bridge rocked from the force of an explosion. Timmerman picked himself up and through the smoke saw that the bridge was still standing. Although holes had been torn in the planking in its center, the footpaths on either side were intact, and Timmerman signaled to his company to move onto it. With a platoon of tanks providing cover against German machine-gun fire that came from towers on the east end of the bridge, the infantrymen rushed forward. Like quarterbacks, they dodged and waved from girder to girder and reached the far side. Timmerman ordered men to clear the towers and another platoon to move to the east end of the bridge. Hoge ordered the remainder of the infantry battalion and Fourteenth Tank Battalion to follow.

Still astonished, Hoge notified his divisional commander, Major General John W. Leonard, that the Ludendorff Bridge over the Rhine was in U.S. hands. Leonard got on a phone to Courtney Hodges at First Army HQ, who called Bradley.

With the same coolness that Hoge demonstrated in giving the order to take the span, Hodges said, "Brad. We've gotten a bridge."

Bradley replied, "A bridge? You mean you've got one intact on the Rhine?"

"Yep," answered Hodges. "Leonard nabbed the one at Remagen before they [the Germans] blew it up."

"Hot dog, Courtney," exclaimed Bradley, "this will bust him [the enemy] wide open. Are you getting your stuff across?"

"Just as fast as we can push it over. Tubby [Barton] has got the navy moving in now with a ferry service and I'm having the engineers throw a couple of spare pontoon bridges across to the bridgehead."

When Bradley notified Eisenhower, Ike said, "Hold on to it, Brad. Get across with whatever you need, but make certain that you hold that bridgehead."

Correspondents flashed news of the capture to their home offices and they sent it out in bulletins to newspapers and radio networks. Referring to a news photograph of the bridge that appeared on the front page of almost every newspaper in the country, a *Time* magazine article observed, "The Ludendorff Bridge at Remagen did not look like a thing of beauty. Its squat towers, like two massive beer mugs, looked typically Teutonic. The picture, taken on a grey day, showed the grey rubble of war in the foreground. But the bridge was intact, and therein lay its exquisite beauty. Every American could see in it an imminent promise of victory in Europe."

But the optimism that bubbled up with the crossing of the Rhine, the article said, was tempered by caution. "The U.S. was through with such bumptious assumptions as it had made after General Patton's dash past Paris last summer," the item continued. "But this time it was not entirely the caution of earlier disappointment that kept down the premature cheering. It was also a more intimate realization of what the end of the war in Europe would mean. In the same week that the Rhine was crossed, the U.S. people learned the full toll of what their might of arms had wrought in Cologne. No one, except the overly sentimental, shed tears. But for the first time the certain chaos of postwar Germany was made graphic. Everyone knew now that, no matter when the war in Europe ends, its end would not bring a cessation of grave problems."

Americans knew that while the war in Europe appeared to be near an end, there was still one going on in the Pacific. Appalling casualties were reported from islands that no one on the home front had ever heard of, and that men who made the travelogues they saw before the main feature at the movies had never visited.

In Germany, an operation called Undertone originally directed the Seventh Army to attack in the Saar, while the First French Army took up defense on General Patch's flank. Though General Devers initiated Undertone on March 15, 1945, Eisenhower proposed that Patton's Third Army attack across the northern portion of Patch's sector. Having been Collins's boss at Guadalcanal, Patch had been shifted to the Mediterranean theater to command an invasion of southern France that was to have immediately followed the Normandy landings, but was delayed until August. Originally called Operation Anvil, it had been renamed for security reasons and proceeded as Operation Dragoon.

Patch's advance in France allowed the Seventh Army to focus more effort on the portions of the Siegfried Line in its zone. It would also create a pincer maneuver, with Patton in an attack to the south and Patch moving north. When asked by Eisenhower if he had any objections to Patton's taking over part of his army, Patch said the object was to destroy Germans, adding, "We are all in the same army."

Patch and Patton worked out the details for the modified Undertone. The Third Army, though stretched, rapidly pushed toward Oppenheim, Worms, Mannheim, and the city of Kaiserslautern. Patch's army captured Saarbruecken. But pillboxes and heavy mining exacted their toll on Patch's and Patton's men. As the German defenses crumbled, Patch's Seventh Army gained momentum and broke through the West Wall defenses on March 20 and was beginning to overrun the Saar-Palatinate triangle. The next day, Seventh Army and Third Army units met. Their pincer destroyed the German Seventh Army and left the First Army as the only German force west of the Rhine. At the same time, Patton reported that all three of his corps had reached the Rhine.

On March 21, a massive Allied ground force lay poised along the Rhine from Arnhem to Switzerland. Eisenhower's armies of 4.5 million personnel included ninety divisions that stood ready for the final drive into the heart of the Third Reich.

CHAPTER THIRTEEN

BEER BRIDGE AND HOMECOMING

Because Third Corps engineers were repairing the important Ludendorff Bridge on March 14, Collins crossed the Rhine by jeep on one of the pontoon spans that had been hastily set up to handle masses of vehicles, equipment, and men being rushed over the river. As a soldier, it was an exciting and triumphant moment, but at the same time a nostalgic one, with memories flooding back of the river when he was a young officer in occupied Germany and trying to make up his mind between staying in the army and quitting to become a lawyer.

"The river was as green and as swift as I remembered it," he wrote to Gladys, "and its terraced vine-clad hills and placid villages as charming as ever. I had intended, like most American soldiers, to spit in the Rhine, but I was too lost in my memories to remember such rudeness. In a minute we were pulling up to the far bank and running along the river road past a carefully trimmed double row of shade trees, not yet in leaf, with their accompanying benches. Only now there were no Germans sitting on them, sipping beer from brown mugs as they half-dozed in complacent contemplation of their beloved Rhine. If they had only had sense enough to sit tight on their benches when the neurotic Hitler awoke them to illusions of grandeur."

When the young Adolf Hitler returned to Germany in 1918 as a former corporal who had been left temporarily blinded by a gas attack, he was permanently scarred by what he believed was the humiliation of Germany in the peace agreement that ended the First World War. As the boiling rage within him erupted in the form of political action in the 1920s, he'd aligned himself with a minor national socialist group, quickly took control of it, and forged it through cunning and brute force, with the swastika as its emblem, into a party that promised to undo the ignominies of the peace treaty and return Germany to the world stage as a mighty power. When the Nazis succeeded in winning a large number of seats in the German parliament in 1932, and Hitler emerged as chancellor to use the office to become the dictator of Germany, Joseph Lawton Collins had just been promoted to major and made executive officer of the Twenty-third Brigade in Manila. The chief concern then for the United States was Japanese intentions in Asia and the Pacific.

Now, reaching the other side of the Rhine, Lightning Joe Collins was the commanding officer of a U.S. Army corps that played a significant role in the crushing of Hitler's dream of a Reich that would survive for a thousand years. Primarily because of the United States, it had lasted less than a dozen, and the Seventh Corps was poised to follow its leader over the Rhine and sweep all the way to Berlin.

Having gained fame as the Big Red One in North Africa and Sicily, the First Division had a new commander. Taking over from Major General Clarence Huebner, Major General Clift Andrus had been Huebner's artillery chief. The First crossed the Rhine on March 15, using Third Corps pontoon bridges and ferries, and took position to the right of the Seventy-eighth Division. Under Major General Edwin P. Parker, it became part of the Seventh Corps when Collins assumed command of the northern sector of the Rhine bridgehead. During the next five days, Seventh Corps engineers built three floating bridges on the river. To engender interest and boost morale among the engineers, Collins told their CO, Mason Young, that he wanted them to break the First Division's record of Rhine River bridge building of twenty-four hours set in 1918.

When Young's men built one bridge in twenty-two hours and a second in seventeen and three-quarter hours, Collins challenged them to set an all-time record by erecting one in ten hours. Their reward, he told the dubious Young, would be beer for the entire engineer battalion. On March 21, the 237th Combat Engineer Battalion, assisted by E Company of the Twenty-third Armored Engineer Battalion and a company of the 239th Combat Engineer Battalion, finished a bridge a short distance south of Bonn that measured 1,308 feet in ten hours and eleven minutes.

Forgiving the overage, Collins found himself and aides scouring the towns along the Rhine to locate enough casks of beer for more than a battalion of thirsty builders. As they quaffed the frothy, tangy payoff, they put up a sign naming their achievement "The Beer Bridge." When Eisenhower learned of the accomplishment, he reported it to George Marshall, but said the reward was champagne. Recording Ike's enhancement of the story in his memoirs, Collins wrote, "I could not have afforded champagne and the men would have preferred beer anyway."

On Saint Patrick's Day, he again crossed the Rhine to check on operations of the First and Seventy-eighth divisions in moving up the Seig. The river was a protective barrier for the Seventh Corps' north flank against counterattacks from the Ruhr region of Germany by the Fifteenth Army of Fritz Bayerlein, who had commanded the Panzer Lehr Division in Normandy. On the day that Collins met with Andrus and Parker, the bridge at Remagen that had been a U.S. windfall in the crossing of the Rhine succumbed to the stresses and strains of the Germans' failed attempt to destroy it, the rushing of tanks, trucks, and men over it, and artillery and bombs exploding close by. Battered and war-weary, it gave way and fell into the river, adding to the U.S. casualty lists twenty-eight engineers killed and ninety-three injured. So welded was the capture of the bridge in American minds that it could be mentioned in Frank Capra's film *It's a Wonderful Life* in 1946 without explanation.

Still in a nostalgic mood during a lull in action on March 23, Collins traveled to the Third Army area to see what the war had done to the city where he'd met, courted, and wed Gladys Easterbrook and that he regarded as a second hometown. "Because Coblenz was an important rail center at the confluence of the Moselle and Rhine," he wrote, "the city had been heavily bombed. [The First World War] Eighth Infantry Strasse barracks was a blackened shell, as was the Festhalle, our billets on Mainzer Strasse, and the palace where Gladys and I were married. As we sped past the Festhalle, we came under observation from the town of Pfaffendorf, across the Rhine, and without any warning a burst of machine-gun fire splattered around us. Luckily none of us was hit, but I did feel annoyed at being shot at in my 'home town.' I felt better when the thought occurred to me to see if there was any wine left in the Dienhart cellars, off Jesuiten Platz. Thanks to a heavy guard of MPs, there was still a goodly supply. When the old German caretakers learned that I had been stationed in Coblenz, they got out their keys and opened a barred section of the cellars where the best Rhine and Moselle wines were stored."

They loaded the jeep with Bemkastel Doktor and Rudesheimer Riesling and a case of fine champagne. The next day, his chief of staff, Dick Partridge, who also loved German wine, persuaded him to allow him to risk a second poaching of the Third Army territory. He came back with a truckload that supplied Collins's staff with after-dinner libations for the rest of the war.

When the Seventh Corps was completely across the Rhine, Collins and General Bradley met to discuss strategy. Collins proposed an immediate attack to the north before the Germans could build a defense along the Seig River. Bradley preferred waiting until they had more troops and that they attempt a breakout from the Rhine bridgehead and drive toward the Lahn River valley for a linkup with Patton's Third Army, a push to the city of Kassel, and a double envelopment of the industrial Ruhr in conjunction with the Ninth Army under Montgomery.

With Hodges's First Army bolstered by four more divisions and the Seventh Corps consisting of the Seventy-eighth and First infantry divisions and a Third Armored Combat Command under Colonel Robert Howze, the force reached a line set by SHAEF and stopped on March 23. That night, Patton made a surprise move across the Rhine that beat Montgomery's force in traversing the river by twenty-four hours, giving the Third Army commander the satisfaction of having twice outpaced Monty to a crucial objective, the first having been in a race to take Messina in Sicily. With key elements of the next phase of the campaign into the heart of Germany in place, Bradley was now ready to attack with the Seventh Corps on the left (north) flank, Huebner's Fifth Corps on the right, and James Van Fleet, now a major general, heading the Third Corps in the center.

The Seventh Corps attack would be led by Maurice Rose's Third Armored Division's "Spearheaders" in conjunction with the First Division. In Collins's recounting of the breakout from the Rhine bridgehead, the Seventh Corps' objective was high ground and a road center at Altenkirchen. The Third Armored was to be prepared to exploit toward Marburg on the upper Lahn. The Seventy-eighth Division was to protect the left flank of the Seventh Corps along the Seig River, relieving elements of the First Division as far east as the town of Merten, thirteen miles from the Rhine, as the attack progressed. The Eighth Division and Fourth Cavalry Group, which was patrolling the Rhine River's west bank between Cologne and the Remagen bridgehead, were to be relieved by the Eighty-eighth Division and reassemble in the vicinity of Bonn in corps reserve. The Fourth Cavalry was prepared to cross the Rhine and take over the defense on the north of the Seventh Corps east of Merten while the Big Red One continued to advance.

The attack of the First Army went off on March 25 against only light resistance except along the Seig, where the First Division repulsed a series of counterattacks. By the twenty-eighth the Third Armored had blazed ahead to Marburg with virtually no damage to its thirteenth-century cathedral or its university, founded in 1527.

"As an indication of how surprised the Germans were at the arrival of our troops," noted Collins, "a trainload of civilians and convalescent soldiers being brought to Marburg for rest and rehabilitation was halted just outside the city by our tanks."

With the fall of Marburg, Bradley decided the time had come to turn the First Army to the north to link up with the Ninth Army in the Kassel-Paderborn area, completing the encirclement of the Ruhr, after which the Ninth Army would again revert to Bradley's command. The Seventh Corps was to make the First Army's main effort. Its east flank would be protected by the Third and Fifth corps, but the Seventh Corps would be responsible for its inside (left) flank, which included its sector along the west bank of the Rhine River south of Cologne and extended almost two hundred miles as the corps neared Paderborn.

To keep in touch with widely separate units, Collins climbed into a Piper Cub and shuttled from one CP to the next. On the second day of the move north of Marburg, all columns ran into small groups of German tanks and infantry armed with antitank weapons (*Panzerfausts*) that advanced in a hastily organized defensive line. The force was manned by students from a training center in Paderborn and an SS tank replacement battalion of about sixty Tiger and Panther tanks.

On the afternoon of the thirtieth, Collins landed in a pasture beside a column of one of the units south of Korbach and flagged down a jeep to drive him into Korbach, where he joined the unit's CO, Truman E. Boudinot. When the town was cleared, night was falling and Boudinot decided to rest his columns for the night.

Collins radioed back to his CP that he would remain overnight with Boudinot.

"We had halted in a sunken part of the road," he recalled, "in which one of the young enemy soldiers who had manned a panzerfaust had been shot through the head and was dying. Our medics had examined him and said there was nothing that could be done to save him. Our minds were temporarily diverted from the wayside tragedy by the unexpected crunch of artillery fire off to our left. We crawled up the bank and were relieved to find that the explosions were coming from a German ammunition train, which the column to the west had set afire. The ruddy glow from the burning train lit up the lowering clouds, brightened from time to time as an exploding shell rocketed skyward, so that as we came back down the embankment we could see that death had come mercifully to the wounded German, whose crumpled body lay at the foot of the opposite bank."

Meanwhile, as the Third Armored Division led off the attack, General Rose and an aide, Major Robert Bellinger, rode in a jeep close behind the leading elements. In a jeep behind them were General Frederick Brown and Lieutenant Colonel Wesley Sweat. Following the jeeps was an armored car with radio communications. When they tried to bypass Paderhorn on a secondary road as the sun was setting, small-arms and tank fire cut them off from a task force led by Colonel John C. Welborn. As Rose began to radio for a unit to respond to the enemy fire, he saw four German tanks coming up the road from the south. Rose had Brown call for artillery, then led the party in a dash to get by the tanks, but one of the tanks swerved and pinned Rose's jeep against a tree.

Waving a submachine gun, the German commander ordered them to get out of the jeep and signaled them to give up their pistols. While the others carried theirs in shoulder holsters, Rose wore a pistol belt around his waist. As he lowered a hand to unbuckle it, the tank commander fired, killing him. Leaving him where he fell, the Germans left with the others as their prisoners without realizing they had killed a general who was not only a divisional commander but a Jew and the son of a prominent rabbi in Colorado. Rose's religion was also not known by most of the men in his Third Armored Division, nor by Collins, many other officers, and reporters. When they found out about his faith, they assumed he had been killed because of it.

In his book *Battle for the Ruhr*, which presented the Rhine campaign from the German point of view, Derek S. Zumbro wrote, "In the fading light, [Rose's] rank insignia would have been difficult to distinguish even under optimal conditions. The nervous German tank commander never realized that he had killed the commander of the U.S. Third Armored Division . . . [Rose] was wearing a standard-issue field uniform with simple stars of rank on his helmet and collars. The Tiger crewman was only familiar with Rose's German counterparts, who were easily distinguished by their distinctive crimson-and-gold tabs, gold-trimmed peaked caps, and riding breeches marked by twin crimson stripes."

Zumbro noted that Americans who believed Rose had been murdered retaliated by shooting Germans who surrendered, and some wounded were shot where they lay or left to die. He cited instances in which the bodies of twenty-seven Germans who had been shot apparently after surrendering were found behind the cemetery of the village of Ettelen, and eighteen executed Germans were found after an American advance in the town of Dorenhagen.

George Patton notwithstanding, Collins in his autobiography hailed Rose as the "top armored commander in the Army when he was killed." He recalled going to Rose's CP in an exposed house at the end of a small town on the Cologne plain. "Maurice," he exclaimed, "do you *always* have to have your CP in the last house in town?"

Rose replied, "General, there is only one way I know how to lead this division, and that's at the head of it."

A war crime investigation later concluded that Rose had been shot in the heat of battle and that the German tank commander had mistaken Rose's action in unbuckling his gun belt as an attempt to draw his weapon.

As the Third Armored neared Paderborn, Field Marshal Walter Model realized his entire army group would soon be trapped in the Ruhr unless he was permitted to withdraw or could receive outside help. Knowing that reserves necessary for such a counterattack were nonexistent, he ignored Hitler's order forbidding withdrawal and attempted to break out of the Ruhr by having Bayerlein's Fifty-third Corps attack from the city of Winterberg south of Paderborn and against the west flank of the First Army.

"We began to get reports from prisoners of preparations for a counterattack from that area," Collins noted. "To meet this threat, which was made more serious because the First was vacating the area as it moved north following the left of the Third Armored, I had the 104th Division take responsibility for the Winterberg sector. Then as the 104th moved north to plug another threatened escape route via Brilon, General Hodges transferred the Ninth Division from the III Corps to the VII Corps. I inserted Craig's Ninth into line opposite Winterberg, behind the 104th. I now had five infantry divisions, the Seventy-eighth, Eighth, Ninth, 104th, and First, plus our Fourth Cavalry Group, strung out in a 175 mile arc from Remagen to the outskirts of Paderborn, boxing in Model's Army Group B. We were thinly spread, even though the Ninth and 104th had beaten back Bayerlein's efforts to break through. But an escape route was still open on the north side of the Ruhr, west of Paderborn, on the front of the Ninth Army, which, as far as I then knew, was still under Montgomery's control."

Eager to close this gap, as well as relieve pressure on the Ninth and 104th divisions, Collins broke the basic rule learned in army schools that a commander never went outside normal command channels. He went directly to General Simpson at Ninth Army headquarters, explained the situation to him, and said, "For God's sake, Bill, get Monty to let you release the Second Armored Division for a drive on Paderborn. I will send a combat command of the Third Armored across to meet the Second at Lippstadt. We will then have the Ruhr wrapped up."

Simpson agreed.

The next day was Easter. Recalling defeating the Second Panzer Division on Christmas Day in the Battle of the Bulge, Collins noted that by going outside the chain of command he had completed the encirclement of the Ruhr. He called the area where the Germans were trapped "the Rose Pocket." In closing the exits, his forces collected more than 300,000 prisoners.

The night before, their commander, Field Marshal Walter Model, said to his officers, "I have led my soldiers in good conscience . . . but for a criminal government."

Rather than surrender, Model killed himself.

With the death of General Rose, command of the Third Armored Division was taken over by the senior combat command leader, Doyle Hickey. With the division for three years, he'd gained distinction in all of the Third's campaigns as part of the Seventh Corps. Although Collins thought he lacked Rose's magnetic personality and drive, he believed he deserved to be the one to succeed Rose.

Learning that Hodges had called Bradley and recommended that the division be given to Ernest Harmon, then commander of the Second Armored Division, and that Harmon already had reported to the Third, Collins protested to Hodges. Stating that he admired Harmon, he argued that fairness required that Hickey be given "a shot at command of the division." He also asserted that because of the rivalry that had grown between the Second and Third, Harmon's taking over of the Third would not "sit too well" with the men. Hodges agreed, as did Bradley, and Harmon returned to the Second with no hard feelings.

By April 1, Collins's Seventh Corps had shifted east for a final drive deeper into Germany as the Red Army pushed westward.

CHAPTER FOURTEEN

THE JOLLY RUSSIAN

Months before the Seventh Corps prepared either to connect with the Russians or push on to Berlin, Franklin D. Roosevelt had disregarded his doctor's worries about the deteriorating state of his health and traveled to the Soviet Union to sit down with Churchill and Joseph Stalin to talk about shaping Europe after Germany's surrender, the defeat of Japan, and how to guarantee that there could never be a Third World War. When the leaders of nations that had become known as "the Big Three" met at Yalta in the Crimea in February, Churchill found that Roosevelt paid more attention to Stalin than to him, and that all of his fears about the Soviet Union taking over Eastern Europe were of little concern to FDR, if any. The conference ended with agreement that conquered Germany would be temporarily divided into four zones, American, British, French, and Soviet, with an equally parceled Berlin in the Soviet zone. As Roosevelt prepared to depart, he shook hands with Stalin and said, "We will meet again soon in Berlin."

In a speech to a joint meeting of the Senate and the House of Representatives on March 1, 1945, Roosevelt declared, "I come from the Crimea conference with a firm belief that we have made a start on the road to a world of peace."

As he spoke, the Red Army was closing in on Berlin.

When Bradley was asked by Eisenhower what it might cost to break through from the Elbe River in Germany to Berlin, Bradley estimated 100,000 casualties. "A pretty stiff price for a prestige objective," he added, "especially when we've got to fall back and let the other fellow take over." Consequently, on March 29, Eisenhower made a military decision that would set off an explosive protest by Winston Churchill and resound in history. Without conferring with the British, he sent a message to Joseph Stalin saying that he was concentrating his forces on the south of Germany and not on taking Berlin.

Stalin cabled back, "Your plans completely coincide with the plans of the Red Army. Berlin has lost its former strategic importance."

Furious, Churchill cabled to Eisenhower, "I deem it highly important that we should shake hands with the Russians as far east as possible."

While the prime minister objected through official channels that Ike had chosen not to reinforce Montgomery with American troops for a drive to Berlin ahead of the Russians, but instead had put the British troops in a secondary role well to the north of the city, the British press howled about what they perceived as relegating the venerated British war hero, and the British people, to a backseat when victory was in sight.

When Churchill protested to Washington, Ike found himself on the receiving end of a series of telegrams, beginning with one from Marshall on March 29, questioning his message to "the Generalissimo." Ike fired back, "Frankly the charge that I have changed plans has no possible basis in fact."

Three years later in *Crusade in Europe*, Ike pointed out that Churchill knew full well that regardless of how far east the U.S. forces drove in Germany, Churchill and FDR had already agreed that the American and British occupation zones would be limited on the east by a line two hundred miles west of Berlin. Recording that he had no idea what Churchill's "true reasons were" in protesting, Eisenhower certainly knew enough about Churchill and world politics by the spring of 1945 to grasp that Churchill was still clinging to his suspicions of the Soviet Union dating to the Bolshevik Revolution of 1917 and his desire to prevent the Russians from imposing Communism on every foot of territory conquered by the Red Army. Less than a year after Ike adhered to the Allied agreement that the Soviets would be allowed to take Berlin, Churchill would give a speech at Fulton, Missouri, in which he recognized the start of the cold war by pointing out that the Soviet Union had erected an Iron Curtain around all the nations the Red Army had occupied during the war.

Despite the flurry of telegrams and second-guessing, Ike held fast and was backed by Roosevelt and the Joint Chiefs of Staff.

The only thing that mattered to Collins at this time was General Bradley's Order No. 20 to the First Army, consisting of the Seventh Corps and Huebner's Fifth Corps. They were to advance east on a line between Kassel and Leipzig "to gain contact with the Soviet forces." With the return of the Ninth Army to his Twelfth Army Group, Bradley had the largest field force to serve under a single commander in American history. He presided over four armies with twelve corps and forty-eight divisions spread over a far wider region and amounting to 1.3 million men. They stood poised to carry out his order to "exploit any opportunity for seizing a bridgehead over the Elbe River" and "be prepared to continue the advance to the east thereof."

As the Seventh Corps moved north of Marburg in its envelopment of the Ruhr, Collins had kept the 1st and 104th divisions positioned so they could quickly follow the Third Armored Division in the push east. Hopes for commencing the drive on April 1, 1945, were dashed when Doyle Hickey's division ran into stubborn resistance.

On April 5, its two veteran combat commands, "A" under Colonel L. L. Doan and "B" commanded by General Truman E. Boudinot, drove for the heart of Germany. By dawn of the following day, another task force took Amelunken on the Weser River to find that the German engineers had systematically blown all of the bridge spans. Task Force Kane's veterans ground ahead in the face of tank and infantry opposition to surround a defending force at Tietelsen. As they bypassed this resistance with one group while pushing another farther south, Combat Command Boudinot and Task Force Welborn knifed south and took Heerbruck. The division was now moving swiftly. Task Force Lovelady (led by William B. Lovelady) cracked through stubborn resistance to clear Manrode. During this period, noted a Third Division pamphlet published in 1945, the "Spearhead" division encountered scattered elements of SS tank and reconnaissance training units that had been stationed in the Paderborn area, as well as several replacement battalions and parts of the 1066th and 661st infantry regiments of the 166th Infantry Division.

"Although the opposition was not of a caliber to be compared with the Ardennes battle groups," a Third Armored historian wrote, "German desperation and fanaticism produced bitterly contested local actions. In addition, the enemy still had a number of 128mm tank destroyers left in the area."

On April 7, all elements of the division had reached the Weser and found that the enemy was now blowing up the bridges. At the river's brink, Task Force Welborn's advance elements received direct fire from both sides of the stream and the town of Herstelle. Another of Welborn's probing spearheads reached Carlshafen, farther east. Task Force Lovelady was slowed by soft terrain, but by the end of the day it had succeeded in taking Helmarshausen. Within the zone of Combat Command Doan, Lieutenant Colonel Clifford Miller and his task force were slowed by a destroyed railway bridge at the town of Godelheim. At the same time, another task force found the river bridge at Wehrden also blown up and noted many barricades in the town. Mopping-up operations along the river consumed a day, and on April 9 a crossing was made. Resistance varied from moderate to stubborn, but half a dozen towns were taken before sunset. Task Force Hogan cleared Hardesen and Northeim as Combat Command Howze relieved Doan on the right. On the far side of the river, another task force encountered twelve Panther and Tiger tanks, but bypassed them and drove toward Nordhausen.

As the Third Armored Division continued advances through April 10, and Task Force Welborn took Epschenrode, Task Force Lovelady, hampered by muddy terrain, advanced beyond Grossbodungen, and Colonel Sam Hogan, a colorful Texan, battled armor and minefields to get to the small town of Zwinge. Within Combat Command Doan, Task Force Kane was hampered by debris in Northeim, but destroyed two Mark IV tanks and a pair of grounded airplanes.

Also on the tenth a platoon of the Eighty-third Armored Reconnaissance Battalion, commanded by Lieutenant Duane Doherty, cleared a V-2 assembly plant at Kleinbodungen. A number of the huge rockets, completed except for warheads, lay where they had been constructed. After taking a number of prisoners, one of Doherty's men found an underground shaft in the assembly plant. A later examination proved that he had uncovered one of the Nazis' underground installations. Reconnaissance soldiers were amazed to find that the tunnels ran more than 640 meters beneath the surface, and radiated off through several kilometers of sandstone and clay. While they found no machinery set up in the tunnels, they were crammed with various types of high explosives.

During this period, the First Infantry Division was coming up to the left rear of the Third. Attached to the armored division were the First Battalion of the Eighteenth Infantry of the First

Division; the Third Battalion of the Forty-seventh Infantry of the Ninth Division; and the Second Battalion of the 414th Infantry of the 104th Division.

"Although the taking of Nordhausen did not constitute the heaviest fighting of April 11," wrote a division chronicler, "that city will live forever in memories of Third Armored Division soldiers as a place of horror." The soldiers found hundreds of corpses sprawled over the huge compound's ragged acres.

"They lay in heaps," said one soldier, "half-stripped, mouths gaping in the dirt and straw: or they were piled naked, like cordwood, in corners of great steel and cement barracks. Most horrible was the sight of the living among the dead. Side by side with bodies of their comrades, sunken-eyed skeletons of men moaned weakly or babbled in delirium. In the filth of their own dysentery, systematically starved, abused, and finally abandoned to die unattended, those who still lived when Combat Command Boudinot sped through Nordhausen were whisked away to emergency hospitals by American medical men. Many were without hope of recovery."

From the concentration camp at Nordhausen, political prisoners worked in an efficient underground factory north of the city called "Dora" and at the V-2 rocket assembly works at Kleinbodungen. Under brutal and unsanitary conditions, they had labored in the labyrinths of underground shafts that had been dug into a hill for a distance of more than two miles. Here they constructed V-1 and V-2 weapons as well as parts for Junkers airplane motors. Although a V-3, a secret antiaircraft device, was undergoing experimentation at Dora, few of the political prisoners were assigned to its development.

Determined that Collins should see the horrors, Hickey went to Seventh Corps headquarters and escorted him to the concentration camp. Recalling that day in his autobiography, Collins noted that in the first building he entered, hundreds of men in striped uniforms lay scattered on the floor. "We took out about six hundred and fifty prisoners still alive," he wrote to Gladys, "but in such miserable stages of starvation that scores of them have since died. Almost three thousand dead were found in the buildings, most of whom had died of starvation or disease prior to the bombing. I directed our military government officer to collect German civilians, members of the Hitler Youth and German prisoners of war, to remove the bodies and inter them. We had the Burgomeisters set aside a plot of ground overlooking the town, and these people were required to dig graves and carry every one of the dead up the hill and bury them. All the local officials disclaimed any knowledge of the camp which, of course, was pure tommyrot. We are going to require them to erect a monument in the cemetery as a memorial to these dead."

While General Hickey chewed angrily on his pipe as he and Collins surveyed the horrors, Combat Command "A" had taken Herzberg. Task Force Kane cleared the town of Osterode in bitter fighting, supported by Thunderbolt bombers attacking the defending tanks.

Between Nordhausen and Osterode, Combat Command Howze swept away defenses of several fortified towns.

As the Third Armored Division's advance elements took Sangerhausen on April 12, at 5:40 p.m. in the United States the bells of teletype machines in newsrooms from coast to coast alerted editors as the tickers typed FLASH. Subscribers to the Associated Press wire service read: PRESIDENT ROOSEVELT DIED SUDDENLY THIS AFTERNOON AT WARM SPRINGS, GA.

The stories that flowed from newsroom teletypes and typewriters told the same shocking facts. Franklin Delano Roosevelt, thirty-first president of the United States and the foremost global war leader, was dead. For months, signs had appeared that the sixty-three-year-old president was not in the best of health, but his death was still a shock. On the Thursday morning of his passing, an attending physician had felt no apprehension over his condition. The president seemed in lively spirits. He was to sit for a portrait. Later on, he was to be the guest of honor at a barbecue given by the mayor of Warm Springs, and then return to the cottage the news media called "The Little White House" on top of Pine Mountain.

Shortly after midday as he sat before a fireplace while the artist worked, he said to the portraitist, "I have a terrific headache."

Within a few minutes, he lost consciousness and did not regain it. He died a little more than two hours later from a massive cerebral hemorrhage. Writers noted the irony that the man who had become to many millions over the earth the pivotal leader of the Allied cause, who had played a mighty role in marshaling most of the nations of the earth against totalitarian regimes, and shaped a worldwide war, died in its closing stages.

Two hours and thirty-four minutes after the White House learned of FDR's death, the vice president, Harry Truman of Missouri, who was largely unknown to the American voters, and had been chosen by FDR over controversial Vice President Henry Wallace to be on the Democratic ticket in 1944, was summoned from the United States Senate, was informed that he was now the president, and took the oath of office with a feeling, he said later, that the weight of the world had fallen upon him.

Where fighting permitted on Pacific islands, in northern Italy, and in Germany as Allied forces smashed eastward, hastily organized memorial services were held and the war resumed.

On April 13, the Third Armored continued to the Saale River and found all bridges blown. The town of Eisleben was declared an open city, and at nearby Polleben men of the Third Armored liberated a British prisoner-of-war camp. Some of the men said they had been prisoners since Dunkirk in 1940, while others had been taken prisoner in the Western Desert of Libya and on the island of Crete. Task Force Lovelady encountered strong 88mm fire during that day and found the bridge blown at Laschwitz. Task Force Richardson advanced to Alsleben and came under direct fire. The force was ordered back to use another bridge, then in the process of being built. Only the task force led by Colonel Sam Hogan found a partially intact span and was able to push infantry across. On April 14, the division crossed the Saale River on two bridges built during the previous night by Lieutenant Colonel Lawrence Foster's Twenty-third Armored Engineers. Task Force Welborn advanced straight to the Mulde River south of Dessau.

"The men of these three divisions were as near to being crack soldiers," said one Third Armored veteran, "as any battle formations committed by the enemy since the Ardennes."

On the same day, Task Force Lovelady struck heavy resistance but continued to advance. Hogan hacked through stiffening lines of resistance to clear an airport in the outskirts of Kothen. German engineers left a wrecked span across the Mulde and forced Task Force Welborn to halt temporarily on April 15 until an infantry force crossed it and secured a bridgehead. Meanwhile, Lovelady's veterans cleared the towns of Thurland and Kleinleipzig, Colonel Hogan cleared all of the northeast, and another task force secured the small town of Frenz, then proceeded to the larger town of Bernburg and ran into stiff resistance in Unterpeissen.

All along the division front, opposition hardened as towns that had been bypassed and were thought cleared suddenly disgorged German troops who harried supply operations in rear areas. Infantry was used to clear Meilendorf, Kornetz, Quellendorf, and Reupzig. These places were defended by troops wielding antitank weapons and small arms. As Colonel Orr's forces occupied towns, the Eighty-third Armored Reconnaissance Battalion sent patrols that took Rendin, Thalheim, and Sandersdorf and discovered that Wolfen and Bitterfeld, near the Mulde, were more strongly fortified. At this time the division was busy holding down a struggling forty-mile front with many uncleared, bypassed towns in rear areas.

The terrain was flat farm country dotted by numerous small towns that were connected by excellent road systems. To the south of Dessau was a large patch of woods through which Task Force Welborn had advanced to the autobahn. To the division's north was the Elbe River, and to the east the Mulde. On this front the armor was facing the greater part of three divisions, each averaging four thousand of Germany's last, well-trained reserves, along with a scattering of other miscellaneous units. The Mulde bridge defenders, meanwhile, continued to confront Task Force Welborn on April 16. Short of infantry, Welborn found German artillery heavy and accurate on the bridging site. After seeing engineering equipment destroyed by the enemy fire, Welborn was ordered to discontinue spanning operations and to withdraw his infantry from the east bank.

While Welborn was holding his bridgehead on the Mulde, Task Force Lovelady cleared enemy resistance from Raguhn, west of the stream that divided the town, while another task force entered Bernburg. This sealed a pocket of the Harz Mountains and resulted in the capture of more than eighty thousand troops.

In its April 16, 1945, issue *Time* magazine noted, "It was a week of almost incredible military events. In six days the western Allied armies took 189,611 prisoners, whereas in all their battles in World War I the Americans had taken less than one-third of that total. In those six days at least 25,000 Germans had been killed or wounded. These were the casualties of a Wehrmacht falling swiftly apart."

On April 12, the Seventh Corps' northern boundary ran through the northwest corner of the Harz Mountains to the junction of the Elbe and Mulde rivers at Dessau. With heights ranging up to thirty-seven hundred feet, the mountains had been ordered held by edict of Hitler as a base from which the largely disorganized Twelfth Army was to counterattack. Meanwhile, Field Marshal Kesselring had managed to assemble a seventy-thousand-man Eleventh Army in the mountains under the command of General Walter Lucht. A veteran corps commander, he made skillful use of wooded terrain that was a reminder to the U.S. First Division of the Hurtgen Forest. Lucht's Harz defenders were a combination of experienced troops and young dedicated Nazis from military schools and other training centers. Setting up roadblocks and demolitions, and fighting from the area's caves and mines, they put up a stubborn resistance.

With the Ninth Division's arrival from the Ruhr pocket on April 14, Collins moved it into the mountains to create what he termed "a triple squeeze" by the Ninth on the north and the First and Eighty-third divisions on the west, south, and east. Although General Courtney Hodges was not enthusiastic about Collins's methodical advance, Collins was reluctant to exert pressure on his divisions and cost needless lives in the waning days of the war. He discerned from his opponent's policy of not waging a scorched-earth defense that General Lucht was also sparing his troops and the civilian population as much as possible.

"After six days of tough delaying actions," Collins recorded, "the end was in sight on April 19, when the First Division captured hill 1142, the dominant height in the mountains. Resistance ended the next day as units began to surrender en masse. On that day the Ninth Division took over 8,000 prisoners and the First Division a like number, including the 100,000th POW captured by the First Division in World War II."

On April 20, Collins marked the twenty-eighth anniversary of his graduation from West Point and also registered the date in memory as the one on which he was informed that the new president of the United States had nominated him to be a lieutenant general. When word got to him that the Senate had confirmed the boost in rank, he also learned that Courtney Hodges had been promoted to four stars. When Collins returned to an airport near his CP, the entire Seventh Corps was there to greet and congratulate him. "I was even more pleased," he recorded, "that many enlisted men individually stopped me in the next few days to add their congratulations."

The date was also the birthday of Adolf Hitler. At the age of fifty-six, he was in a bunker built deep beneath the marble-clad chancellery designed by his architect, Albert Speer, as a symbol of the immortality of the Third Reich. But the marble-encased concrete and steel-reinforced walls and ceilings were not thick enough to shield its few occupants from the earthshaking thumps of Red Army artillery. That night, Berlin radio admitted that the capital was "burning with unrest" and that red flags flew on all buildings in workers' districts, signifying solidarity with international workers whom the Soviet Union claimed to champion. The twentieth of April was also the day that the U.S. Army captured the city of Nuremberg, where the Nazi Party held its annual meetings to venerate their führer with upraised right arms and shouts in chorus, *"Heil Hitler!"*

In 1932, when Adolf Hitler was plotting to grab power in Germany, Collins had been a captain teaching tactics at the Infantry School. Now he was putting army theories into practice to seal off the Harz Mountains. His Seventh Corps' Third Armored Division was closing in on the town of Dessau on the Elbe, an easy drive to Berlin on one of the autobahns that Hitler had built for his army. While Hitler's propaganda chief, Joseph Goebbels, went on the radio to exhort Berliners to "fight to the death," tanks of the Red Army's Marshal Georgy Zhukov were rumbling through the capital's suburbs and the men of the 173rd Regiment of the Russian Fifty-eighth Guards Division of the Thirty-fourth Corps were about to meet the Sixty-ninth Division of Huebner's Fifth Corps, to the right of Collins's Seventh Corps, at the Elbe.

On April 25, two Soviet forces met in Berlin. As one observer recorded the event, their rocket-firing trucks rumbled down streets where boys of thirteen and fourteen were given guns and commanded to use them against the Bolsheviks. From upper-story windows and rooftops, cellars, and subways Germans fought back with machine guns, pistols, and grenades. The fight for Berlin by this impromptu force became house to house and street to street. To no avail.

The next day, two mighty armies from half a world apart, representing two nations that held opposite views on the role of government and the worth of the individual, came together on the banks of a German river that few Americans knew existed. The forces linked the Eastern and Western fronts to stand astride the ruins of a Germany that would remain split for nearly five decades.

In Moscow, the linkup along two hundred miles of the Elbe was saluted with twenty-four salvos from 324 guns, and from the Kremlin to villages on the distant Russian steppes the people of the U.S.S.R. celebrated victory. From the banks of the Elbe, the Associated Press correspondent Hal Boyle reported that the American and Russian commanders who met at the river tried to make their encounter "a grand opera event but it ended like the finale of a circus performance."

Boyle reported, "There was just too much good will and wine flowing to keep up the military formalities." The ordinary GI and his Russian counterpart sat in warm sunshine, drinking champagne from beer mugs, clapping one another on the back, and toasting each other.

A dispatch that combined the prose of Boyle and AP reporter Don Whitehead stated, "It was a celebration unlike anything seen before in this war. One great party, with doughboys and Russians singing, laughing and dancing and trying to talk to each other in sign language. A few Americans who spoke Russian interpreted for their friends. A Russian sat on a stone wall playing an accordion while an American sergeant joined in the Red Army song, 'If war should come tomorrow we will be prepared on land, at sea and in the air.' A Russian woman in uniform sang in a sweet, throaty voice. It was pleasant on the waterfront in the warm sun."

Whenever an American approached a group of Russians, they smiled broadly, saluted, and shook hands. Some of the more enthusiastic, who "liberated" stores of German champagne and cognac, elaborated on the greeting with a hug. At the U.S. command post, the Americans and Russians sat at tables loaded with fried eggs, bread, sardines, salmon, and spaghetti. A major of Marshal Ivan Stepanovich Konev's Fifty-eighth Division welcomed the Americans by saying to the soldiers, "Today is the happiest day in all our lives. The most difficult for us were those days when the Germans were at Stalingrad. Now we meet one another and this is the end of our enemy. Long live your great leader! Long live your great leader!"

The AP men wrote, "The entire day was a fantastic, memorable one, crammed with emotional outbursts from the time a column of the Sixty-ninth Infantry set out for Torgau on the Elbe, where contact had been made with the Russians the previous day. As doughboys marched along the road from the Mulde River to the Elbe they met thousands of German civilians fleeing before the Russians, hoping vainly to find safety within American lines. The pain and misery of defeated Germany were etched in their faces. On the east bank of the Mulde thousands of civilians were gathered, their belongings stacked into little carts. Bedding, food, clothing, pots, pans and huge bundles burdened the carts. Women stumbled along with huge bundles on their backs in the choking dust, just as the frightened people of Belgium and France fled before the Nazis five years ago."

Columns of German soldiers marched along the road to the west without anyone to guard them. Many still carried their sidearms.

A result of the expected linkup was implementation of a plan for the Seventh Corps to take over for the Fifth Corps in a zone being held by the Sixty-ninth, Second, and Ninth divisions. While on a visit to the Sixty-ninth, Collins was informed that a

Russian officer in Torgau wanted to meet an American general. Curious to see firsthand what was going on at Torgau, and intrigued by the prospect of meeting a Russian officer, Collins and his aide, Jack Walsh, traveled by jeep.

The encounter recalled by Collins in his autobiography was indeed a memorable one. He wrote, "He was a chunky, powerfully built man, dressed in a rumpled field uniform and customary Russian boots that showed signs of rough campaigning. He looked more like a tough non-com than an officer, but he had 'fighter' written all over him. We had an interpreter with us whose English was understandable, but unfortunately I have no record of his name or rank, but he must have been the commander of the regiment opposite Torgau. He greeted us warmly and invited us into the cafe for the inevitable toasts. He lifted his glass to President Roosevelt, whom he praised as a friend of Russia, to which I replied, of course, in a toast to Marshal Stalin. Eisenhower, Koniev, Montgomery, and others were drunk to in turn. Each time my Russian host would jump to his feet and deliver an impassioned speech. What interested me was that he paid tribute to our aid, particularly to our trucks, without which he said the Soviet army would never have reached the Elbe. There was no political commissar present to dampen his enthusiasm."

When the toasting was finished, Collins, Walsh, and the Russians drove up to the Elbe, where Collins watched in amazement as a group of Russian soldiers, using a hand-operated pile driver, drove freshly cut logs into the muddy river to serve as pilings for a footbridge. As they stood watching this primitive building and a woman MP efficiently directing traffic on the far bank, Collins asked the Russian about the disposition of his troops. With none of the secrecy Collins associated with the Russians, the officer pulled a wrinkled map from inside his tunic and pointed out the location of all his troops. Collins did likewise.

The Russian asked, "Are you digging in?"

Collins replied, "Of course not."

The Russian turned to an aide and barked, "Tell the men not to dig in."

For Collins, the fact that the Russians had been digging in suggested that they were wary of American intentions and wanted to be prepared to fight if it came to that. Such a fear was preposterous, of course, because he knew his troops were already wondering how soon they would be going home.

After moving Seventh Corps headquarters to Leipzig on April 30, Collins was visited by the commanding officer of the Soviet Thirty-second Corps, General Baklanov, his divisional generals, and members of his staff. At a hastily arranged luncheon attended by Seventh Corps generals and staff, Collins estimated that Baklanov was no older than thirty-five, indicating that he had proven his ability as a combat leader. Speaking neither English nor French, the Russian general relied on an interpreter and came across in translation as stodgy, but as gin flowed abundantly in the absence of vodka, Collins noted that Baklanov relaxed and was more at ease. He repeatedly said how glad he was to be in Leipzig and how he had scarcely believed it was possible a week before.

The next day, Germany's Grand Admiral Karl Doenitz announced from Hamburg that Hitler was dead, that Doenitz had taken over the rule of the Third Reich, and that the fight "to save the German people from the advance of the Bolshevist enemy" would continue. On May 2, the German army in northern Italy and southern Austria surrendered and Stalin stated that Berlin had fallen.

After a twelve-day siege that was the most savage and bloody in the history of combat, the Red Army had conquered the largest city ever subdued in the annals of warfare.

Along the Elbe, the U.S. Ninth Army and the British Second Army had their hands full as more than 150,000 Germans laid down their arms.

At 2:41 in the morning of May 7, 1945, in the ancient cathedral city of Reims, France, where Eisenhower had established his headquarters, Field Marshal Alfred Gustav Jodl, chief of staff of the German army, stiffly signed the Allied surrender terms in the presence of General Walter Bedell Smith, as well as British and French witnesses. Jodl asked if he could speak. Told he might, he stiffened and said, "With this signature, the German people and armed forces are, for better or worse, delivered into the victors' hands. In this war, which lasted more than five years, both have achieved and suffered more than any other people in the world. In this hour, I can only express hope that the victor will treat generously with them."

The ceremony lasted four minutes. He was then admitted to Eisenhower's office. Having chosen not to elevate the proceedings by accepting the capitulation himself, Eisenhower asked Jodl through a translator if he understood the terms he had just signed.

Jodl replied, *"Ja."*

Eisenhower said icily, "You will, officially and personally, be held responsible if the terms of this surrender are violated, including its provisions for German commanders to appear in Berlin at the moment set by the Russian High Command to accomplish formal surrender to that government. That is all."

Jodl saluted and left.

The official proclamation of the surrender was to be held up for a day and announced at the same time in Washington, London, and Moscow, but a report of the end of the fighting in Europe was flashed around the globe by the Associated Press chief in France, Edward Kennedy, for which he had his war correspondent's credentials revoked. His scoop was followed by a flood of announcements from other sources.

While the news was spreading, Eisenhower called into his office all the Allied officers who had taken part in the surrender. Flashing the smile that had become the most famous grin in the world for newsreel cameras, he held up the fountain pens used in the surrender to form a V for victory. At 3:19 a.m. he went into the war room and made a speech for the cameras.

In a "Victory Order of the Day" he told the troops, "The crusade on which we embarked in the early summer of 1944 has reached its glorious conclusion. It is my special privilege in the name of all nations represented in this theater of war to commend each of you for your valiant performance of duty. Though these words are feeble, they come from the bottom of a heart overflowing with pride in your loyal service and admiration for you as warriors."

From D-day to V-E Day, the forces he commanded had driven seven hundred miles, liberating France, Belgium, Holland, Luxembourg, Denmark, and Norway, and overran most of Germany, much of Austria, and part of Czechoslovakia. They had endured the Hurtgen Forest, deflated the Ardennes bulge, shattered the Western Wall and the Siegfried Line, crossed the Rhine, and trapped more than 300,000 Germans in the Ruhr in the greatest double envelopment in military history. They had driven to the Elbe River and shaken hands with the Red Army over the corpse of Hitler's Third Reich.

In all of these campaigns and battles, Joseph Lawton Collins had led the Seventh Corps.

On the day of the announcement of Hitler's suicide, Seventh Corps headquarters received word that the First Army was to be transferred to the Pacific. On May 6, as Courtney Hodges prepared to leave for the United States, the Seventh Corps was passed to the control of the Ninth Army. It was the first time since D-day that the Seventh Corps was not part of the First Army.

For Collins the departure of Hodges meant presiding over a ceremony to present U.S. decorations to Russian officers marking the linkup at the Elbe, including General Baklanov and another general, Jadov. Arrangements had been made for the Russians to fly to Leipzig, where a band and honor guard would welcome them. When they did not arrive at ten a.m. as planned, Collins and the welcome party waited and worried that something had happened to the Russians' plane. Finally a small craft arrived carrying the message that the Russians were on their way by car in several groups, with their arrival to be expected by four thirty p.m.

What was to have been a luncheon now became plans for dinner, but when four thirty came there were still no Russians in sight. By the time they appeared in what Collins called "driblets," it was dark. Medals were presented and the group headed for dinner at a hotel. As they all sat down, more Russians straggled in. Before, during, and after the meal, the Americans served gin, and when that ran out switched to Scotch. Having waited most of the day for the Russians to show up, the hosts were eager to call it a night, but the Russians didn't want to leave. Even when the two Russian generals got up to depart, the others showed no signs of following them. Collins pleaded to Baklanov through an interpreter for help. Standing on a chair, Baklanov bellowed something in Russian that Collins assumed to be the Russian equivalent of "Charge!" With that, the Russians rushed to the door and out to their cars, sweeping the generals with them.

"We could only stand in amazement on the sidewalk and wave goodbye," Collins wrote, "wondering how such an outfit ever licked the Germans."

The evening was not his last experience with his happy Russian general. When Baklanov invited him to a luncheon at his headquarters near Pilsen in Czechoslovakia, the Russian staged a welcome at an inn with townspeople who Collins suspected had been ordered to exhibit a show of enthusiasm over being occupied by the Red Army. A presentation by a pretty Czech girl in native costume with a bouquet of red roses, wrapped tightly in cellophane, was followed by a program of acrobatics, singing, and dancing by a professional troupe of Soviet artists, flown in for the occasion. Recalling it two decades later in his autobiography, he wrote, "It is indeed sad that these friendly exchanges of visits between American and Soviet military forces right after World War II could not have been followed by equally friendly political exchanges."

For the next two decades, Joseph Lawton Collins would find himself on the front lines of a confrontation called the cold war between the United States, Great Britain, and other allies on one side of an Iron Curtain and the Soviet Union and countries it had conquered on the other.

CHAPTER FIFTEEN

JUST DON'T READ HIM

From D-day to Germany's surrender, according to the War Department, American ground forces had suffered 79,795 killed, 334,919 wounded, and 58,501 missing in action, for a total of 473,215 casualties. In the war with Germany on all fronts, the United States had more than three-quarters of a million casualties, with 150,000 dead. The war in the European and African theaters had involved as many as 27 million men. At the peak of their supremacy, the Allies had slightly more than 16 million men under arms, including approximately 600,000 underground fighters in Nazi-occupied countries. Of these 16 million, according to the War Department, 4 million were Americans, Russians totaled 10 million, the British a million, and the French 600,000. German army strength in late summer of 1944, including men of occupied nations who were forced to serve or volunteered, reached 8 million. Allied forces in Italy had contended with 1.3 million enemy troops.

The day of the German surrender was officially recognized as May 8, 1945. Twenty-four hours later, the War Department announced that how soon soldiers in Europe would come home would be determined by a point system based on their length of service, days in combat, if they had been wounded, and parenthood. At the Pentagon, General George Marshall decided that the American people should be able to meet some of the officers he had chosen to lead the army against Germany and Italy. When orders were given to bring many of them back to the United States for ceremonies in cities across the country, Collins found himself on a plane with General Patch, General Lucian K. Truscott, Jr., and others headed for Texas and a welcome home by the people of San Antonio, primarily for Texans but including officers from adjacent states. Patch was a native of Arizona. Truscott was born in Texas but had grown up in Oklahoma. Patch had been overall commander of the August 1944 invasion of southern France (Operation Dragoon), and Truscott had been pulled out of the war in Italy to command the Dragoon ground forces. As Patch commanded forces driving up from the French Riviera to link up with Patton's Third Army, Truscott was sent back to Italy to take over command of U.S. forces in northern Italy and crush the retreating German army.

Attending the San Antonio celebration meant that Collins would see Gladys for the first time since he covered up his recurrence of malaria and flew to England to meet with Ike and Bradley to learn what they had in mind for him in the European theater. His order to go to the San Antonio festivities included a thirty-day furlough. Although the thousands who lined the city streets wholeheartedly cheered the generals who rode past them in open cars, they went wild for a young man who'd gone to war as a private and became the most decorated GI hero of the war, including the Medal of Honor. Shy and looking embarrassed by the adulation, Audie Murphy had been promoted to lieutenant and had his picture on the cover of *Life* magazine. When the movie star James Cagney saw it, and read the details of Murphy's heroism, he decided Murphy belonged in the movies and opened the gates of Hollywood studios, giving Murphy a career on the silver screen.

Following the San Antonio welcome, Collins and Gladys returned to Washington, D.C. A few days later, he learned that in a meeting with Marshall, Courtney Hodges had told Marshall that Collins had been "the outstanding corps commander" in Europe and requested that he be sent to the Pacific to continue as the Seventh Corps commander with Hodges's First Army. Remembering that MacArthur had dismissed Collins as "too young" to head a corps, Marshall on May 28 told the acting head of the War Department's Operations Division to inform MacArthur that his opinion on what corps commanders he desired would not be welcome. The cable to MacArthur listed Collins as Seventh Corps commander. He and all others but one were younger than most of the corps commanders then serving under MacArthur.

Marshall arranged for Collins to spend two weeks of his month's furlough with Gladys in Lake Placid, New York, at an army facility. While they were relaxing and riding horses in hills and woods, atomic bombs were dropped on Hiroshima and Nagasaki. As Japan's government considered the effects of the bombs and weighed a U.S. demand for an immediate surrender, Collins left Lake Placid for California on the first leg of a journey to the Pacific. A few days after he reached San Luis Obispo, Japan surrendered. He then received a phone call from General Jacob Devers, who had taken command of Army Ground Forces, directing him to return to the nation's capital to be his chief of staff.

Both had commanded forces in Europe during the war and they were at West Point as instructors at the same time, but Collins did not know Devers well. As a cadet at the Academy in 1929, Devers had been a star baseball player and then an enthusiastic horseman in the Field Artillery. At the end of the European war, he'd commanded the Sixth Army Group in the south flank of the

Allied front. As head of Army Ground Forces, he was contending with pressures from the public and from Congress for rapid demobilization. Expecting Devers to assign him to assist in dealing with cries of "Bring the boys home," Collins found himself diverted from becoming Devers's chief of staff to assist Marshall in developing a plan to merge the army and navy and their separate air forces into a single department before Marshall retired from active duty. Although the attack on Pearl Harbor demonstrated a lack of coordination of plans and operations of the army and navy, and the growth of airpower during the war had forced its integration into strategic and tactical operations of the older services, Collins appreciated that any plan to combine the services into one department invited fierce opposition from the services and their champions in the Congress.

Nothing proved this more than the case of Brigadier General Billy Mitchell. In 1927, when Collins was at the Field Artillery School in Oklahoma, the World War I aviation hero and airpower proponent Mitchell had been charged with insubordination for publicly criticizing the army and navy for opposing creation of a separate air force. Tried by court-martial, he was forced to resign from the army. World War II had forced better interservice coordination by expansion of the Joint Chiefs of Staff to include a chief of staff for the president and a representative of the Army Air Forces and by the establishment of unified field commands in each war theater.

The first steps toward giving airpower the equal status with land forces that Billy Mitchell advocated had been taken on March 2, 1942, when the Army Air Corps was made semi-independent of the Army Ground Forces. Its commander, General Henry A. "Hap" Arnold, became a member of the JCS on an equal footing with Marshall, Chief of Naval Operations Ernest King, and Admiral William D. Leahy, chief of staff to President Roosevelt. These organizational and operational changes were accomplished under the war powers of the president. Permanent status would have to be confirmed by Congress.

In 1943, General Marshall initiated studies on postwar organization of the armed services by the Special Plans Division (SPD) of the War Department under Brigadier General William Tompkins. The SPD recommended a Department of War with a presidential cabinet secretary and four subdepartments of army, navy, air, and supply, each headed by an undersecretary. A single chief would supervise a joint general staff, which would consist of chiefs of staff of the three combat services and a chief of supply. Marshall approved the study and sent it to the JCS. They appointed a special committee of army, navy, and air officers with Admiral James O. Richardson designated chairman. After visiting all theaters of operations and consulting most senior combat commanders, the committee recommended a single defense department. Admiral Richardson submitted a lone dissenting opinion that established a pattern for negative U.S. Navy testimony to Congress on the subject of unification. Meanwhile, Senate and House advocates of a department of defense introduced bills to create it.

Familiar with this history, Collins was designated by Marshall to serve as spokesman for the army to present to the Senate Committee on Military Affairs the Marshall unification plan. The core of the proposal was based on a history of the army and navy submitting to Congress separate budgets and argued that unification would mean wiser and more economical budgeting. Although the Marshall plan did not assert the much later phrase "more bang for the buck," that was the gist of the proposal. While Marshall and others testified on the subject, Collins was the one who presented the details of the army's proposal. As a result, the navy began calling the proposal "the Collins plan."

On December 12, 1945, navy officials told Congress that the Collins plan was inferior to the navy's proposal to keep the navy an independent service. A week later, President Truman called for approval of a single department of defense with the air forces equal to the army and navy. To a Congress controlled by Republicans since the elections of 1946, he said that any further studies of the issue "would serve no useful purpose."

After the Senate committee adjourned for the Christmas and New Year holidays without reaching a conclusion, additional hearings dragged on for a year and a half. The result was the enactment of the National Security Act of 1947. It created the Department of Defense with a secretary of defense as the civilian head of the coequal departments of the army, navy, and air force, but with the navy and Marine Corps having their own air wings. Two years later, the act was amended to make it clear that the defense secretary had supreme authority over the three services and creating a chairman of the Joint Chiefs of Staff.

By 1947, George C. Marshall had retired from the army and had been sent to China to mediate an end to fighting between the forces of the government of Chiang Kai-shek and those of Mao Tse-tung's Communist rebels. His successor as army chief of staff was Eisenhower.

Soon after Ike settled into his office in the Pentagon, Collins learned that his former boss was considering him for the new post of chief of information for the War Department and went to see him, in Collins's words, to "head off this assignment."

Three years after he'd traveled to London in hopes of persuading Ike to give him command of a corps, he was greeted by the same Eisenhower grin and watched it change into a frown as he said that he "didn't want any part" of the job.

"I thought," Collins said, as the frown turned to a scowl, "that my métier was commanding troops."

Eisenhower exclaimed, "Joe, what in hell have you been doing for the past two years?"

The next day, December 16, 1945, an Eisenhower order confirmed the appointment.

Five days later, Collins, Eisenhower, and the world learned that George Patton was dead.

Having led the Third Army from Normandy in 1944 to Czechoslovakia in the spring of 1945, he had been put in charge of the occupation of the German province of Bavaria and ordered by Ike to remove all Nazi party members from government. When Patton was slow in carrying out "denazification" because he felt he needed experienced people to run the government, he answered a question on the matter from a reporter by saying that the Nazi Party was really no different from the Democratic and Republican parties at home. When the story unleashed a firestorm of protests back in the States, Ike fired him and put him in charge of the Fifteenth Army, with the task of supervising a compilation of the history of the army in the war.

On December 9, Patton's chauffeur-driven car was hit by a truck and Patton suffered a broken neck. Suddenly, Americans who despised him because of his brash and often profane demeanor joined in an outpouring of sympathy. Members of Congress who had said he needed "a general buttoning up" made speeches of "grave concern." Church congregations that had excoriated him for telling children that they would grow up to be soldiers and nurses prayed for him. Men of his Third Army who mocked his nickname of "Old Blood and Guts" by saying, "Yeah, our blood and our guts," abruptly spoke of him affectionately. At a military camp in Massachusetts, 1,739 men and officers awaiting transportation overseas started a "Prayers for Patton" campaign. Immobilized in a hospital bed in Heidelberg, Germany, he soon developed pulmonary complications and died four days before Christmas. On a cold and rainy day, he was buried in a U.S. Army cemetery.

For Joseph Lawton Collins, the abiding memory of Patton would be the day they'd run into each other at Bradley's CP in France. Patton had lamented about being in the doghouse and longed to be able to do something spectacular to get him out of it.

By V-E Day, Patton was in command of half a million troops in twelve infantry and six armored divisions. The Third Army had captured 81,522 square miles of territory and liberated or captured an estimated twelve thousand cities, towns, and communities, including twenty-seven cities of more than fifty thousand in population. His troops had taken 765,483 prisoners of war, with 515,205 surrendering during the last week of the war for a total of 1,280,688 POWs processed. From France to the end of the war, the Third Army's toll on the enemy was an estimated 1,280,688 captured, 144,500 killed, and 386,200 wounded, adding up to 1,811,388.

Although Patton's personality and competition with Montgomery added to Eisenhower's problems, at war's end Ike told him and his troops, "Working and fighting together in a single indestructible partnership, you have achieved perfection in unification of air, ground, and naval power that will stand as a model in our time."

Desirous of avoiding Patton-like public relations problems as the army chief of staff, Eisenhower had commandeered Collins to take on the challenge of dealing with a press corps in Washington that was under none of the constraints of military censorship that had been imposed both by army censors and their personal commitment to victory. In the nation's capital city, members of the Fourth Estate were fiercely competitive and looked on the government with critical and frequently suspicious eyes. In this superheated atmosphere, no newspaperman was more feared, admired by many, and despised by others than the columnist Drew Pearson.

Born Andrew Russell Pearson in 1897, he graduated from Swarthmore College in the 1920s and served as a foreign journalist for newspapers in Europe, Australia, India, and South Africa. He later wrote for the *United States Daily* and other smaller newspapers. During the 1930s, he became best known as a journalist for the *Baltimore Sun* and gained fame reporting news of a Cuban revolution. His reporting garnered honorable mention for the Pugsley Award for the best journalistic reporting of the year.

In 1931, Pearson and Robert S. Allen, the Washington bureau chief for the *Christian Science Monitor*, anonymously published a book, *The Washington Merry-Go-Round*. A collection of gossipy news items concerning key figures in public service, it was derided as scandalous, but Pearson and Allen brought out *More Merry-Go-Round* the next year. Exposed as the authors, they were forced to resign from their newspapers, but Pearson was soon hired as head of the *Baltimore Sun's* Washington bureau and, with Allen, began the "Washington Merry-Go-Round" column. By 1940, syndication of the column included 350 newspapers nationwide.

A dapper figure with a toothbrush mustache and a rapid-fire way of talking that reminded those who heard him of New York's Broadway and celebrity gossip Walter Winchell, Pearson at the time Collins became the chief spokesman for the army was preparing to publish a charge that the army was guilty of malfeasance, or at best bureaucratic bungling, in failing to procure proper-quality coffins for war dead being brought home. When one of Collins's three deputies, each in charge of an information agency, got wind of Pearson's intent, he alerted Collins.

Believing that if the allegation was true the army should acknowledge it and take corrective steps, Collins asked the quartermaster general to get the facts. He reported back that the coffins were not defective. Collins went to Eisenhower and suggested that he (Collins) talk to Pearson, set him straight, and ask that Pearson not publish his charge. Eisenhower agreed and proposed that he accompany Collins to the meeting with Pearson. Collins persuaded Ike that if he met with Pearson, he would leave himself open for a Pearson interrogation. Eisenhower agreed and Collins saw the columnist alone.

"After I laid the facts before Pearson at a meeting in my quarters," Collins recalled, "he decided to drop the story. During our talk I told him that General Eisenhower and I were determined to see that the army did an honest, forthright job during this difficult time of demobilization, and I offered to cooperate with him in running down any future alleged delinquencies, an offer Eisenhower had approved. Pearson accepted our offer, and as long as I was Chief of Information he lived up to our agreement."

Not long after defusing the Pearson charge, Collins found himself at a capital dinner party and seated next to a woman who had read the latest Pearson column. Outraged, she exclaimed, "Isn't Drew Pearson terrible?"

Collins agreed.

The woman asked, "Isn't there something we can do about him?"

"Certainly."

The woman leaned forward eagerly and asked, "What?"

Collins replied, "Just don't read him."

As chief of information for the army, Collins found himself buffeted by criticism in the press, from Capitol Hill, and by a public outpouring of impatience with the rate at which their men were coming home as the United States dismantled, in Collins's words, "the finest military force ever assembled."

"The pell-mell demobilization of American armed forces after the war," wrote the historian Robert A. Pollard, "demonstrated the underlying strength of neo-isolationism. [Secretary of Defense James] Forrestal and Secretary of War Robert R. Patterson, who had replaced [Henry] Stimson in September, warned Truman in October 1945 that demobilization jeopardized the American strategic position in the world. Truman agreed, but felt that he could do nothing to stop it. In January 1946, Forrestal had noted in his diary, the 'Under Secretary [of State Dean Acheson] said [demobilization] was a matter of great embarrassment and concern to his own Department in their conduct of our foreign affairs.'"

The Truman administration found itself facing overpowering

public and congressional pleading, accompanied by riots at some overseas military bases in January 1946, for the early return home of American soldiers. Nothing drew the attention of the American people to the problems faced by soldiers, sailors, and airmen coming home from the war more than a movie that won the Academy Award for best picture in 1947. In *The Best Years of Our Lives*, film audiences were presented with the stories of three veterans trying to cope with the transition to civilian life. Fifty-three years old, Collins settled with Gladys and their children in a house that they expected to be permanent for the first time in his thirty-three years of army service. This meant that the two girls would not have to move and adapt to a new school. Jerry was serving in the army. He had graduated from West Point in June 1945. At a booming command, some forty-eight hundred white-gloved hands snapped twenty-four hundred rifles to present arms. Front and center marched the 853 members of the class of 1945, the largest in West Point history. In Washington on the same day, an event took place that made the display at West Point more broadly significant than ever.

That day, in the first of a series of hearings, the Postwar Military Policy Committee of the House opened debate on a universal military training bill that would require all able-bodied young men to serve one year in training under arms. It was an issue that would linger unresolved for many months and eventually become as controversial as the "Collins plan" for creation of the Department of Defense. Meanwhile, as the army's chief of information, he was receiving what he called "many a lesson in public relations." He also discovered that the American press was no longer in a mood to accommodate the government, as it had been during the war. As CO of the Seventh Corps, he had been able to persuade and, if he had to, order a war correspondent to cooperate by either not reporting something or writing a story that would be helpful to the army. The new attitude of the press was made abundantly clear in a meeting Collins had with the publisher of the *Philadelphia Bulletin*, Robert McLean, who was also the president of the Associated Press.

When Collins proposed that McLean arrange a panel discussion between journalistic leaders on the topic "The Responsibility of the Press in the Cold War," McLean refused and stated that the press had no responsibility other than to abide by the tenets of good journalism. But he did agree to arrange for Collins to address a session of the AP's managing editors at their next meeting. The speech would be made at a time when the army was under increasing public pressure to speed the process of bringing home from Europe and the Pacific soldiers who had been drafted.

What happened next was embarrassing to Collins and Eisenhower and a searing lesson in the power of the press. Just before his scheduled address to the AP, he accompanied Eisenhower to Capitol Hill, where Ike was to testify before the House Military Affairs Committee. "When he arrived," Collins recalled, "he was handed a message from the committee chairman, Andrew Jackson May of Kentucky, to the effect that May first would like to see the General in the Chairman's office. As we opened his door, cameras clicked and light bulbs flashed, revealing Chairman May poised in front of a table, beyond which a bevy of middle-aged women, with a banner that proclaimed them as members of the 'Bring-the-Boys-Home Mothers Club,' gazed wistfully at a pile of baby shoes in the center of the table. That picture of a startled and furious Eisenhower, glowering across the stack of baby shoes at the smug-faced chairman, with the mothers as backdrop, went all over the United States."

Enlarged to life size, the photo was displayed prominently near the dais when Collins addressed the managing editors. "I seized on it," he wrote, "as exemplifying the problem of the army in trying to overcome the irrational approach of a large segment of Congress and the press to the army's complex problem of demobilizing over a million men, scattered around the problem of trying to maintain some semblance of ability to check the Soviets' ruthless takeover of much of Eastern Europe. I pointed out the destructive effect on our combat units, which in addition to being stripped of key personnel were forced to leave much of their equipment, worth billions of dollars, untended in open fields in Europe and the jungles of the Pacific Islands, to rust and rot. But all the efforts of the army, even with some belated support from some of the press, could not slow the incessant demands to bring the drafted men home."

Hoping to establish cordial relations with the Washington press establishment, Collins found a friendly reception from editors of the *Post, Star,* and *Herald* and reporters assigned to cover the Pentagon, but when Eisenhower sent him to Europe to find out why the army was getting critical stories on the occupation forces in Germany, he ran into a far different set of newsmen than he'd known during the war. At a press conference in Frankfurt, he was asked if the American people were aware of the complex problems of the occupation. He replied, "No."

The reporter who posed the question asked, "Why not?"

"Because you fellows," he said, "spend most of your time concentrating on scandal instead of the important aspects of the Cold War being fought between the Russians and Allied forces of occupation."

He soon learned a lesson that countless government officials and generals had taken to heart and those like Patton, who did not, came to rue: that it is never wise to be totally frank or to pick a fight with anyone who bought printer's ink by the barrel. With the rebuke resounding in the minds of every American journalist in Germany, Collins was invited to a dinner by the Berlin Press Club. After cocktails and the meal, Kendall Foss, the chairman of the Correspondents Association of Berlin, informed him bluntly that as long as there was scandalous conduct among the officers and men of the occupation the press would report it. With that, one reporter told Collins that he had sent home several stories about difficulties with the Russians that never made it into his newspaper, but when he filed a racy item about pregnant army nurses, his editor had cabled, "Send us more of the same."

Having seen that the nature of news reporting of the army had changed, Collins also found that after three years in combat he had come back to a capital city that had undergone dramatic changes. A federal government that swelled to contend with the demands of the war now faced a new threat from the nation's former ally, the Soviet Union. While the total strength of the army was being drastically cut, but not fast enough for the public, the Soviet Union was turning countries it occupied in the war into satellites. Communist regimes were first imposed in Poland and then in Hungary. To counter Soviet intentions, the United States began broadcasting the U.S. point of view behind the Iron Curtain on the Voice of America. Concerned about threats of possible Soviet takeovers of Greece and Turkey, President Truman declared a policy in March 1947 of "containment" of the spread of Soviet Communism.

Known as the Truman Doctrine, it would remain the policy of the United States until the 1980s, when President Ronald Reagan committed his administration to winning the cold war with increased defense spending and an expansion of the military that the Soviet Union could not match. Asked before he was elected in 1980 what his policy would be regarding the Soviets in the cold war, Reagan had answered, "We win, they lose."

In June of 1947, George C. Marshall, now the secretary of state, as part of the policy of thwarting Soviet inroads, unveiled a bold plan for economic assistance to the war-shattered countries of Europe that came to bear his name. In the same year, the House Committee on Un-American Activities, alarmed over possible Communist inroads in the motion-picture industry, turned its attention toward the movie capital and probed for influence of Communists or their sympathizers in movies. The committee eventually cited ten screenwriters and directors for refusing to testify and the "Hollywood Ten" went to jail.

At cocktail parties and dinners to which Collins found himself invited, the guests who only two years earlier talked about defeating Nazis, Fascists, and Japan now fretted about the Red Peril. An occasional guest he encountered at these affairs was Matthew Ridgway, looking ill at ease and eager to get back to commanding troops. His compatriot in the airborne, Maxwell Taylor, was head of the European Command and was keeping a wary eye on the Russians and their intentions in divided Berlin. James Van Fleet was in Greece, helping the Greeks to prevent Communism from getting a foothold in the birthplace of democracy. Courtney Hodges was still in command of the First Army, but based on Governors Island in New York Harbor. Terrible Terry Allen was biding time until retirement. The man who had been boss of all of them during the war, Omar Nelson Bradley, was the head of the Veterans Administration.

With the increasing tensions about Soviet-American relations in the autumn of 1947, Dwight Eisenhower called Collins into his office and offered him a new job. He was to be Ike's assistant with the title Deputy Chief of Staff of the Army. As chief of information, he and Ike had seen each other almost daily and had gotten to know one another on a personal as well as on a business basis. But Collins wrote in his memoirs that the deputy chief of staff proposal "came out of the blue." When he answered that he would be delighted to accept the post, he asked if Eisenhower might be better served by "someone less outspoken." Eisenhower replied with a dismissive wave of his hand. The appointment became effective on September 1, 1947.

Five months later, Eisenhower retired from the army to become president of Columbia University. President Truman selected Omar Bradley to succeed him. Bradley chose to keep Collins on as his deputy, with responsibility for reorganizing the office of chief of staff to meet the challenges to the army imposed by the militancy of the Soviet Union. Collins proposed and Bradley accepted creation of the posts of Vice Chief of Staff and Deputy Chiefs for Plans and Administration and Operations. When they were authorized by Congress, Bradley named Collins as vice chief of staff. The job entailed not only advising Bradley but making trips to inspect army installations and troops at home and overseas and report on their readiness to react to any threat involving the Russians.

At the start of 1948 the U.S. military governor in Germany, General Lucius Clay, had scoffed at the possibility of war with the U.S.S.R. Then he began to notice a serious change in the attitude of the Soviets. He reported that they all acted "faintly contemptuous, slightly arrogant, and certainly assured." In March, he cabled to Bradley, "For many months, based on logical analysis, I have felt and held that war was unlikely for at least ten years. Within the last few weeks, I have felt a subtle change in Soviet attitudes which I cannot define but which gives me a feeling that it may come with dramatic suddenness."

On March 31, the Soviets told the Allied powers that effective April 1 military passenger trains en route to Berlin from the West would be stopped and baggage and passengers checked by Soviet troops. With Washington's support, Clay continued to move the American trains to Berlin. The Russians responded by shuttling them onto side tracks. Within days, the trains were drawn back, the Soviets lifted restrictions, and some traffic resumed by the end of April.

Congress reacted to Soviet bellicosity by approving a $22 million increase in the air force budget to permit expansion to seventy air groups, and the Joint Chiefs of Staff submitted an integrated plan for war with the Soviet Union that was acceptable to the service chiefs. When Truman again pushed for a Universal Military Training Act at a cost of $4 billion, Congress decided the cost was not only prohibitive but politically distasteful. Some members also said it wasn't clear how expanding the army could bolster the U.S. military position in Europe.

On May 19, the Joint Chiefs of Staff adopted an emergency war plan called Halfmoon. It assumed that atomic weapons would be used if war commenced with the U.S.S.R. Fears of a Third World War heightened on June 24 when the Soviets closed all Allied access to Berlin. The crisis came when the army that had crushed Germany had only two divisions in Europe, and the forces available to defend against a Soviet move to take all of Berlin consisted only of the Third Battalion of the First Division's Sixteenth Infantry Regiment. Surveying the situation, Bradley found the army in Europe in such a "shockingly deplorable state" that it "couldn't fight its way out of a paper bag."

Because a ground response was impossible, Truman ordered a fleet of long-range B-29 bombers to England, with the implication that the type of plane that had carried atomic bombs to Japan could easily reach Moscow. He then turned to the air force to mount an airlift of food, fuel, and other supplies to West Berlin and waited to see if and how the Soviets reacted. When the first planes arrived at Tempelhof Airport unmolested, the air force launched Operation Vittles, and for the rest of 1948 and into the summer of 1949, with planes landing at better than one a minute, the Berlin Airlift saved the city from starvation.

Defeated in the first daring gambit of the cold war, Josef Stalin called off the blockade and Berlin continued as the most likely flashpoint of the cold war.

With the crisis over, Collins found himself in the role of chief army spokesman in the long-simmering controversy over universal military training (UMT) that Truman had rekindled by calling the Republican-dominated Eightieth Congress into an extraordinary special session on March 17, 1948. He asked for an extension of the selective service system that was due to expire and enactment of a UMT measure.

As early as 1944 the army had favored one year of compulsory training for every able-bodied eighteen-year-old to provide it with a constant force-in-being of a half million trainees. For emergencies the army would have at hand a pool of ex-trainees to be mobilized by the draft. After the first year of training, citizen soldiers would get the chance to become reserve officers, either through the Reserve Officer Training Corps or at officer candidate schools. The graduates of officers' schools would have to spend another year on active duty and keep alert from then on with correspondence courses and short annual periods of soldiering in the field. Most would go on the inactive list at thirty, although the army would hang on to top reserve officers until age sixty-four. Backing its reserve force, the army also wanted a permanent regular force (including the air force) of several times the size it had been before World War I. Around this would be a professional core able to organize 4 million troops almost overnight, the minimum that the army believed necessary if the nation was to survive.

At the time of the proposal, *Time* magazine asked, "Slim Chance? Already entrenched against some phases of the Army's plan is the National Guard Association. Reason: the Guard fears the Army would scrap it as superfluous and no longer practical (except possibly as state militias set up for police and disaster work). Stoutly on record as favoring universal military training, the politically potent Association will nevertheless fight any attempt to wash out their organization. Major General Ellard A. Walsh, Association president, said, 'The chances of the Regular Army to impose its ideas of a military establishment on the nation are probably slim.'"

Educators resisted any government attempt to go into what they considered their sole domain, the training of the country's youth. The navy also looked dimly on the plan. But the most powerful opponent was the Federal Council of the Churches of Christ in America, claiming to represent 26 million U.S. Protestants. It made a public appeal for deferment of any action by the Congress until after the war.

When Collins went to Capitol Hill to testify about UMT in 1948, he had become one of the most familiar faces and voices in the corridors of the Congress. Never having been portrayed by war correspondents as a "political general," such as Eisenhower, MacArthur, and Patton, he exhibited no indications that he affiliated himself with a political party or that he ever voted. As a result, he was able to present himself to both the Republicans and Democrats as a man with no agenda or aspirations, but only as an advocate of army policy.

A means of communicating government policy and proposals that had not existed when Collins left the United States for the Pacific in 1942, television was rapidly burgeoning as he carried the banner for universal military service to Capitol Hill in 1948. A few months earlier, the National Broadcasting Company's television station in Washington had presented the first broadcast of a program titled *Meet the Press*, on which a panel of reporters questioned a newsworthy guest on current political issues. Originated on radio in 1945, and produced by Lawrence Spivak and moderated by Martha Rountree, the program was soon extended to the entire NBC television network, consisting at that time of two other stations. As *Meet the Press* and other news interview programs reached a nationwide television audience in the mid-1950s, Collins would be a guest as army chief of staff during the Eisenhower presidency. But his UMT testimony in 1948 was of interest only to Capitol Hill reporters for wire services and newspapers and newsreel cameras. Despite his appearances before congressional committees and support by a presidential panel of advisors, the secretary of defense, secretaries of the army, navy, and air force, and the Joint Chiefs of Staff, the same interests that opposed UMT in 1944 persuaded the already reluctant congressmen to reject it.

As a case in point, Collins cited House Armed Services Committee member Dewey Short. In the middle of Collins's testimony, he abruptly left the committee room. He later explained, "Lightning Joe, you were about to convince me, so I *had* to walk out on you."

Universal military training would lie dormant until 1951, when it was revived as a small National Training Corps as part of an extension of the draft. What motivated Congress to enact both was a military attack by Communist forces that left Americans in a state of alarm and some of them scratching their heads and asking where on earth a place called Korea was.

CHAPTER SIXTEEN

COMMAND DECISIONS

W hen the National Security Act of 1949 created the post of chairman of the Joint Chiefs of Staff, President Truman placed Omar Bradley in the job and named Collins to succeed him in an office that had been held by the nation's most distinguished generals. It was Black Jack Pershing after World War I, MacArthur in the mid-1930s, Marshall all through World War II, and then Eisenhower and Bradley. Except for MacArthur, Collins had served under all of them. He was under Pershing in 1920, Ike and Bradley before and after D-day, and would have been in MacArthur's command in the Central Pacific if Admiral Nimitz hadn't shifted the Twenty-fifth Division to the Southwest Pacific Command to relieve the marines at Guadalcanal. Now, as chief of staff, he was at the head of the army and a member of the Joint Chiefs at a time of confrontation with the Soviet Union around the globe.

While the United States carried out the swiftest demobilization ever witnessed, the Red Army troops who embraced the soldiers of the Seventh Corps at the Elbe with pledges of enduring Soviet-American amicability stayed in Germany and in countries

★ *241* ★

of Eastern Europe, where the Kremlin imposed puppet govern-
ments from the Baltic to the Adriatic, as Winston Churchill had
said in his Iron Curtain speech in March 1946. In reaction to Soviet belligerency a month before Collins was elevated from deputy to chief of staff, the United States had joined Great Britain,
France, Canada, Belgium, Italy, the Netherlands, Luxembourg,
Portugal, Norway, Denmark, and Iceland in an alliance designed
as a military bulwark against the Soviet Union. Signed by the
United States on April 4, 1949, the North Atlantic Treaty went
into effect on August 24, 1949. The parties agreed that an armed
attack against one or more of them in Europe or North America
would be considered an attack against them all. Each pledged to
assist any member attacked, including the use of armed force to
restore and maintain the security of the North Atlantic area.

Because the United States had never belonged to such a peacetime codefensive alliance, no head of the U.S. Army had ever
faced the challenge presented by the North Atlantic Treaty Organization (NATO). The alliance came at a time when the
strength of the American military that had borne the major effort
in the defeat of Germany and the Japanese had been drastically
cut. If a Soviet attack occurred, Collins would be responsible with
the Joint Chiefs of Staff for mobilizing the army's response and at
the same time for assuring its combat readiness through training
and maintaining of troop morale and unit cohesiveness.

In a controversial executive order (No. 9981) signed on
July 26, 1948, President Truman decreed a policy, the effect of
which on army morale no one could predict. As commander in
chief of an army that was overwhelmingly made up of white draftees, he ordered a policy of "equality of treatment and opportunity
for all persons in the armed services without regard to race, color,
religion or national origin." The surprise order was to be put into
effect "as rapidly as possible, having due regard to the time required to effectuate any necessary changes without impairing efficiency or morale."

To determine how to implement the order, Truman appointed a Committee on Equality of Treatment and Opportunity in the Armed Forces. As chief of staff, Collins used his testimony before the board to relate his observations on the role of blacks in the army both before and during the war. Recalling that blacks had been organized under white officers to fight for the Union in the Civil War, and that they had been segregated before World War II, he noted that his first encounter with them had been as Seventh Corps commander in maneuvers in Arkansas in 1941. Because a few blacks belonged to the Thirty-third Division, he had found himself dealing with how to handle their presence in the racially segregated state. Although he was able to arrange for them to use bathing facilities in some black school gymnasiums, several towns refused to open their white schools. This meant finding either black schools or using the army's limited number of mobile bath units. His most serious and potentially dangerous problem arose when a black National Guard company from Illinois was marching down the main highway between the towns of Prescott and Hope. As a state police car carrying two white troopers and a pair of vagrant white women they had arrested passed by, black troops shouted obscenities. When this was reported to Collins, he suggested to his Seventh Corps superior, General Robert C. Richardson, that he (Collins) drive at once to the scene.

"As I passed through a small town," Collins recorded, "a little group of wild-eyed men, armed with squirrel rifles and shotguns, was gathering at a crossroads on the highway. Without stopping, I proceeded a mile or so until I came upon the company, the men of which were sitting quietly on the grass to one side of the road. The company commander, a black captain, reported to me that as the police car had driven by his marching company at a high speed, some of his men had called out in protest. The state troopers stopped a distance beyond the company, then drove back, and with drawn pistols, ordered the company off the road. By the time I reached the scene the police had departed without further incident. I told him to get the company back on the road, but suggested that he bypass the next town on the road en route to his camp. I did my best to assure him that his unit would not be further molested."

When he drove to the town, he found the excited group of citizens had quieted down. He identified himself and spoke to a man who seemed less agitated than the others. He told him the story as recounted by the company commander, which differed radically from the one told by the state troopers. Collins explained quietly but forcefully that the soldiers were federal troops participating in official maneuvers and had every right, which the army meant to maintain, to move freely on the highways. He also said that he could guarantee that the units were very well disciplined and would cause no trouble. He appealed to the townspeople's common sense and suggested that they return to their homes and put away their weapons. They accepted his suggestion with no argument, offered no threats, and dispersed.

Collins's next experience with black troops was during the war. Although none were in the Seventh Corps, the acute need for replacements faced by Eisenhower and Bradley resulted in an appeal to blacks in service, supply, and transportation outfits to volunteer to become combat infantrymen. Under white officers and sergeants, they received six weeks of training and went into action. Reports of their performance, Collins noted, were uniformly unfavorable, but he learned that many whites who had been reluctant to fight side by side with blacks found that they performed better in mixed units than in wholly black outfits. Eventually, black units performed as well as white ones, and in some instances individual black soldiers became heroes.

After the war, the War Department and then the Defense Department policy was that the number of black draftees assigned to the army could not exceed 10 percent, the approximate percentage of blacks in the American population.

As chief of staff in 1948, Collins had the responsibility of seeing that Truman's order to desegregate the army was implemented, but he recorded in his autobiography that there was little enthusiasm for making the armed services into an instrument of change. He wrote, "The attitude of most senior officials of the Army, both civil and military, during World War II and in the early post-war period, was that the Army was not designed or intended as an instrument to accomplish social and political changes in American society. Its mission was to provide for the military security of the United States. Many senior officers, and I was one of them, felt that the military services should move ahead to provide equal opportunity to all soldiers for training and advancement, but that the lead in eliminating segregation, as distinct from discrimination in the ranks, and in the social aspects of Army life, should be political and accord with the state and federal laws and social customs."

Despite Truman's executive order, the pace of integrating the armed services was slowed by a combination of resistance by Southern members of Congress and much of the public, north and south, and a reluctance by the navy and air force to accept black draftees whom they deemed to be below their educational standards. When it appeared that racial integration was to be left solely to the army, Collins appealed to the secretary of defense to direct all services to accept blacks equitably.*

---

*Author's note: Eleven years after Collins was given the responsibility for integrating the army, I witnessed the persistent difficulty of assuring that whites and blacks served together amicably. As I was undergoing basic training at Fort Bragg, North Carolina, in the fall of 1957, my company's first sergeant and his assistants were from Arkansas and all the recruits were white. Although I had enlisted in Pennsylvania, they were draftees from Southern states. While I and a couple of my newly made buddies were at a movie on the post on the Friday evening after President Eisenhower sent troops of the 101st Airborne Division to carry out a Supreme Court order that North Central High School in Little Rock, Arkansas, be integrated, a group of white recruits from another company leaving the movie voiced racial insults to several black draftees from another company who were from Philadelphia. When I and my buddies got back to our barracks, we found that it had been ransacked in a raid by black recruits. Lockers and bunks were overturned, some with men in them, and personal items stolen. In a demonstration of racial equality, the commanding officer of the training unit chose to punish everyone, guilty or not, with an order that we all go on marches at double-time for a week.

Because the army chief of staff's responsibilities extended beyond the United States and Europe to the Far East and the Pacific, Collins's first venture outside the country as chief of staff was to Japan to meet with MacArthur and inspect troops of the Eighth Army. His intent was not only to survey U.S. readiness in the region but to smooth any of MacArthur's feathers that might have been ruffled because he had not been visited by a member of the JCS since Eisenhower called on him in 1946. He also wanted to assure MacArthur that although Lightning Joe Collins had left the Pacific in 1942, Chief of Staff J. Lawton Collins maintained a great interest in the Far East. If MacArthur resented that the man he'd rejected as too young to head a corps in 1942 was now his superior in office but not in rank (Collins had four stars, MacArthur had five), he spared no effort in welcoming him. He arranged a full-scale military review on the grounds adjacent to the palace of the Japanese emperor, quarters in a splendid guesthouse close to MacArthur's in a high-walled American compound, and a lavish dinner with MacArthur and his wife.

Briefings on the situation in the Far East and the status of U.S. military preparedness were presented by his staff, most of whom Collins had known before the war. This amicable and useful visit was cut short by a call to Collins to return to Washington to testify before the House Armed Services Committee on a dispute between the navy and the air force over allocation of funds in the 1952 budget.

The crux of the conflict was termination by the secretary of defense and the JCS of a project to build a supercarrier, the *United States*, while approving the air force's acquisition of additional B-36 intercontinental bombers. While Collins had nothing to do with either decision, he was angered by erroneous testimony by the commandant of the Marine Corps about the role of the army in the battle of Guadalcanal.

Of far greater importance to Collins than a squabble about a supercarrier versus the B-36 or rehashing Guadalcanal was pending legislation to revise and update statutes that predated unification of the War and Navy departments into the Department of Defense. If they were not changed, the army would revert to its pre–World War II organization. Hearings were to begin on March 1 by a subcommittee of the House Armed Services Committee. They went smoothly until the committee took up a section of the old statutes that required the army chief of staff to report to undersecretaries of the army rather than directly to the secretary and granted him no powers to command combat troops, as Marshall had commanded none in the war. Collins proposed that the chief of staff report only to the secretary of defense, and have the sole responsibility for planning and ensuring combat readiness.

During the war, he had made it clear to artillery officers that as a divisional and corps commander he would have the final say in the use of their cannons. As the chief of staff, he recognized that the nuclear age required an examination of how the United States and NATO could fight a ground war with the Soviet Union in Europe. Believing that the army could not match the millions of troops and fleets of tanks the Russians could put in the field, he reasoned, along with most senior military experts, that war in Europe with the Red Army ruled out the use of nuclear bombs that would leave the continent in radioactive rubble. The answer to a tide of Soviet troops and armor, he felt, had to be artillery firing shells equipped with nuclear warheads with destructive power limited to the confines of a battlefield. The challenge was in producing a nuclear shell small enough to fit in the barrel of the army's largest cannon (240mm) and rugged enough to withstand being loaded and fired without going off prematurely. When nuclear weapons experts and ordnance engineers came up with a 280mm nuclear shell, three years were needed to produce an artillery piece and carriage to handle it. The big gun firing a nuclear punch of ten to twenty kilotons of TNT was tested on the Atomic Energy Commission's Frenchman Flats proving ground north of Las Vegas, Nevada, on May 25, 1953.

Two years and five months before a shell from an atomic cannon vaporized snakes and other wildlife in the desert, and rattled the gambling casinos in Las Vegas, the hot war that the Defense Department planners expected to begin with a Soviet grab for Berlin broke out on the other side of the globe. On Saturday night, January 25, 1950, in Washington, D.C., an evening not unlike the one of George Marshall's dinner for General Eisenhower at the Alibi Club, Collins answered a phone in the house he and his wife had shared since the spring of 1945. The caller informed him of an attack by forces of Communist North Korea across the thirty-eighth parallel, which since the end of World War II divided the Korean peninsula and marked the border with the Republic of South Korea.

At eleven thirty on Sunday morning, Collins and deputy chief of operations Brigadier General Thomas J. Timmerman attended a meeting at the State Department with Secretary of State Dean Acheson, Undersecretary James Webb, and Assistant Secretary Dean Rusk. As the senior official, Acheson proposed a program of action "to provide a measure of U.S. support" for South Korean forces. Consultations with the Joint Chiefs of Staff chairman, General Bradley, and navy and air force members of the JCS resulted in suggestions to be presented to Truman that American air and naval forces establish a protective corridor around the South Korean capital of Seoul, the airport at Kimpo, and the harbor at Inchon. MacArthur's command was to be authorized to send to Korea any equipment recommended by the U.S. mission in Seoul, and MacArthur was to have operational control of all U.S. military activities in Korea. Military advisors were to remain with South Korean forces. Although these proposals were to be presented to Truman at a meeting in Blair House (the White House was being renovated) upon his return from a long vacation in his hometown of Independence, Missouri, the proposals were sent to MacArthur in Tokyo with the caveat that they had to be approved by Truman. MacArthur responded, "Come over and join the fight. We are delighted with your lines of action and this aid should turn the trick. Thank you."

At the Blair House meeting, Bradley asserted, "We must draw the line somewhere."

On June 27, South Korean president Syngman Rhee appealed to the United Nations Security Council for assistance. Because Soviet representative Jacob Malik was boycotting the UN and could not use the Soviet veto power, the council called on UN members to aid South Korea in repelling the invasion. The next day, North Korean troops broke through the last line of South Korean defense north of Seoul.

As a member of the JCS, Collins joined in reviewing the situation with Dean Acheson and Defense Secretary Louis Johnson in a conference with Truman. They agreed that General Mac-Arthur should be authorized to use troops to secure the South Korean port of Pusan and undertake other measures, including the use of air and naval assets, to prevent the North Koreans from overrunning South Korea. By Friday morning, it became clear that the South Koreans were being driven back by the North Korean invaders and that the Korean peninsula was in danger of going Communist. In a two-thousand-word cable to Washington, General MacArthur stated, "The only hope of holding the present line is through the introduction of U.S. ground combat forces in the Korean battle area." He proposed moving a regimental combat team (RCT) of twenty-two hundred men to Korea and the authorization of a buildup of U.S. Army strength in Japan to two divisions.

Since Collins became army chief of staff in August 1949, he and every senior officer in the Pentagon had been expecting and planning for a cold war showdown in Europe. Suddenly, all eyes were looking to a peninsula in the Far East that no one, including MacArthur, had ever suggested as a likely place for the United States to make a stand against Communism. This had been expressed in a memorandum from Eisenhower as chairman of the

JCS to the secretary of defense, James Forrestal, on September 25, 1947. Stating that keeping bases and troops was of "little interest" to the United States because of limited resources, the memo was endorsed by the president's National Security Council and accepted by Truman. The result had been a phased withdrawal of forty-five thousand American troops in Korea that Forrestal advised could be better used elsewhere and "would not impair the [U.S.] military position in the Far East Command."

The only contrary voice was MacArthur's. In October 1948, he told President Syngman Rhee, "Personally, I will do anything I can to help the [South] Korean people and to protect them." Although the JCS decided to leave about seventy-five hundred troops in South Korea, they also made it clear that the American commitment would last only through the first month of South Korean independence. In a speech at the National Press Club in Washington on January 5, 1950, the secretary of defense, Dean Acheson, stated that the U.S. "defense perimeter" in the Far East did not include Korea. Following the outbreak of war in Korea, Republicans interpreted Acheson's declaration as an invitation to the North Korean Communists to move south.

With the North Korean invasion and MacArthur pushing hard for a commitment of U.S. troops, Collins had doubts about the wisdom of American involvement in the fighting and was worried that MacArthur might take actions without President Truman's approval.

On July 1, a combat team of the First Battalion of the Twenty-first Infantry, commanded by Lieutenant Colonel Charles B. Smith, was on the ground at Pusan, and MacArthur had issued orders to the Twenty-fourth Division to go to Korea.

Collins would later say that he wished he'd spoken more forcefully against intervention.

After a meeting that Truman convened to brief members of Congress on the Wednesday after the North Korean invasion, the Republican leader in the Senate, Robert A. Taft of Ohio, complained that rather than being consulted, they had been told of a fait accompli and blamed the Korean crisis on a "bungling and inconsistent foreign policy." He said that he did not wish to see "a complete usurpation by the president of [congressional] authority to use the armed forces of this country" and the termination "for all time [of] the right of Congress to declare war, which is granted to Congress alone by the Constitution of the United States."

Taft's protest against the executive branch's unilateral decision to go to war would be echoed by antiwar activists, most of whom were Democrats, during the Vietnam War against President Lyndon B. Johnson, and again by Democrats against President George W. Bush's launching of a war to depose Saddam Hussein in Iraq. Like President Bush's justification for the Iraq war, Truman cited a UN resolution authorizing the use of force. He committed troops to Korea after the Security Council's vote, with the Soviets still boycotting its sessions, asking all UN members to give assistance to South Korea. When Truman was asked at a press conference if the United States was at war, he replied, "We are not at war."

Perhaps intending a tone of sarcasm, a correspondent asked, "Mr. President, would it be correct under your explanation to call this a police action under the United Nations?"

"Yes," said Truman, "that is exactly what it amounts to."

Collins recorded in his autobiography, "Thus, for the first time in our history, the United States embarked in peacetime on a major war in a far-off country that many Americans had never heard of, a war that began without a congressional declaration and ended without a peace treaty. It was unique also because, although the United States furnished the bulk of the troops, equipment, supplies, and leadership, it was fought by an international force under the aegis of the United Nations."

Although the United States did not have complete freedom of action in the conduct of the war, Army Chief of Staff Collins had the duty to assure that the soldiers in Korea had his full support in a war that he personally believed was the wrong one in the wrong place at the wrong time. On July 13, 1951, he arrived in Tokyo with U.S. Air Force general Hoyt Vandenberg and members of the JCS staff to seek more information on exactly how MacArthur planned to defeat the North Korean invasion. Describing MacArthur as being "cool and poised" as he spoke of his aims while constantly pacing the floor, Collins observed, "He always gave me the impression of addressing not just his immediate listeners but a larger audience unseen."

Having previously called the North Korean army ill-trained Oriental rabble, MacArthur conceded that it was a "tough opponent, well led," with the expertise at infiltration shown by the Japanese and tactics of Russian tank units in World War II. Stating that what he had done so far to fight them was a desperate rearguard action by American troops that were "tailored for occupation duty" rather than for combat, he said that how well he could turn rout into counterattack depended on how many troops he received and how rapidly he received them. Success, he said, would be in direct proportion to the degree of speed with which he received reinforcements.

According to notes of the conference, MacArthur planned to destroy North Korea, block relief by the Russians or Red China, and unify the Korean peninsula. Collins asked when MacArthur could begin a counteroffensive. MacArthur replied that he could stabilize the situation when he had three divisions.

Collins left Tokyo to visit the U.S. ground commander in Korea, Lieutenant General Walton H. "Johnny" Walker. Head of the Eighth Army based in Japan since 1948, he was born in Texas and graduated from West Point one year before Collins's brother James served on the Mexican border. In World War I, Walker was promoted on the battlefield to lieutenant colonel. He became a tank commander under George Patton in World War II and received Patton's highest praise as "my toughest son of a bitch." His CP in Korea was at Taegu, north of Pusan. On tours of his front lines, he traveled by jeep and carried a Colt .45 and a repeating shotgun. "I don't mind being shot at," he told a subordinate, "but these bastards are not going to ambush me." Two days before Christmas 1950, he was killed when his jeep wrecked, and his body was taken home by his son Sam Sims Walker, commander of a battalion of the Nineteenth Infantry, and interred at Arlington Cemetery.

Characterizing Walker for a Combat Studies Institute seminar in 1983, Collins said, "He was a fine commander in the field. He irritated a lot of people. He was not the type of man you would mix with. He had an abrasive sort of temperament. But so far as his command responsibilities went, he did a fine job in Korea."

Before leaving Korea, Collins and Vandenberg were briefed on MacArthur's plan to cut off the North Koreans with a landing on the west coast of the peninsula far to the north of the Pusan perimeter. The place he chose was the port of Inchon, which was close to the South Korean capital, Seoul, and Kimpo Airport. In audacity, the scheme matched that of Anzio in Italy, but Collins knew enough about Douglas MacArthur to trust him not to let Inchon be a repeat of the bloody Anzio debacle and stalemate. This confidence was not replicated by the Joint Chiefs of Staff, nor by Truman, who was sensitive to having taken the country to war without asking Congress's consent, and keenly aware that the war would be an issue raised by the Republicans in the 1952 presidential election. Having defeated Thomas E. Dewey in a historic upset in 1948, Truman appreciated that the Republicans would feel they had a score to settle, not only because of their 1948 disappointment but because of Truman's decision to go to war without approval by the Congress they controlled.

When Collins returned to Washington to urge the JCS and Truman to okay the reinforcements MacArthur wanted, he reported on the Inchon plan that MacArthur had revealed in only the sketchiest way. Consequently, the Joint Chiefs decided to send Collins back, accompanied by Admiral Forrest P. Sherman, to review the details with MacArthur. They arrived in Tokyo on August 21.

After a tour of the Korean battlefront with Walker, Collins returned to Tokyo for a briefing on the Inchon plan by MacArthur. He described MacArthur puffing on his corncob pipe and expressing confidence that difficulties, hazards, and problems would be overcome, that a landing south of Inchon would outflank the North Korean forces, and that the JCS's fears were unfounded. Collins quoted MacArthur as saying, "By attacking as [British general James] Wolfe did at Quebec [in 1777], where the enemy thought it impossible, he would gain surprise and a decisive victory." Collins reported that MacArthur closed with "a dramatic peroration in which he staked his reputation that Inchon would not fail." Collins was "favorably impressed," but still had some reservations. There was more at stake than MacArthur's reputation, great as that was.

When MacArthur said he wanted to be given two additional divisions, Collins said, "You are going to have to win the war out here with the troops available to you in Japan and Korea."

"Joe," said MacArthur, "you are going to have to change your mind."

At a meeting with MacArthur's staff later that day, Collins noted again that resources were scarce and told them, "Don't get too grandiose."

On Collins's return to Washington, he briefed Truman, the secretary of defense, and the other chiefs. For the first time they were informed about the attack plans, the risks involved, and MacArthur's personal confidence in the outcome. After hours of debate and soul-searching among the JCS, and continuing doubts by Collins, MacArthur's greatly reduced equivalent of Eisenhower's D-day was approved. The planning proceeded, as one official historian wrote, "sustained only by hope, credit, and promises." At no time during his planning did MacArthur feel he had the men and guns he would need. The Joint Chiefs of Staff frequently told him that with the military resources of the United States at rock bottom and because of the short target date in September that MacArthur adamantly insisted on, the men and guns might not arrive on time. Disagreements over time, place, and method of landing stemmed in part from this reality. MacArthur knew that even with the support by the JCS in Washington he might not have enough trained men and equipment to breach enemy defenses and exploit a penetration. Trained men, especially those with amphibious training, were at a premium in the United States as well as in the Far East. To gather, assemble, equip, and move them secretly and swiftly to the area by the September 15 deadline would require an enormous, finely coordinated effort by everyone involved.

At the age of seventy, MacArthur also knew that Inchon was his last opportunity as a commander to do something great, and that a failure would be the first line in his obituary. Defeat would overshadow all that he had accomplished in World War I and all the battles he had masterminded on the route to victory over Japan in World War II. But victory at Inchon could be the capstone of his career and reputation.

In a military and naval stroke with troops under the banner of the UN, Inchon not only succeeded but was hailed as one of the great achievements of warfare, trapping the entire North Korean army in a pincer movement that would permit its destruction and allow the UN forces to sweep north of the thirty-eighth parallel and push all the way to the Red Chinese border.

In his 1969 book reflecting on Korea, *War in Peacetime*, Collins wrote, "The success at Inchon was so great, and the subsequent prestige of General MacArthur was so overpowering, that the Chiefs hesitated thereafter to question later plans and decisions of the general which should have been [questioned]."

Motivated by the war in Korea, the Congress authorized rapid expansion of the army and by December 1950 the number of troops Collins had at hand had doubled. The need for manpower also sped up integration of the races. The 10 percent draft quota was abandoned and black enlistments tripled. By June 1953, the ratio of blacks going to Korea was 22 percent and they were placed in Eighth Army combat units without regard to ratios. Fed into the manpower pipeline, they and the men who went to Korea before them were in a new kind of war in which decisions were not made only by generals in the field but by men in Washington, D.C., and at the UN headquarters in a place in New York with the encouraging name of Lake Success.

Although George Marshall had been required to be as much a political figure as he was army chief of staff during World War II, he'd had to consider only the opinions of Roosevelt, Churchill, and Stalin, with Charles de Gaulle and the French as factors as well. Collins and the Joint Chiefs had to contend with the members of the UN Security Council and General Assembly, to which the problem of Korea had been handed as a means of getting around vetoes by the Soviet delegate, who had been hastily sent back to the UN by Josef Stalin, alarmed by the reaction of the rest of the world to the aggression of a Soviet puppet.

Wary of possible Soviet or Red Chinese intervention in Korea, the JCS sent a directive to MacArthur on September 27, 1950, that he must report to them any sign of a Chinese Communist or Soviet threat "to the attainment of your objective." In the second paragraph, that goal was stated as the destruction of the North Korean armed forces, for which MacArthur was authorized to use amphibious, airborne landings, or ground actions north of the thirty-eighth parallel, provided there was no major intervention by Chinese or Soviet forces. If so, he was to go on the defensive. This order ruled out crossing the Manchurian border.

In the conduct of the Korean War, Army Chief of Staff J. Lawton Collins had the power and the direct means of communication to do what George C. Marshall had not been able to do in World War II. Collins was not only able to take a direct role in strategic and tactical decisions but talk with MacArthur and subordinates through television linkups. While Marshall had been mostly kept in Washington by FDR, in the Korean War Collins was able to get on an airplane and meet with MacArthur and make visits to the front.

In one of the twists and turns that marked Collins's rise to army chief of staff in the Korean War, Marshall was again above him in the chain of command. Having retired from the army only to be sent to China by Truman to try to fashion a peace between Chiang Kai-shek and Mao Tse-tung, then named secretary of state, Marshall had been appointed secretary of defense in September 1950. On September 29, he sent a message for MacArthur's eyes only. It said, "We want you to feel unhampered tactically and strategically to proceed north of the thirty-eighth parallel."

MacArthur's reply said in part, but an important part, that he regarded "all of Korea open for our military operations."

How the General Assembly felt about MacArthur crossing the thirty-eighth parallel was expressed on October 8, 1950. Undoubtedly emboldened by the success of Inchon, the members adopted a resolution recommending all "appropriate steps be taken to ensure conditions of stability throughout Korea" and for "establishment of a unified, independent, and democratic government" in Korea.

MacArthur planned another landing to take the city of Wonsan and operations to capture the North Korean capital, Pyongyang, that would trap and destroy North Korean forces that had managed to escape north of the parallel. "Perhaps awed by the stunning success of the Inchon operation," Collins speculated, "the JCS, Secretary of Defense Marshall, and President Truman approved the plan in spite of some doubt about the command arrangements."

Collins studied Korea's terrain, which he termed "a jumble of high mountains and tortuous mountains," with only a single-track railroad and one highway between Wonsan and Pyongyang, and saw "a formidable barrier." The western half of Korea was cut by a succession of rivers flowing into the Yellow Sea. The most important of these streams was the Yalu River, forming Korea's northwest boundary with the territory of Manchuria. Beyond the river stood the Red Chinese army with scores of infantry divisions that Chinese foreign minister Chou En-lai had warned would enter the war if the UN forces crossed the line into North Korea.

Analyzing MacArthur's performance as commander for students at the Combat Institute in the spring of 1983, Collins faulted him for rarely visiting the front. "His forte was the strategic field," he said. "He never got into combat that I knew of in modern times. He'd done a good job in World War I as a brigade commander of the Rainbow Division. He was competent at that stage of the game, but he never did pay too much attention to the troops, the fighting men at the front. He was a lofty and theoretical commander, far removed from the dirt, dust and mud of a commander of frontline troops. He tried to coordinate the fighting in Korea between [General] Edmond Almond on one side of the mountain range and Johnny Walker on the other side, with a practically impassable mountain chain between. At the end, when things were going badly, all he did was issue an order."

Although MacArthur was running the Korean War from Tokyo, his commander in chief was in Washington, D.C. Harry Truman informed him that he wanted to sit down with his top general somewhere convenient to both and get MacArthur's views on how the war was going, and how soon he expected to win it. They agreed to meet at Wake Island. In the election year of 1944, President Roosevelt had traveled a much shorter distance to Hawaii for a meeting with MacArthur and Admiral Chester Nimitz to discuss strategy for defeating the Japanese. Nimitz wanted the next step to be a largely naval operation to capture the island of Formosa as a base for attacking the Japanese homeland. MacArthur wanted to fulfill his pledge to the people of the Philippines to return to the islands leading an army of liberation. He won the debate by privately telling Roosevelt that if he did not choose the Philippines, the voters would penalize him at the polls. Although Truman and the Democrats would not have to face the voters until 1952, MacArthur knew they were already taking a beating in the press from Republicans, that some leaders in the Grand Old Party were talking about MacArthur as an attractive GOP candidate, and that Truman desired a victory in Korea as soon as possible.

Going with Truman on the more than four-thousand-mile journey to Wake Island were concerns of the JCS over the possibility of Red China getting into the war. Traveling only nineteen hundred miles, MacArthur brought his reputation as a hero in two world wars and supreme confidence that he was about to roll back the Red Tide in Asia.

As the president, a former artillery captain, and the five-star general shook hands on October 15, 1950, Truman said, "I've been a long time meeting you."

"I hope," said MacArthur, "it won't be so long next time."

In an account of the meeting that Truman wrote for the State Department a few months later, Truman said that MacArthur assured him that Red China would not attack and that the war was won. Army secretary Pace told Marshall that MacArthur had said the war would be over by Thanksgiving and the troops home by Christmas.

Nine days after the Wake Island meeting, a unit of the South Korea (ROK) Sixth Division reached Chosan on the Yalu River. They fired on the North Koreans fleeing across a pontoon bridge. The next morning, Chinese troops crossed the river undetected, attacked the ROK Second Corps, and drove it back in a rout. In his Pentagon office, Collins read reports of U.S. efforts to fill gaps in the front as two Chinese divisions attacked. With the right flank of the U.S. corps exposed by the collapse of the ROK First Division, General Walker replaced the Koreans with the First

Cavalry Division, commanded by Major General Hobart R. Gay, who had been Patton's chief of staff, but a battalion of its Eighth Cavalry was surrounded and decimated.

As the Eighth Army struggled to hold off repeated assaults in winter weather, reminding Collins of the Battle of the Bulge, he noted that MacArthur was in Tokyo, four hundred miles from the front, and still discounting Chinese intervention. When they withdrew into hills to the north of the UN front on November 6, Collins had no doubt they would be back. East of the mountain range separating the UN-American forces, General Almond ordered an attack by a force under the command of Major General David Barr toward the Yalu. With the U.S. Army waging its fiercest fighting since the Ardennes in 1944, it was clear that MacArthur was wrong about the war being won by Thanksgiving. Barr's troops reached the Yalu on November 21. A week earlier, the First Marine Division, which Collins's Twenty-fifth Division had relieved at Guadalcanal in 1942, had moved up a mountain pass to the Chosin reservoir and driven off a Chinese regiment.

On November 25, the Chinese Fourth Field Army, the Thirteenth Army Group, and the Ninth Army Group, totaling twelve divisions and 300,000 men, counterattacked and sent the UN forces reeling.

MacArthur radioed to the JCS, "We face an entirely new war."

Korea was also a new war in terms of how the American people were informed about what was happening at the front. With many homes having television sets, Americans watched news programs showing pictures of the war that had been shot the day before, rather than the week or more that it took for World War II newsreels to arrive in movie theaters. Nightly, homes were being provided with reports of a war that MacArthur promised would be over by Thanksgiving, but continued past Christmas with no end in sight.

Collins had been almost entirely unknown to the American

public in World War II, but since becoming chief of staff he had gotten accustomed to mentions of his name in newspapers, on radio news programs, and occasionally on television in connection with postwar demobilization, congressional testimony on UMT and integration, and the Soviet threat in Europe. He had even been featured in a news story in the *New York Times* on March 20, 1950, for being awarded the University of Notre Dame's Laetare Medal as a distinguished Roman Catholic. Following the outbreak of war in Korea, his journeys to see MacArthur garnered front-page headlines. On December 3, 1950, one in the *New York Times* announced, "Collins on His Way to Meet M'Arthur; Army's Chief May Visit Korea Also."* A December 4 headline that had the name in full read, "Collins Is Welcomed by MacArthur."

After the formal greeting, Collins headed for Korea to see General Walker at his headquarters in Seoul. Walker briefed him on the Chinese attack and warned that if they were able to drive across the thirty-eighth parallel it was doubtful that they could be stopped from reaching Seoul. He expressed confidence that the original U.S. toehold at Pusan could be maintained indefinitely. It was the last time Collins saw Walker. Informed at the Pentagon on December 23 that Walker had been killed when his jeep collided with a truck south of Seoul, Collins found his death an inglorious and sad end for a gallant officer.

From Seoul, Collins flew to an airstrip near Hungnam. Met by Almond, he was taken to Almond's CP for a review of the action in his zone, then on to the Third and Seventh divisions' command posts. Almond assured him that his troops could hold at Hungnam as long as needed.

Back in Tokyo, he listened to MacArthur ask for reinforcements to keep him from being forced to withdraw from Korea. Collins didn't agree, but elected not to argue the point. Before

---

*How Collins felt about General MacArthur's name being abbreviated went unrecorded.

leaving Tokyo, he assured reporters that he saw no value in using the atom bomb in Korea. Back in Washington on December 9, he and the Joint Chiefs went to the White House and Collins updated Truman on the views of MacArthur and the frontline commanders.

With Walker's death, MacArthur requested that Collins replace Walker with Matthew Ridgway. Collins agreed and recommended him to Truman, Marshall, Pace, and the JCS. All approved. Having chafed at being stuck behind a desk as Collins's deputy for operations, with brief inspection trips to Japan and Korea, Ridgway gave up Christmas with his family and arrived in Tokyo shortly before midnight on December 25. The appointment proved to be not only timely for the fortunes of the American and UN efforts in Korea but beneficial to the advancement of Ridgway's army career.

Shocked by the performance of field officers and their failure to carry out his orders, Ridgway informed Collins he intended to be "ruthless" with the generals who failed "to measure up." Soon, commanders were replaced. By late February, he had a new set of division commanders. The effects were reflected on the battlefield. News stories about the new Eighth Army chief noted that he went around with a brace of hand grenades clipped to his field jacket. To make it easier for newsmen to report from his front, he installed a phone bank in their quarters and had a soundproof room built for radio reporters. He was also alert to the new element of journalism in the form of television news reporters and their cameramen, whose reports would be on the air in the United States as early as the next day.

As army chief of staff, Collins was also keenly attuned to the new technology of communications that gave him an advantage in influencing the conduct of a war, technology that was not available to General Marshall in World War II. When the Germans broke out of the Ardennes, Marshall had recognized that all he could do to help Eisenhower was to keep quiet and rely on Ike's

judgment. In Korea, everything that MacArthur did was subjected to immediate review by the Joint Chiefs of Staff, with attention to the policies laid out by Truman and the diplomats at
the UN. Nor had Marshall been required to worry about reining
in a commander who felt he was more qualified to set policy than
his military and political superiors. In deciding not to drive on to
Berlin, and leave it to the Russians, Eisenhower had adhered to
an agreement by the Big Three. In declaring that Chinese intervention in Korea constituted "a new war," MacArthur had
opened a can of worms that resulted in a great deal of squirming
in the capitals of the Western world.

Worries that MacArthur might trigger a wider war with
China that could bring in the Russians deepened when he proposed a naval blockade of Chinese ports. He also recommended
acceptance of an offer of troops by Chiang Kai-shek on Formosa,
where he had been driven in the wake of Mao Tse-tung's victory
in China. The JCS rejected these proposals. When he warned the
Joint Chiefs that troop morale was at a low ebb, they decided it
was time for another face-to-face talk with the Far East commander and sent Collins and General Vandenberg back to Tokyo.
They arrived on January 15, 1951, and MacArthur explained that
JCS directives were not clear as to how long and under what conditions he was expected to keep his forces in Korea. He also said
that his directives did not explain clearly enough his responsibility for defending Japan. He read to Collins and Vandenberg a letter from Truman that he interpreted as a directive to remain in
Korea indefinitely.

Collins replied that the message was not a directive and that
at a conference with the president before he and Vandenberg left
Washington it was agreed that a decision to evacuate Korea
should be delayed as long as possible without creating a situation
that endangered the Eighth Army in Korea or the security of
Japan. The United States' objective, Collins asserted, was to permit the longest possible time for political action by the United

Nations and the best opportunity to inflict a maximum punishment on the Chinese.

If a decision was made to send the reinforcements to Japan that MacArthur wanted, Collins said, it would take at least six weeks for them to arrive, and in the interim MacArthur's basic mission of defending Japan would remain unchanged.

MacArthur responded by declaring that according to Collins, his command should not be held responsible for the defense of Japan and still be required to hold a line in Korea. He maintained that Soviet forces had the capability of attacking Japan, and because this threat was always present, he urged sending four National Guard divisions to Japan to help in its defense. Collins pointed out that MacArthur had been advised that the divisions were not called up for that purpose and refused to make any commitment on sending the requested units.

The day before Collins arrived in Tokyo, an enemy buildup was discovered north of the Eighth Army's defensive line. Ridgway responded by ordering an armor-supported coordinated attack against the concentration. Declaring his intention to kill as many enemy soldiers as possible and withdraw to main positions, he began an operation named Wolfhound to prove that the Eighth Army was no longer on the defensive. Eager to assess the offensive, Collins spent two days with Ridgway. They toured the front lines and talked with corps and division commanders. Collins told reporters, "As of now, we are going to stay and fight." Ridgway said, "There is no shadow of doubt in my mind that the Eighth Army can take care of itself."

When Collins returned to Tokyo on January 17, he sent a report to his fellow members of the Joint Chiefs of Staff telling them that the Eighth Army was in good shape and was improving daily under Ridgway's leadership. He reported that he had found U.S. troop morale very satisfactory, but that the weakest link in the United Nations team was the Korean army. He considered this force still capable of holding off North Korean units, but believed it lacked confidence and feared the Chinese. He said he saw no signs of dissatisfaction or collapse in the ROK army, but warned that both could develop quickly if there was a serious reverse. He also stated that what he had seen of the enemy made him optimistic. The Chinese had made no move to push south from the Han River, and when counterattacked they had usually fled. He detected signs of Chinese supply difficulties and indications of lowered morale.

"On the whole," he said, "the Eighth Army is now in position and prepared to punish severely any mass attack."

Collins and Vandenberg met with MacArthur again in Tokyo before leaving. Collins read to MacArthur a message that he had sent to JCS chairman Bradley that forecast a more favorable future for the United Nations Command. MacArthur agreed that the situation looked brighter and stated that his forces could hold a beachhead in Korea indefinitely. He felt that with continued domination of sea and air, and with the enemy's lengthening lines of communication, the Chinese would never be able to bring up enough supplies to be able to drive his forces from Korea. He also said that a decision to evacuate Korea was a purely political matter and should not be decided on military grounds. The effect of the Collins report was that for the first time since the Chinese attacked in November, Washington saw reasonable hope that catastrophe might be averted in Korea. For Collins, the reason for this turnaround was Ridgway.

When he began an offensive by the Eighth Army on January 25, noted Collins, Ridgway made no grandiose promises of success. "He did not care about real estate," said Collins, "he wanted Chinese bodies." In the first week, the enemy toll was twenty-three hundred. When Chinese resistance stiffened, a South Korean regiment broke ranks and the result was a slaughter. A U.S. artillery unit caught in the Chinese counterattack was surrounded. "There was shooting all over the place," reported a corporal who was sent with fourteen riflemen to secure the guns. Only three of them survived.

Although groups of UN soldiers broke under superior fire and resisted orders to return to combat, the Americans stood their ground and the Chinese broke off the fight. The next day, Ridgway assessed the outcome and found that the Eighth Army had bested the Chinese in a head-to-head fight that boded well for the future, if the policy makers chose to settle the fight militarily, as MacArthur urged them to do, rather than negotiate a truce.

Despite repeated MacArthur appeals to be allowed to broaden the objectives of the war that came across in Washington as demands, the State Department and the JCS agreed that the goal was a cease-fire with restoration of the prewar status quo. By late February 1951, Collins recorded, Ridgway's offenses had "straightened the UN line across the waist of Korea."

The army historian James F. Schnabel described the front as having "no gaping holes, no soft spots, and no enemy salients threatening to tear it in two." Until the intervention by Chinese Communist armies, MacArthur had confined his views on the war to official communications with Washington or in the meetings he had with Collins. After the Chinese moved across the Yalu, he began speaking publicly.

In a chronicle of the war for the Center for Military History (its director was Collins's nephew, James Lawton Collins, Jr.), Schnabel wrote that "smarting from the defeat his forces had suffered," MacArthur spoke out sharply in his own defense, and in published statements in early December charged that limitations on his operations were an enormous handicap "without precedent in military history."

MacArthur intimated that selfish interests in Europe were causing support to be withheld from his forces. To some extent this was true. Leaders of Western Europe believed that they faced the most acute threat of Communism and feared the United States was so consumed with Korea that it would not be able to respond with a sufficient force to a Soviet move across the Iron Curtain. They also fretted that the Chinese intervention in Korea would escalate into a U.S. war with China that would allow Stalin to make a move in Europe.

MacArthur's statements were widely assessed as a criticism of the UN policy of "limited war" in Korea and as an oblique criticism of the Truman administration in its conduct of the war. "They were probably not so intended," Schnabel surmised. "General MacArthur pointed out quite rightly that at no time had he asked for authority to retaliate beyond the inviolate northern boundary of Korea. His statements, issued at a time when the administration was trying earnestly to reassure uneasy allies, were nonetheless of great concern to President Truman and his advisers."

MacArthur's insistence on blaming operational restrictions for the situation was taken in Washington as a reflection on the judgment of the Joint Chiefs of Staff for imposing them, but the JCS believed that MacArthur was partly responsible for his own predicament. This was also President Truman's view. He was irritated by MacArthur stating publicly that Washington had not let him do things his own way, and the result was a defeat of his November 24 attack and Chinese intervention.

Truman said later that he should have relieved MacArthur of command at that point, but that he had not done so because he didn't want it to appear that MacArthur had been fired because the offensive had failed.

As a result of MacArthur's statements, Truman ordered government officials to clear public statements concerning foreign policy with the Department of State and those concerning military affairs with the Department of Defense. Although the order was sent to all executive branches, it was clearly aimed at Mac-Arthur.

Meanwhile, MacArthur had proposed to Collins that the

United States should carry the war to China through bombing, blockade, and other means. Throughout December, January, and February, he insisted on these measures, but always through channels. But on February 13, he issued a statement to the press contending that if he was not allowed to reduce materially the superiority of the Chinese through attacks upon their "sanctuary" beyond the Yalu, he could not seriously consider conducting major operations north of the thirty-eighth parallel. In a press statement on March 7, he said that vital decisions, yet to be made, must be provided on the highest levels. Because neither statement had been cleared by the Department of Defense, they were in violation of Truman's directive.

The most explosive statement came on March 24. In addition to offering to negotiate with enemy leaders in the field, MacArthur said that the enemy "must by now be painfully aware that a decision of the United Nations to depart from its tolerant effort to contain the war to the area of Korea through expansion of our military operations to his coastal areas and interior bases would doom Red China to the risk of imminent military collapse."

This was too much for Truman. Finding the public statement to be "a most extraordinary" statement for a military commander of the United Nations to issue on his own responsibility, he saw it as defiance of his orders as commander in chief and a challenge to his authority. While he felt he could no longer tolerate instances of MacArthur's insubordination, he delayed a final decision on relieving him of his command. This self-restraint ended on April 5, 1951, when the Republican leader of the House of Representatives, Joseph W. Martin, released to the press a letter from MacArthur written on March 20 that was a reply to a Martin letter.

In a commentary on U.S. foreign policy, MacArthur said that Asia was fully as important as Europe and that the United States must prosecute the Asian war until victory was achieved. On April 6, Truman summoned his special assistant, Averell Harriman, who had been an FDR advisor throughout World War II; Secretary of State Acheson; Secretary of Defense Marshall; and Joint Chiefs chairman Bradley, and asked for their advice. Harriman said MacArthur should have been fired two years ago. Marshall was concerned about possible political repercussions that might follow the dismissal of MacArthur. He advised caution in firing a hero of two world wars who was popular with the general public and Republicans with eyes on the 1952 elections who had the power in Congress to affect pending military appropriations. Secretary of State Dean Acheson believed that MacArthur should be relieved, but only after a unanimous decision to do so by the Joint Chiefs of Staff. Bradley said he believed MacArthur had acted in an insubordinate manner and deserved to be fired, but he told Truman he wished to talk with Collins before making a recommendation.

Truman asked all of his advisors to return the next day for more discussion, and directed Marshall to restudy all messages exchanged with MacArthur in the past two years. The next morning, the group met again in Truman's office. Marshall told the president that after reading all the messages he agreed that MacArthur should have been relieved two years earlier. Before this brief meeting ended, Truman told Bradley to obtain the views of the remaining Joint Chiefs of Staff and to be prepared to make a final recommendation on April 9.

Bradley, Collins, General Vandenberg, and Admiral Sherman met on the afternoon of April 8 in the Pentagon and discussed military aspects of MacArthur's relief. At the end of this conference, they conferred briefly with Marshall. All of the Joint Chiefs of Staff agreed that from the military viewpoint the relief of MacArthur should be carried out. There was no vote, but their unanimous view that MacArthur had violated policies was conveyed to Truman.

Collins said, "It was not easy to be a party to the dismissal of a distinguished soldier." He testified during a congressional hearing on the removal that he based his belief on two factors. He was convinced that MacArthur had not been in sympathy with policies governing the operation of United Nations forces in Korea. "I felt," he explained, "that the President, as our Commander in Chief, was entitled to have as a commander in the field a man who was more in sympathy with the basic policies and more responsive to the will of the President as Commander in Chief." He also felt that MacArthur had failed to comply with instructions directing him to clear any public statement that involved matters of policy, particularly on foreign policy.

After receiving the views of his principal advisors on April 9, Truman made the decision to relieve General MacArthur of his command in the Far East. Ridgway was to replace him, and on Collins's recommendation Lieutenant General James Van Fleet was to become the new commanding general of the Eighth Army.

Truman originally intended to notify MacArthur of his relief at 8:00 p.m. Washington time on April 11 (10:00 a.m. Tokyo time on April 12). A message was sent to Secretary of the Army Pace, then visiting in Korea, telling him to deliver the relief message to MacArthur at his residence at the time indicated. Unfortunately, a breakdown in a communications power unit in Pusan kept Pace from receiving the instructions. By this time, there were indications in Washington that the firing of MacArthur had gotten beyond the walls of the White House and Pentagon. Truman decided to accelerate MacArthur's official notification by approximately twenty hours. It didn't matter. In Tokyo, MacArthur learned that he had been relieved from his wife, Jean. One of his aides heard the news on a radio broadcast, told her, and Jean told MacArthur half an hour before the official word arrived. When he read it, he said to her, "Jeannie, we're going home."

He had not been in the United States since he went to the Philippines in 1935. His return would not be that of a disgraced general; rather, he returned to a hero's welcome that began when his airplane, *Bataan*, landed after midnight in Honolulu, Hawaii, where World War II started for Americans. When he reached the nation's capital, once again past midnight, the Joint Chiefs of Staff, on Truman's order that MacArthur get the full military honors, met him with salutes and handshakes. Truman also gave government employees the day off, adding them to the crowd that lined the way to the Capitol, where both houses of Congress waited in a joint meeting to hear the address that Joseph Martin had invited MacArthur to give. In the galleries above the floor of the House of Representatives, television cameras of every network were positioned to carry the speech to the largest audience in television's brief history.*

In answer to those who had said he wanted a wider war, MacArthur said that he knew war "as few other men living know it, and nothing to me is more revolting."

In a deep and rolling tone, he continued, "But once war is forced upon us, there is no alternative than to apply every available means to bring it to a swift end. War's very object is victory."

Mindful of pressures on Washington by European leaders who worried that the United States was diverted by Korea and Communist expansion in Asia, he warned, "Don't scuttle the Pacific."

Telling Congress and the American people at the end of the speech that he was an "old soldier who tried to do his duty as God gave him the light to see that duty," he said he was closing his military career and intended to "just fade away."

New Yorkers decided that he couldn't disappear until they'd given him their traditional salute with a parade.

There had been none like it.

---

*Author's note: In my high school in my hometown of Phoenixville, Pennsylvania, all classes were suspended and students and faculty gathered in the assembly hall to watch the drama on television. This happened in schools and workplaces from coast to coast. Stores that sold TVs were crowded with people who came in just to see MacArthur.

The procession with MacArthur in a convertible stretched through nineteen and a half miles of the island of Manhattan. From the tip at the Battery to midtown and back again, seven and a half million admirers cheered amid ticker tape, confetti, and flags. The welcoming was twice the size of the one the city gave for Eisenhower in 1945 and exceeded the welcome given in 1927 to the aviator Charles Lindbergh after his unprecedented solo flight across the Atlantic. For a brief period there was a "MacArthur for president" movement.

For Joseph Lawton Collins, the firing of MacArthur meant giving testimony in hearings held by the Senate. Asked about the performance of South Korean troops, he replied in a New Orleans drawl, "Every time they were hit by the Chinamen, they just plain run." Even as he testified, he appreciated that Korea had ceased to be a war run by generals, but had become an embarrassment for Truman's administration that would be settled by talking to an enemy that was receiving orders from Peking while China was being directed from the Kremlin by Joseph Stalin. With Ridgway's forces under the UN banner, they were constrained by global political factors, with the result that the battlefield settled into a stalemate that lasted for two years after MacArthur's departure. On July 27, 1953, Stalin was gone, having died in March, Eisenhower was president, and the Chinese were seated opposite the American and UN representatives at a conference table, the size and shape of which had been agreed upon after lengthy negotiations. When they got up, an armistice was in place that would be the closest thing to a peace treaty well into the new millennium and leave Korea divided with American troops standing guard at the thirty-eighth parallel for six decades and no end in sight.

A month after the armistice, Collins reached the end of his four-year term as army chief of staff. Although he was eligible to retire, and planned to do so happily with Gladys, he was presented with another twist of fate by the inauguration of the nation's thirty-fourth commander in chief.

CHAPTER SEVENTEEN

AT THE PLEASURE
OF THE PRESIDENT

I n the autumn of 1950, President Truman had asked Eisenhower to leave the presidency of Columbia University and don his uniform to take the reins of NATO. He served from December 19, 1950, until he was implored by moderate to liberal Republicans to seek the GOP presidential nomination in 1952. Mostly from eastern states, they hoped to block a bid by the conservative Ohio senator Robert A. Taft, known as "Mr. Republican." Persuaded that he could not only become the GOP standard-bearer but the first Republican president since Herbert Hoover lost to FDR in 1932, Ike left NATO. After an intense battle for the majority of delegates at the Chicago convention, he won the nomination. Because Truman decided not to run again, the Democrats picked Illinois governor Adlai E. Stevenson. The outcome of a campaign Ike called "a crusade" was another Eisenhower victory.

As the NATO Supreme Allied Commander in Europe (SACEUR), he had not been satisfied with the support he received from a group of French, British, and U.S. military advisors called the "Standing Group." Desirous of "putting more drive" into it, and persuading NATO members to fulfill their troop commitments, he asked Collins to remain on active duty and accept appointment as the U.S. member of the Standing Group for two years in order "to get things done."

Acceptance of the assignment required Collins to move to Paris and visit each of the European members of NATO that failed to live up to its obligations to provide troops. He found that he'd known most of the defense ministers and their staffs in World War II, but he discovered that he had little influence with them on the issue that concerned Eisenhower. Appeals for fuller support of NATO delivered with all the good-old-boy Southern charm Collins could muster were answered with excuses that cited a host of "economic difficulties" resulting from the war. No one stated that their real reason for not bolstering NATO's military strength was their recognition that the main deterrent to a Soviet attempt to take over Europe was the U.S. Army in Germany and the U.S. Air Force's long-range bombers loaded with nuclear weapons.

After a year of frustration, Collins received a new assignment that plunged him into a cauldron of political intrigue. An adventure in high-stakes cold war strategy that would take him halfway around the world began on Saturday night, October 30, 1954. Having gone to Oklahoma City to address a civic group luncheon, he was spending a quiet evening as the guest of General and Mrs. Ray McLain. Their conversation was interrupted by a phone call for Collins from an Eisenhower aide, who told him in a mysterious tone that he was to return to Washington the following day for a meeting with Secretary of State John Foster Dulles.

The aide added in a whisper worthy of an Alfred Hitchcock spy thriller that Collins would be going on a special mission to meet with "Iron Mike." Collins knew immediately that he referred to Lieutenant General John W. "Iron Mike" O'Daniel. A tough combat commander in World War II, he was the head of an American military assistance group in Vietnam.

In May 1954, as French colonial forces at Dien Bien Phu fought the Vietminh Communists under Ho Chi Minh, France had appealed for U.S. intervention with air strikes. Eisenhower had declined. In his account of his years as president, *Mandate for Change*, he wrote that air attacks at Dien Bien Phu would have been ineffective, but he said that "the strongest reason" for the United States' refusal to respond to French pleas was the American tradition of anticolonialism. With the French having collapsed in Indochina, a conference was held in Geneva to formally bring an end to the fighting. Vietnam was divided at the seventeenth parallel, with the Communists given the north and the south given to the government of Ngo Dinh Diem, pending the holding of a plebiscite in two years on the question of whether the country was to be reunited. Appointed as president by the former emperor, Bao Dai, living in exile in France, Diem had a tenuous relationship with the French while the Communists posed a military threat to the south.

When Collins arrived at Bolling Field in Washington on Sunday, October 31, 1954, he was told to go to Secretary of State John Foster Dulles's home. During the meeting, Dulles explained to Collins that because the U.S. ambassador in Vietnam, Donald R. Heath, was due for a change of station, and his replacement's nomination had yet to be sent for approval by the Senate, Eisenhower had suggested that in the meantime Collins was the perfect choice to go to Saigon "to take a fresh look at the situation" and recommend an assistance program that would "reinforce the political and economic stability" of the Diem government. Collins would have the rank of Ike's personal ambassador. The title designation meant that he would not have to be confirmed by the Senate and could retain his army commission. He would relinquish his membership on the NATO Standing Committee temporarily.

Having been to Vietnam in 1951 as army chief of staff, Collins had kept up his interest in the country and followed attempts by the French to retain Indochina as a colony. While in Paris with NATO, he had met the present French commissioner general in Saigon, General Paul Ely, when Ely served on the NATO Standing Group.

During the conference at Dulles's home, the secretary of state stated that he thought Collins's chance of success on his Vietnam mission was one in ten, but he and Eisenhower believed that the importance of checking the spread of Communism in Southeast Asia was worth the effort.

At a press conference, Eisenhower had stated a U.S. policy in Southeast Asia that would be followed by Presidents John F. Kennedy, Lyndon Johnson, and Richard Nixon. He called it the "falling domino" principle. He said, "You have a row of dominoes set up, you knock over the first one, and what will happen to the last one is the certainty that it will go over very quickly. So you could have a beginning of a disintegration [in Asia] that would have the most profound influences."

Noting that the region had already lost 450 million people to a Communist dictatorship in China, he said, "We simply can't afford greater losses. But when we come to the possible sequence of events, the loss of Indochina [Vietnam], of Burma, of Thailand, of the [Malaysian] Peninsula, and Indonesia following, now you begin to talk about areas that not only multiply the disadvantages that you would suffer through the loss of materials, sources of materials, but now you are talking about millions and millions of people. Finally, the geographical position achieved thereby does many things. It turns the so-called island defensive chain of Japan, Formosa, of the Philippines and southward; [and] it moves in to threaten Australia and New Zealand."

The consensus of the conferees at Dulles's home was that Collins should leave for Saigon as soon as possible. Dulles estimated that he would be there for sixty to ninety days. Taking it for granted that he would gladly serve "at the pleasure of the president," as such appointments were customarily accepted, no one asked him if he would take the assignment. After numerous meetings, briefings, and consultations with Dulles and others with knowledge of Vietnam and problems facing the Diem regime, he went with Dulles to the White House to see Eisenhower. The president read a letter aloud that described Collins's objectives. After signing it, Eisenhower told Collins he was pleased that the appointment gave him broad authority to direct, use, and control all of the agencies and resources of the United States in Vietnam, and to speak with full authority of the U.S. government in support of maintaining a free government in Vietnam. He would also assist Diem in developing forces solely for its internal security.

On November 3, 1954, the *New York Times* carried an Associated Press story on Collins's appointment as a presidential "special aide in Vietnam" and recorded Eisenhower's concern about "the dangerous forces threatening South Vietnam." Three days later, the *Times* headline on an AP report from Saigon read "Task in Vietnam for Collins Hard." The dispatch stated that he was heading to Vietnam "at a critical moment in the struggle to prevent Communism from grabbing another big chunk of Southeast Asia." Collins and five members of his special mission arrived in Saigon in midmorning on November 8 and were met at the airport by Iron Mike, the embassy chargé d'affaires, Randolph A. Kidder, embassy staff, and Tran Van Don as Diem's representative. Told that Paul Ely was at the summer residence of the French high commissioner in Dalat, 150 miles from Saigon, Collins realized that the French "were not happy" about his mission.

After meetings at the U.S. embassy, Collins went to the Norodom Palace to meet Diem. Wearing a white sharkskin suit, the black-haired, pudgy, pleasantly smiling, ascetic-looking president who greeted him at the head of a marble staircase appeared self-conscious and not quite sure of himself. Like most first impressions, it proved wrong. Collins soon realized that Diem possessed a steely tenacity and had a stubborn character that would infuriate the elder statesmen of Eisenhower's inner circle, such as

John Foster Dulles and his brother Allen at the helm of the Central Intelligence Agency, and later younger men surrounding President Kennedy, whom the reporter and author David Halberstam in his book on Vietnam would call "the best and the brightest."

When Collins met with Ely, the French general's mood was a cool formality that conveyed his government's lack of enthusiasm for America's intrusion into the affairs in Saigon and the Eisenhower administration's support of Diem. A Catholic president in an almost wholly Buddhist country, Diem won the support of Catholics in Congress, including Senators Mike Mansfield and John F. Kennedy and Congressman Walter Judd, as well as New York City's influential Francis Cardinal Spellman.

Although Diem was president of the governing Council of Ministers, the real power was held by his brother, Ngo Dinh Nhu, and his wife, known as Madam Nhu. In language that reads like a passage in a mystery or spy novel, Collins wrote that he rarely saw Nhu but was always conscious of his influence in the background. His beautiful wife was "highly visible" as Diem's official hostess and was described by Collins as a "vixen" who constantly meddled in politics. Other members of the Ngo family held offices in the government. One of the brothers was an archbishop who worked for Catholic support abroad, and another was ambassador to the United Kingdom. That Collins was Catholic was less important to them than his lofty rank as Eisenhower's personal envoy with authority to shape American policy in Vietnam.

For the vast majority of the American people at this time, Vietnam was not a concern. They had elected Eisenhower to bring an end to the war in Korea and were relieved that the guns were silent and no more draftees would be sent into combat. They felt confident that the general who had commanded the army that ended the war with Germany would keep the Russians at bay and make sure that Asian countries would not topple one by one like dominoes into Communist control. So what if Ike liked to get away from the White House to golf and fish? Or that the liberal elite took a swipe at him and those who elected him by calling him "chairman of the bored."

If stopping the Reds in Asia meant handing the South Vietnamese government a U.S. Treasury check for $25,571,428 to aid refugees who'd fled the Communist north, as Collins did on December 21, 1954, Americans thought it was a humane and noble thing to do, especially at Christmastime.

While Collins gladly demonstrated American generosity to the Vietnamese people, he had come to the conclusion that support for Diem was no longer a viable policy because Diem was unwilling to give up control of the armed services, thereby jeopardizing Iron Mike O'Daniel's mission to develop an effective army. In a cable to Secretary of State Dulles, who was in Paris to confer with the French president and Anthony Eden of the U.K. on Vietnam issues, Collins proposed that the United States should either find a reliable replacement for Diem or withdraw support for the South Vietnamese. Dulles replied that Collins should review the situation in mid-January. On January 20, 1955, he reported his opinion that "free Vietnam" could not match the military capability of the Communist Vietminh to overrun all of Vietnam. He also harbored suspicions of French objectives.

Summoned back to Washington on January 22, 1955, for meetings at the State Department and the JCS at the Pentagon, he also met with Eisenhower and learned that Diem had asked that the Collins mission be extended. Ike discussed this with Collins and on February 3 replied to Diem that Collins would stay for another two months. After a respite with his family at a cottage that Collins had bought on the shore of Chesapeake Bay, he returned to Saigon on February 9 and stepped into a hornet's nest. Diem had decided to crack down on various sects that had their own military units and ran lucrative businesses, including the Grande Monde gambling casino in the Cholon district. On the night of March 29, Collins was awakened by the sound of machine-gun fire and mortars from Cholon. Standing on an upper porch, he watched tracers rising over the district and the flashes of explosions in the direction of Norodom Palace. In the morning, he was told that in a battle that took place at the police headquarters between a sect force and the government, ten Vietnamese were killed and forty wounded.

On March 31, a truce was arranged and the French were recommending that ex-emperor Bao Dai meet in Paris with all sides. The State Department rejected the plan and told Collins to make it clear that Washington remained committed to Diem. On April 7, Paul Ely informed Collins that France would no longer support Diem. After pondering the situation, Collins reluctantly came to the conclusion that he must also propose to Washington that it might be time to cut ties with Diem. He sent a cable to Dulles saying that he felt Diem was "not indispensable" and that to save South Vietnam from Communism, the United States should look elsewhere for a leader in Saigon.

On April 17, Collins was called back to Washington with the cover story that he was to discuss the budget. At a meeting with Eisenhower and Dulles at the White House, a decision was made to notify U.S. diplomats in Paris to inform Bao Dai that the United States was still supporting Diem, but was open to any suggestion by Bao Dai regarding a replacement for Diem as president. Collins saw this as "wavering." While in Washington, he learned of renewed fighting in Saigon and that Diem had brought in the army to suppress the sects responsible. Meanwhile, Diem's allies on Capitol Hill heard about the likelihood that Diem would be removed. Senator Mike Mansfield warned that if Diem went, so would any further Senate action on military aid to Vietnam. When a large number of House members echoed the threat, Dulles ordered his men in Paris to ignore his previous instructions.

Advised that Eisenhower's nomination of C. Frederick Reinhart to be the new ambassador to Vietnam would soon obtain Senate approval, Collins returned to the turmoil in Saigon and began working on his final estimation of the situation and his suggestions for future American policy. Sent to Dulles on May 5, 1954, it said that as soon as the current crisis was over, "decisive efforts must be made to persuade or otherwise force Diem to reorganize his government." If Diem did not, the United States should join with France and Bao Dai in assisting liberal nationalists to set in place "a competent government."

He concluded, "No matter who heads the government here, free Vietnam will not be saved unless sound political, economic, and military programs are promptly and effectively put into action. This will require wholehearted agreement and coordination between the Vietnamese, Americans and French. Difficult as this may be to achieve, it is possible, in my judgment. If this tripartite approach is not secured, we should withdraw from Vietnam."

The three-sided solution Collins proposed never happened, leaving Vietnam solely an American problem. Upon the arrival of the U.S. ambassador, Collins left Saigon on May 14, 1954. Meeting with Eisenhower and Dulles, he said to the man who had put him in command of the Seventh Corps in 1944, "I hope, Mr. President, that you and Secretary Dulles do not feel that I have let you down in Vietnam."

Dulles answered, "By no means, Joe. When you went out, we thought there was a ten percent chance of saving Vietnam from Communism. You have raised that figure to at least fifty percent."

The next day, Collins was again the U.S. representative on the NATO Standing Group and remained in the job into the last year of Eisenhower's second term.

When John F. Kennedy inherited Vietnam, France had abandoned its former colony and the North Vietnamese had launched a war against the South. Eisenhower had spent a billion and a half dollars supporting South Vietnam and provided a small number

of military advisors. A believer in the domino theory and determined not to allow a Communist victory in Vietnam, Kennedy
sent his military advisor, General Maxwell Taylor, to South Vietnam to assess the situation. He proposed that a task force of seven
thousand combat troops be sent to demonstrate American resolve
to keep South Vietnam free and to bolster Diem.

By May 1963, Saigon was aflame with opposition to Diem,
including the deaths of several Buddhist monks who publicly set
themselves on fire. Madam Nhu called the immolations "Buddhist bonfires." When her husband blamed the unrest on generals, they plotted to overthrow Diem, Nhu, and all of his family.
Disenchanted with Diem, Kennedy gave his blessing to Ambassador Henry Cabot Lodge to open secret talks with the generals.
Encouraged by this official American approval, they moved to
seize control of the government.

As fighting raged, Diem phoned Lodge and demanded to
know the position of the United States. Lodge said he was "not
acquainted with all the facts," but that he had a report that "those
in charge of the current activity" offered Diem and Nhu safe conduct out of the country if Diem resigned.

By the time the rebels captured the presidential palace on November 1, 1963, Diem and Nhu had fled to the Cholon section.
Contacting the generals, they were assured of safe passage from
the country. Believing they were safely on their way to exile, they
boarded an armored personnel carrier.

Moments later, they were murdered.

Although Kennedy and his men had no way of knowing that
Diem would be killed, by showing that they were not against
overthrowing him the United States had in effect taken over South
Vietnam and the conduct of the war. Three weeks after Diem's
death, Kennedy was assassinated and Lyndon Johnson inherited
Vietnam with a determination to defeat the Communists by increasing the levels of U.S. troops in increments that opponents of
the war called "escalation."

Writing his autobiography in 1979, with the Vietnam War having ended four years earlier with a Communist victory, and the first U.S. defeat in a war in its history, Collins wrote, "Unfortunately, my forecast of Diem's inability to overcome the vast obstacles that beset him proved to be largely correct. Despite his, and our, failures in Vietnam, he was a dedicated Vietnamese patriot whose brutal murder was despicable and wholly unwarranted. He deserved a better fate at the hands of his countrymen."

"GOOD LUCK TO YOU, BOY"

O n March 23, 1956, after forty-three years in the U.S.
Army, Collins submitted retirement papers to become
effective eight days later. He departed the Pentagon and crossed
the Potomac River to the White House to bid official farewell to
Eisenhower. Amid a cluster of reporters, press photographers,
and television news cameras, Ike turned on the famous smile,
shook Collins's hand, gave his shoulder a fatherly squeeze, and
said, "Good luck to you, boy."

No one had called him a boy since his childhood in New Orleans, and no one since then could have gotten away with it but
the general who had done so much to advance the army career of
Lightning Joe Collins. Although George C. Marshall had brought
him from the Pacific theater and suggested that Eisenhower consider him for a command in Europe, it was Ike who entrusted the
Seventh Corps and the outcome of the Utah Beach landing and
capture of Cherbourg to him. In command of the corps from then
to the finish of the Third Reich, he had been at the center of the
toughest fights of the European war and proven MacArthur was
wrong in saying he was too young to head a corps. It was Ike as

chief of staff who had tapped him to be his deputy and successor, then his eyes and ears in Vietnam.

Following the meeting with Eisenhower in the Oval Office, Collins went to Fort McNair for a last salute from the army. Standing beside him for a last review of troops were two other World War II vets, General John E. Dahlquist and Lieutenant General Floyd L. Parks. A *New York Times* editorial on March 24, 1956, said, "These men and their peers deserve the honors richly. They had served their country and their fellow men in the best sense of the term. They—and others of their generation now unfortunately nearing retirement age—provided the leadership in World War II for the greatest army the United States has ever raised, and they furnished the command echelons in Korea. They have fought the good fight and deserve well of their country."

When Collins wrote his autobiography in 1979, he reflected on nearly half a century of army life. He wrote, "Forty-eight years ago, with my eyes wide open, I decided to forgo a career as a lawyer and to stick to the profession of soldier that I had chosen as a youngster in 1913. I have thought over that decision many times since and always with the same result—I have no regrets, though I have had to make some philosophical adjustments along the way. The lack of roots in a permanent home community, which I and my wife have felt, has been compensated for by our association with the wonderful, dedicated people who make up the corps of officers of the United States Army."

Two days after his official retirement date, he and Gladys sailed from New York on the German ocean liner *Bremerhaven* for six months of vacationing on the continent he had helped liberate and protect from a Soviet invasion. They planned to drive through parts of Europe he had not seen in the war, including Spain, Provence in France, and the Italian lake region, in a Renault sedan he bought while in Paris with NATO that he left with Gladys's brother, Major General Ernest Easterbrook. After a nine-thousand-mile odyssey, they returned to Washington and settled for the first time in an apartment.

A new building at 4000 Massachusetts N.W., it was near the home of his brother James. Also retired after a long army career, he had a son, James Lawton Collins, Jr., who had led a battalion of the North Dakota National Guard onto Utah Beach and served in Korea. A graduate of West Point in 1939, the younger James had two daughters, Corrine and Suzanne, and two sons, James III and Michael (Mike), who had chosen to serve his country in the air force.

The decision to join the air force was based on a lifetime interest in aviation and to avoid any accusations of nepotism if he joined the army while his uncle was chief of staff. After entering the air force, he completed his flight training and was chosen for advanced day-fighter training in jets. This was followed by assignment to a wing of nuclear bombers. Relocated to Chaumont, France, where his father had been Pershing's aide-de-camp in World War I, he took part in a training exercise in the summer of 1956 and was forced to eject from an F-86 after a fire started behind the cockpit. He was safely rescued and returned to Chaumont. While in France, he met Patricia Finnegan working in an officers' mess. Mike was Episcopalian because his father left the Catholic Church when he married a Protestant. After getting engaged, Mike had the same dilemma that faced his uncle Joe. He asked Patricia's father for his permission to marry her despite the religious difference, but the wedding was put off because Mike was sent to West Germany as U.S. forces in Europe went on alert following the outbreak of a rebellion against Soviet domination in Hungary in the fall of 1956.

As Russian tanks occupied Budapest and other Hungarian cities and towns to put down the uprising, Britain, France, and Israel attacked Egypt and seized control of the Suez Canal, which Egyptian president Gamal Abdel Nasser had nationalized. The dual invasions left President Eisenhower in the awkward position in which cold war allies were carrying out a surprise attack at the same time the Russians were crushing Hungarian rebels. All he could do was denounce both and help thousands of Hungarians who had fled from the Russians to Austria by creating a committee of prominent Americans to supervise a program for admitting some of the refugees into the United States.

When Collins heard about the committee on the radio, and that a former undersecretary of the army and friend, Tracy S. Voorhees, was chairman, he called him to offer his services. That very morning, Voorhees named Collins as vice chairman and director. Although the committee was not a U.S. government entity, it was backed by Eisenhower and closely coordinated with federal agencies and the Department of Defense. The army provided a World War II troop-handling center, Camp Kilmer, New Jersey, close to the port of New York, to receive and process refugees, and the Military Air Transport Service handled air force and navy flights from Europe. The Red Cross formed a motor corps to take refugees from Camp Kilmer to the railroad stations and airports to settle in cities and towns from coast to coast.

In one of the great humanitarian achievements of the twentieth century that has been all but forgotten since 1956, and eclipsed by other cold war events, more than thirty-two thousand Hungarians were taken in by the United States, including engineers, doctors, teachers, musicians, writers, lawyers, and skilled craftsmen. On May 14, 1957, the committee reported to Eisenhower that its work was completed and recommended its own dissolution.

Five months before Collins ended his role in assisting victims of the Soviet Union's grip on Eastern Europe, he began work with a group that was forming as a result of Eisenhower having called a conference in Washington, D.C., as part of a "people to people" program that Eisenhower hoped would promote understanding between Americans and the rest of the world and thereby show that democracy, freedom, and capitalism were superior to Communism. Asked to be chairman of the Foreign Student Service Council (FSSC), Collins accepted. The purpose of the organization was to assist foreign students enrolled in universities in the Washington area to adapt to the city and meet with members of Congress, the heads and staffs of federal agencies and departments, and private citizens.

This association resulted in Collins being invited to become a member of the board of directors of the Institute of International Education (IIE). The nonprofit private organization developed and administered educational exchanges for other groups, including foundations, corporations, and U.S. colleges and universities. With headquarters in New York and offices across the country and around the world, the IIE assisted more than seven thousand students, teachers, technicians, and specialists from 125 countries to study or train, and to learn about the United States and carry favorable impressions of America and its peaceful intentions home to counter Soviet propaganda to the contrary. After assuming chairmanship of the IIE advisory committee in Washington in 1958, Collins remained with the IIE until 1965.

"Worthwhile as these volunteer activities were," Collins wrote, "they added nothing to the family coffers. Gladys and I had acquired six grandchildren with more in prospect, who someday would need help with their education. So my ears pricked up when I received a phone call in mid-January 1957 from General Ed Hull, then president of the Chemical Manufacturers Association, inquiring if I would be interested in joining the board of directors of Charles Pfizer and Company."

At a meeting with Pfizer executives, Collins made it clear that he would do no lobbying or other business on behalf of the drug development and manufacturing firm with the Department of Defense and that he wished to continue to reside in Washington. He also said that he expected Gladys to be allowed to accompany him on any foreign travels for the company. He signed a contract on April 1, 1957, and was elected to the Pfizer board on April 15. The relationship with the firm that took him and Gladys on numerous trips to Europe and Asia continued until he retired in April 1969.

At the end of March 1969, he was an honorary pallbearer, along with Omar Bradley and Alfred Gruenther, at Eisenhower's funeral in Washington and for the interment at Abilene, Kansas.

That year, Houghton Mifflin published his reflections on the Korean conflict in *War in Peacetime*. On July 20, 1969, he and Gladys sat before a TV screen, as did the nation and much of the world, while astronaut Mike Collins, now a captain in the air force, became the family's best-known member by piloting the command module of Apollo 11 in orbit around the moon while Neil Armstrong and Buzz Aldrin went down to the lunar surface to collect rocks and soil, take pictures of themselves with the earth in the background, and erect a pole bearing the American flag.

It was an achievement not seen by Collins's brother and Michael's father. On June 30, 1963, James Lawton Collins had died of a heart attack at Walter Reed Army Hospital in Washington, D.C., at the age of eighty. With his passing, only five of the ten children of Jeremiah Collins and Catherine Lawton Collins remained. Peter lived in New York and Bernard was in Montgomery, Alabama. Agnes was unmarried and Margaret was Mrs. McDonald. Both lived close enough to Joe in Washington, D.C., to visit him and Gladys regularly and to spend time with them in the cottage they'd named Jayhawk Rest on the Chesapeake shore.

From 1959 to 1962, James Lawton Collins's other son and namesake had been commanding officer of the U.S. Army Language School at Monterey, California, and became the first director of the Defense Language Institute in Washington. In both posts, James, Jr., was able to hold conversations with the students in French, Italian, German, Spanish, and Russian. Having acquired a taste for German wines while serving in Germany, he would retire from the army in 1982 and become a member of a wine cooperative in Virginia and a grower of vinifera grapes at his Middleburg home, harvesting as much as two tons a year. In the Vietnam War, he was a special assistant to General William Westmoreland. As a military historian, he wrote articles on the Vietnam War and coedited the *D-Day Encyclopedia*, containing articles by more than one hundred military historians, including the story of Joseph Lawton Collins's Seventh Corps, and his nephew James's account of leading artillerymen onto Utah Beach. More than fifty years after the war, James Lawton Collins, Jr., was still making trips to North Dakota for 975th Field Artillery Battalion reunions. He died of a pulmonary embolism on May 6, 2002.

Having written about the Korean War, Joseph Lawton Collins decided that it was time to set down in a book his experiences and thoughts on World War II. He titled it *Lightning Joe*. It was published in 1979 to acclaim by military historians and reviewers for the general public.

On May 17, 1983, the Fort Leavenworth Hall of Fame, established to honor American soldiers whom a panel of historians chose for contributing significantly to the defense of the United States, recognized Lightning Joe Collins as "the best corps commander during World War II." Informing the organizers that he didn't want to travel to Kansas "just for a ceremony," he asked to talk with students and faculty of the Command and General Staff School. He reminded them that he had also taken the course, but declined to accept a teaching post because he wanted to lead troops.

As a general who had been in combat in both the Pacific and Europe, he was asked to compare Japanese and German soldiers. He replied, "The Japanese were very gallant men. They fought very, very hard, but they were not as skillful as the Germans. But the Germans didn't have the tenacity of the Japanese."

In June 1984, he was President Ronald Reagan's personal

representative at Normandy for fortieth-anniversary ceremonies remembering D-day, at which Reagan delivered a memorable speech on June 6 atop the cliffs of Point du Hoc above Omaha Beach. For Collins on that day, the memories that flooded back were of the men of the Seventh Corps at Utah Beach.

Three years, three months, and eleven days later, their commander died of cardiac arrest at home with Gladys. At ninety-one years of age, Collins had outlived Marshall, Ike, Bradley, Montgomery, Patton, Terrible Terry Allen, Tubby Barton, Courtney Hodges, and MacArthur. Among his decorations were the Distinguished Service Medal, two Silver Stars (one for Guadalcanal), Order of the Crown of both Italy and Belgium, the Legion of Honor, the Croix de Guerre, the Russian Order of Sukorov, and the British Companion of the Order of the Bath.

On the day of Collins's death, his son, Colonel Joseph E. "Jerry" Collins, was retired from the army and living in Lewiston, Idaho. Nancy's married name was Rubino and she resided in Bethesda, Maryland. Gladdie (married name Stenger) made her home in Potomac, Maryland. There were seventeen grandchildren and eight great-grandchildren. After a Mass of Christian Burial at Fort Myer Chapel, he was given all the military honors available to every American soldier at the Arlington National Cemetery. When Gladys died two years later, she was buried next to him.

COLLINS CHRONOLOGY

- Born in New Orleans, Louisiana, on May 1,1896
- Graduated from the United States Military Academy in 1917, and commissioned a second lieutenant and assigned to the Twenty-second Infantry, April 1917
- Promoted to first lieutenant, May 1917, and temporary captain, August 1917
- Attended the Infantry School of Arms at Fort Sill and served with his regiment at various locations, 1917–19
- Promoted to captain, June 1918, and to temporary major, September 1918
- Commanded the Third Battalion, Twenty-second Infantry, in France, 1919
- Reverted to captain, 1920
- Assistant chief of staff of American forces in Germany, 1920–21
- Married Gladys Easterbrook, 1921
- Instructor in the department of chemistry at West Point, 1921–25

- Graduated from the company officer course at Infantry School, Fort Benning, 1926
- Graduated from the advanced course at the Field Artillery School, Fort Sill, 1927
- Instructor in weapons and tactics at the Infantry School, 1927–31
- Promoted to major, August 1932
- Executive officer, Twenty-third Brigade, Manila, and assistant chief of staff of the Philippine Division, 1933–34
- Graduated from the Army Industrial College, 1937
- Graduated from the Army War College, 1938
- Instructor at the Army War College, 1938–40
- Promoted to lieutenant colonel, June 1940
- Chief of staff of the Seventh Corps, 1941
- Promoted to the temporary rank of colonel, January 1941
- Promoted to brigadier general (temporary), February 1942
- Promoted to major general (temporary), May 1942
- Chief of staff of the Hawaiian Department, 1941–42
- Commanding general, Twenty-fifth Infantry Division, on Oahu and in operations against the Japanese on Guadalcanal, 1942–43
- Commander of the Seventh Corps, 1944–45
- Promoted to temporary lieutenant general (April) and permanent brigadier general (June), 1945
- Deputy commander and chief of staff, Ground Forces, August–December 1945
- Director of information (later chief of public information), 1945–47

- Deputy (later vice) chief of staff of the United States Army, 1947–49

- Promoted to temporary general and permanent major general, January 1948

- Chief of staff of the United States Army, August 16, 1949–August 15, 1953

- Representative of the United States to the Military Committee and Standing Group of NATO, 1953–54

- Special representative of the United States in Vietnam with ambassadorial rank, 1954–55; returned to his NATO assignment

- Retired from active service, March 1956

- Director, Hungarian refugee relief, 1956–57

- Chairman, Foreign Student Service Council, 1957

- Board of Directors, Institute of International Education, 1957

- Board of Directors, Charles Pfizer and Company, 1957–69

- Published *War in Peacetime*, 1969

- Published autobiography, *Lightning Joe*, 1979

- Died in Washington, D.C., on September 12, 1987

CHAIN OF COMMAND AND ORDER OF BATTLE,

June–August 1944

SUPREME ALLIED COMMANDER,
Gen. Dwight D. Eisenhower

COMMANDER, TWENTY-FIRST ARMY GROUP,
Gen. Sir Bernard L. Montgomery

COMMANDER, FIRST ARMY,
Lt. Gen. Omar N. Bradley

COMMANDER, SEVENTH CORPS,
Maj. Gen, J. Lawton Collins

UNIT	COMMANDER
FOURTH DIVISION	Maj. Gen. Raymond O. Barton
EIGHTH INFANTRY	Col. James A. Van Fleet
TWELFTH INFANTRY	Col. Russell P. Reeder; Lt. Col. James S. Luckett (June 11)
TWENTY-SECOND INFANTRY	Col. Herbert Tribolet
NINTH DIVISION	Maj. Gen. Manton S. Eddy
THIRTY-NINTH INFANTRY	Col. Harry A. Flint
FORTY-SEVENTH INFANTRY	Col. George W. Smythe
SIXTIETH INFANTRY	Col. Frederick J. de Rohan
SEVENTY-NINTH DIVISION	Maj. Gen. Ira T. Wyche
313TH INFANTRY	Col. Sterling A. Wood
314TH INFANTRY	Col. Warren A. Robinson
315TH INFANTRY	Col. Porter P. Wiggins; Col. Bernard B. McMahon (June 24)
EIGHTY-SECOND AIRBORNE	Maj. Gen. Matthew B. Ridgway
505TH PARACHUTE INFANTRY	Col. William E. Ekman

UNIT	COMMANDER
507TH PARACHUTE INFANTRY	Col. George V. Millett, Jr.; Col. E. D. Ruff (June 15)
508TH PARACHUTE INFANTRY	Col. Roy E. Lindquist
325TH GLIDER INFANTRY	Col. Harry L. Lewis
NINETIETH DIVISION	Brig. Gen. Jay W. MacKelvie; Maj. Gen. Eugene M. Landrum (June 13)
357TH INFANTRY	Col. Philip D. Ginder; Col. John W. Sheehy (June 13); Lt. Col. Charles M. Schwab (June 15)
358TH INFANTRY	Col. James V. Thompson; Col. Christian H. Clark, Jr. (June 12); Col. Richard C. Partridge (June 16)
359TH INFANTRY	Col. Clarke K. Fales
101ST AIRBORNE DIVISION	Maj. Gen. Maxwell D. Taylor
501ST PARACHUTE INFANTRY	Col. Howard R. Johnson
502ND PARACHUTE INFANTRY	Col. George H. W. Mosley; Lt. Col. John H. Michaelis (June 6)
506TH PARACHUTE INFANTRY	Col. Robert F. Sink
327TH GLIDER INFANTRY	Col. George S. Wear; Col. Joseph H. Harper (June 10)
FOURTH CAVALRY GROUP	Col. Joseph M. Tully
FOURTH CAVALRY SQUADRON	Lt. Col. E. C. Dunn
TWENTY-FOURTH CAVALRY SQUADRON	Lt. Col. F. H. Gaston, Jr.
SIXTH ARMORED GROUP	Col. Frances F. Fainter
SEVENTIETH TANK BATTALION	Lt. Col. John C. Welborn
746TH TANK BATTALION	Lt. Col. C. G. Hupfer

SEVENTH CORPS BATTLE CASUALTIES REPORT,

June 6, 1944–July 1, 1944

UNIT	TOTAL	KILLED	WOUNDED	MISSING	CAPTURED
All Units	21,119	2,811	13,564	5,663	79
Fourth Div.	5,452	844	3,814	788	6
Ninth Div.	2,438	301	2,061	76	0
Seventy-ninth Div.	2,376	240	1,896	240	0
Ninetieth Div.	2,339	386	1,979	34	0
Eighty-second AB Div.	4,480	457	1,440	2,573	12
101st AB Div.	4,670	546	2,247	1,907	0
Corps Troops	304	37	157	49	61

Source: Seventh Corps Reports, June 1944

SEVENTH CORPS STATISTICS

- Number of days in combat: 337
- Total miles traveled across Europe: 1,200
- Greatest advance in one day: 90 miles
- Enemy divisions encountered: 51
- Enemy divisions destroyed: 14
- Enemy tanks and armored vehicles destroyed: 1,164
- Enemy trucks and other motor transport destroyed: 4,697
- Enemy aircraft destroyed and probably destroyed: 415
- Bridges built in footage: 33,292
- Personnel casualties suffered (approximate): 90,000
- Rations issued: 39,993,084
- Gasoline issued: 29,964,832 gallons
- Water purified and issued: 39,313,800 gallons
- Ammunition expended: 100,000 tons
- Value of ammunition fired: $100,000,000
- Small arms and mortar ammunition used: 69,967,135 rounds
- Artillery and tank ammunition used: 4,193,976 rounds
- Telephone calls processed at headquarters: 2,041,800; daily average: 6,000
- Troops served doughnuts and coffee by Red Cross Club-mobiles: 1,409,500

UNITS THAT SERVED WITH SEVENTH CORPS
June 6, 1944–May 31, 1945

Combat Divisions

- First Infantry Division
- Second Infantry Division
- Second Armored Division
- Third Armored Division
- Fourth Infantry Division
- Fifth Armored Division
- Seventh Armored Division
- Eighth Infantry Division
- Eighth Armored Division
- Ninth Infantry Division
- Ninth Armored Division
- Thirtieth Infantry Division
- Thirty-fifth Infantry Division
- Sixty-ninth Infantry Division
- Seventy-fifth Infantry Division
- Seventy-eighth Infantry Division
- Seventy-ninth Infantry Division
- Eighty-third Infantry Division
- Eighty-fourth Infantry Division
- Eighty-sixth Infantry Division
- Ninety-sixth Infantry Division
- Ninety-ninth Infantry Division
- 104th Infantry Division

Paratroops

- Eighty-second Airborne Division
- 101st Airborne Division

Armored Units

- Third Armored Group
- Sixth Armored Group
- Ninth Armored Group
- Tenth Armored Group
- Seventieth Tank Battalion
- 705th Tank Battalion
- 709th Tank Battalion
- 737th Tank Battalion
- 738th Tank Battalion
- 740th Tank Battalion
- 741st Tank Battalion
- 743rd Tank Battalion
- 744th Tank Battalion (Light)
- 745th Tank Battalion
- 746th Tank Battalion
- 750th Tank Battalion
- 759th Tank Battalion (Light)
- 771st Tank Battalion
- 774th Tank Battalion
- 777th Tank Battalion
- 786th Tank Battalion

Cavalry Units (Mechanized)

- Fourth Cavalry Group
- Fourteenth Cavalry Group
- 102nd Cavalry Group
- 113th Cavalry Group
- Fourth Cavalry Reconnaissance Squadron
- Eighteenth Cavalry Reconnaissance Squadron
- Twenty-fourth Cavalry Reconnaissance Squadron
- Thirty-second Cavalry Reconnaissance Squadron
- Thirty-eighth Cavalry Reconnaissance Squadron
- 102nd Cavalry Reconnaissance Squadron
- 113th Cavalry Reconnaissance Squadron
- 125th Cavalry Reconnaissance Squadron

Chemical Units

- Twenty-third Chemical Smoke Battalion
- Sixtieth Chemical Depot Company
- Seventy-ninth Chemical Smoke Generator Company
- Eightieth Chemical Smoke Generator Company
- Eighty-fourth Chemical Smoke Generator Company
- Eighty-sixth Chemical Mortar Battalion, Companies A and B
- Eighty-seventh Chemical Mortar Battalion
- Ninetieth Chemical Mortar Battalion, Company B
- Ninety-second Chemical Mortar Battalion (less Company B)
- 113th Chemical Processing Company, Detachment

Engineer Units

- 1106th Engineer Combat Group
- 1110th Engineer Combat Group
- 1111th Engineer Combat Group
- 1120th Engineer Combat Group
- 1121st Engineer Combat Group
- First Engineer Special Brigade
- Forty-ninth Engineer Combat Battalion
- Fifty-first Engineer Combat Battalion
- Sixty-first Engineer Combat Battalion
- Seventy-second Engineer Light Pontoon Company, Platoon
- Eighty-sixth Engineer Heavy Pontoon Battalion
- 112th Engineer Combat Battalion
- 146th Engineer Combat Battalion
- 148th Engineer Combat Battalion
- 164th Engineer Combat Battalion
- 181st Engineer Heavy Pontoon Battalion
- 207th Engineer Combat Battalion
- 237th Engineer Combat Battalion
- 238th Engineer Combat Battalion
- 246th Engineer Combat Battalion
- 291st Engineer Combat Battalion
- 294th Engineer Combat Battalion
- 296th Engineer Combat Battalion
- 297th Engineer Combat Battalion
- 298th Engineer Combat Battalion
- 299th Engineer Combat Battalion, Company B

- 300th Engineer Combat Battalion
- 467th Engineer Maintenance Company
- 501st Engineer Light Pontoon Company
- 505th Engineer Light Pontoon Company
- 507th Engineer Light Pontoon Company
- 508th Engineer Light Pontoon Company
- 512th Engineer Light Pontoon Company
- 582nd Engineer Dump Truck Company
- 602nd Engineer Camouflage Battalion, Company D
- 610th Engineer Light Equipment Company, Platoon
- 612th Engineer Light Equipment Company
- 631st Engineer Light Equipment Company
- 663rd Engineer Topographical Company
- 962nd Engineer Maintenance Company
- 966th Engineer Maintenance Company
- 988th Engineer Treadway Bridge Company
- 989th Engineer Treadway Bridge Company
- 990th Engineer Treadway Bridge Company
- 991st Engineer Treadway Bridge Company
- 994th Engineer Treadway Bridge Company
- 501st Engineer Water Supply Company, Detachment
- 2892nd Engineer Technical Intelligence Team
- 2944th Engineer Technical Intelligence Team

Field Artillery Units

- Headquarters Seventh Corps Artillery
- Thirty-second Field Artillery Brigade

- Eighteenth Field Artillery Group
- Seventy-ninth Field Artillery Group
- 142nd Field Artillery Group
- 179th Field Artillery Group
- 188th Field Artillery Group
- 205th Field Artillery Group
- 224th Field Artillery Group
- 258th Field Artillery Group
- Third Field Artillery Observation Battalion, Battery B
- Thirteenth Field Artillery Observation Battalion
- Seventeenth Field Artillery Observation Battalion, Battery A
- 285th Field Artillery Observation Battalion
- Fifty-eighth Armored Field Artillery Battalion (105mm Howitzer Self-propelled)
- Sixty-second Armored Field Artillery Battalion (105mm Howitzer Self-propelled)
- Sixty-fifth Armored Field Artillery Battalion (105mm Howitzer Self-propelled)
- Eighty-third Armored Field Artillery Battalion (105mm Howitzer Self-propelled)
- Eighty-seventh Armored Field Artillery Battalion (105mm Howitzer Self-propelled)
- 275th Armored Field Artillery Battalion (105mm Howitzer Self-propelled)
- 400th Armored Field Artillery Battalion (105mm Howitzer Self-propelled)
- Eighteenth Field Artillery Battalion (105mm Howitzer)
- Seventy-sixth Field Artillery Battalion (105mm Howitzer)

- 153rd Field Artillery Battalion (8-inch Gun)
- 172nd Field Artillery Battalion (4.5-inch Gun)
- 174th Field Artillery Battalion (155mm Gun Self-propelled)
- 183rd Field Artillery Battalion (155mm Howitzer)
- 188th Field Artillery Battalion (155mm Howitzer)
- 193rd Field Artillery Battalion (105mm Howitzer)
- 195th Field Artillery Battalion (8-inch Howitzer)
- 196th Field Artillery Battalion (105mm Howitzer)
- 240th Field Artillery Battalion (155mm Gun)
- 258th Field Artillery Battalion (155mm Gun Self-propelled)
- 266th Field Artillery Battalion (240mm Howitzer)
- 268th Field Artillery Battalion (8-inch Gun)
- 283rd Field Artillery Battalion (105mm Howitzer)
- 551st Field Artillery Battalion (240mm Howitzer)
- 552nd Field Artillery Battalion (240mm Howitzer)
- 635th Field Artillery Battalion (155mm Gun)
- 660th Field Artillery Battalion (8-inch Gun)
- 666th Field Artillery Battalion (155mm Howitzer)
- 690th Field Artillery Battalion (105mm Howitzer)
- 746th Field Artillery Battalion (8-inch Howitzer)
- 751st Field Artillery Battalion (155mm Howitzer)
- 768th Field Artillery Battalion (155mm Howitzer)
- 951st Field Artillery Battalion (155mm Howitzer)
- 957th Field Artillery Battalion (155mm Howitzer)
- 965th Field Artillery Battalion (155mm Howitzer)

- 980th Field Artillery Battalion (155mm Gun)
- 981st Field Artillery Battalion (155mm Gun)
- 987th Field Artillery Battalion (155mm Gun Self-propelled)
- 991st Field Artillery Battalion (155mm Gun Self-propelled)

AUTHOR'S NOTE

Before I began working on this book, the image of J. Lawton Collins in my memory was not of a World War II general in combat uniform and helmet on a battlefield but of a soft-spoken, distinguished gentleman on TV news interview programs in the early 1950s. Perhaps he had stuck in my mind because like me he wrote his signature with an initial instead of a first name. Although I had a vague remembrance of him from reading newspaper reports of the war in Europe when I was in elementary school, and in high school at the time of the Korean War when he was in headlines as army chief of staff, it was not until very much later that I realized he became chief of staff because of his outstanding record as a combat commander during the Second World War. Just how significant he had been in the planning of the Utah Beach landing as the Seventh Corps commander on D-day became clear when I began research for the first biography of Brigadier General Theodore Roosevelt, Jr. When I discovered later that no one had published a biography of Collins, I decided to delve more deeply into his World War II service to see if he warranted one.

I began with his autobiography, *Lightning Joe*, and was astonished by the story of how a New Orleans youth had risen in army officer ranks to command combat troops on Guadalcanal and moved to Europe to lead the Seventh Corps from D-day to the end of the war in Europe, then became the army's top officer in the Korean War and Eisenhower's fact finder in the initial stage of U.S. involvement in Vietnam. In pursuit of more knowledge about Collins, I looked in histories of World War II in Europe and the Pacific and memoirs by Eisenhower and Bradley. As I read the passages describing his accomplishments from Guadalcanal to Seventh Corps engagements on D-day, during Operation Cobra and the breakout from Normandy, in the march to the Roer River, in the awful fight in the Hurtgen Forest, at the Battle of the Bulge, in the taking of Cologne, crossing of the Rhine, and linking up with the Russians at the Elbe, I became convinced that a biography was woefully overdue.

The indispensable main Collins source was his autobiography, followed by Omar Bradley's *A Soldier's Story*, and the Eisenhower memoir, *Crusade in Europe*. He was cited in many volumes on histories of Guadalcanal, of Utah Beach, of the Hurtgen Forest, the German surprise counterattack through the Ardennes forest, the Ruhr Valley and Rhine campaigns, the meeting with the Russians, and the German surrender. I turned next to his and other books on the Korean War and the portions of histories of Vietnam dealing with the Eisenhower administration's role in the 1950s. I discovered that references to Collins in accounts of World War II in contemporary newspapers and magazines were scarce, but there was an explosion of coverage of him as the army chief of staff during the Korean War and as Eisenhower's envoy to Saigon in 1954. Useful insights and rich details of the European campaigns and battles from D-day onward were found in several publications of the army's Center of Military History. Collins's World War II papers and records, including correspondence, field records, and other materials are archived at the Eisenhower presidential library in Abilene, Kansas.

As always when undertaking a writing project, I had the encouragement of my literary agent, Jake Elwell. I'm grateful to my editor, Brent Howard, on this and previous books on the World War II commanders William O. Darby and Lucian K. Truscott, Jr., and for the moral support of friends Sid Goldstein, Bill Restivo, Judy Cusano, and John Bogdanovic, my sisters Jean and Arlene, my niece Ginny, and Dr. Hussein Awini, all of whom helped me through a hospitalization while I was writing this book. A nod of thanks is also due to Janet Holsinger and the staff of History Associates for finding photos in the National Archives.

The more I write about a war that raged when I was a kid, the more I become indebted to the young men and the intrepid combat leaders like Lightning Joe Collins who won what President Franklin D. Roosevelt promised in his address to Congress on the day after Pearl Harbor would be "an inevitable triumph."

BIBLIOGRAPHY

Acheson, Dean. *Present at the Creation: My Years in the State Department.* New York: W. W. Norton and Company, 1969.

Ambrose, Stephen E. *Eisenhower and Berlin 1945.* New York: Norton, 1945.

———. *The Supreme Commander.* New York: Doubleday, 1970.

———. *D-Day June 6, 1944: The Climactic Battle of World War II.* New York: Simon & Schuster, 1994.

Appleman, Roy E. *South to the Naktong, North to the Yalu.* Washington, D.C.: Office of the Chief of Military History (OCMH), U.S. Army, 1960.

Astor, Gerald. *The Greatest War: Americans in Combat, 1941–1945.* Novato, CA: Presidio Press, 1999.

Babcock, Robert. *War Stories: Utah Beach to Pleiku.* Baton Rouge, LA: St. John's Press, 2001.

Balkoski, Joseph. *Utah Beach.* Mechanicsburg, PA: Stackpole Books, 2005.

Blair, Clay. *Ridgway's Paratroopers: The American Airborne in World War II*. Exeter, England: Lee Publishing, 1991.

Blumenson, Martin. *Breakout and Pursuit: The European Theater of Operations*. Washington, D.C.: OCMH, U.S. Army, 1961.

Bradley, Omar N. *A Soldier's Story*. New York: Henry Holt, 1951.

Chandler, David, and James Lawton Collins, eds. *The D-Day Encyclopedia*. New York: Simon & Schuster, 1994.

Clark, Mark W. *From the Danube to the Yalu*. New York: Harper, 1954.

Cole, Hugh M. *The Ardennes: Battle of the Bulge*. Washington, D.C.: OCMH, U.S. Army, 1965.

Collins, J. Lawton. *War in Peacetime*. Boston: Houghton Mifflin, 1969.

———. *Lightning Joe*. Baton Rouge, LA: Louisiana State University, 1979.

D'Este, Carlo. *Decision in Normandy*. London: William Collins, 1983.

Department of the Army. *Utah Beach to Cherbourg*. Washington, D.C.: Historical Division, 1947.

Eisenhower, Dwight D. *Crusade in Europe*. Garden City, NY: Doubleday and Company, 1948.

———. *Mandate for Change*. Garden City, NY: Doubleday, 1963.

Eisenhower, John S. D. *The Bitter Woods: The Battle of the Bulge*. New York: G. P. Putnam's Sons, 1969.

Frank, Richard B. *Guadalcanal*. New York: Random House, Gr1990.

Goulden, Joseph C. *Korea: The Untold Story of the War*. New York: Times Books, 1982.

Harrison, Gordon. *Cross-Channel Attack*. Washington, D.C.: OCMH, U.S. Army, 1951.

Hastings, Max. *Overlord: D-Day and the Battle for Normandy*. New York: Simon & Schuster, 1984.

Higgins, Trumbull. *Korea and the Fall of MacArthur*. New York: Oxford University Press, 1960.

Jeffers, H. Paul. *Theodore Roosevelt, Jr.: The Life of a War Hero*. Novato, CA: Presidio Press, 2002.

Lewis, Nigel. *Exercise Tiger*. New York: Prentice Hall, 1990.

MacDonald, Charles B. *The Battle of the Hurtgen Forest*. New York: Lippincott, 1963.

McManus, John C. *Alamo in the Ardennes*. Hoboken, N.J.: John Wiley & Sons, 2007.

Miller, John T. *Guadalcanal: The First Offensive*. Washington, D.C.: OCMH, U.S. Army, 1949.

Morgan, Frederick Edgeworth. *Overture to Overlord*. Garden City, NY: Doubleday, 1950.

Morison, Samuel E. *The Invasion of France and Germany, 1944–1945*. Boston: Little Brown, 1962.

Neillands, Robin. *The Battle for the Rhine*. Woodstock and New York: The Overlook Press, Peter Mayer Publishers, Inc., 2007.

Parker, Danny S. *Battle of the Bulge*. Cambridge, MA: DaCapo Press, 2004.

Perry, Mark. *Partners in Command*. New York: The Penguin Group, 2007.

Pogue, Forest. *The Supreme Command*. Washington, D.C.: OCMH, U.S. Army, 1954.

Pugsley, Christopher. *Battle Zone Normandy: Operation Cobra*. Gloucestershire, UK: Sutton Publishing, 2004.

Rees, David. *Korea: The Limited War*. London: Macmillan, 1964.

Ridgway, Matthew. *Soldier: The Memoirs of Matthew B. Ridgway*. New York: Harper, 1956.

———. *The Korean War*. Garden City, NY: Doubleday, 1967.

Ryan, Cornelius. *The Longest Day*. New York: Simon & Schuster, 1959.

Schnabel, James. *Policy and Direction: The First Year*. Washington, D.C.: OCMH, U.S. Army, 1971.

Taylor, Maxwell D. *Swords and Plowshares*. New York: Norton, 1972.

Tregaskis, Richard. *Guadalcanal Diary*. New York: Random House, 1943.

United States Army. *Mission Accomplished: The Story of the Campaigns of the VII Corps, United States Army, in the War Against Germany, 1944–1945*. Leipzig, Germany: J. J. Weber, 1945.

Weigley, Russell. *Eisenhower's Lieutenants: The Campaigns of France and Germany, 1944–1945*. Bloomington, IN: Indiana University Press, 1981.

Zumbro, Derek S. *Battle for the Ruhr*. Lawrence, KS: University of Kansas Press, 2006.

INDEX